I0812854

THEN & NOW

PORTSMOUTH

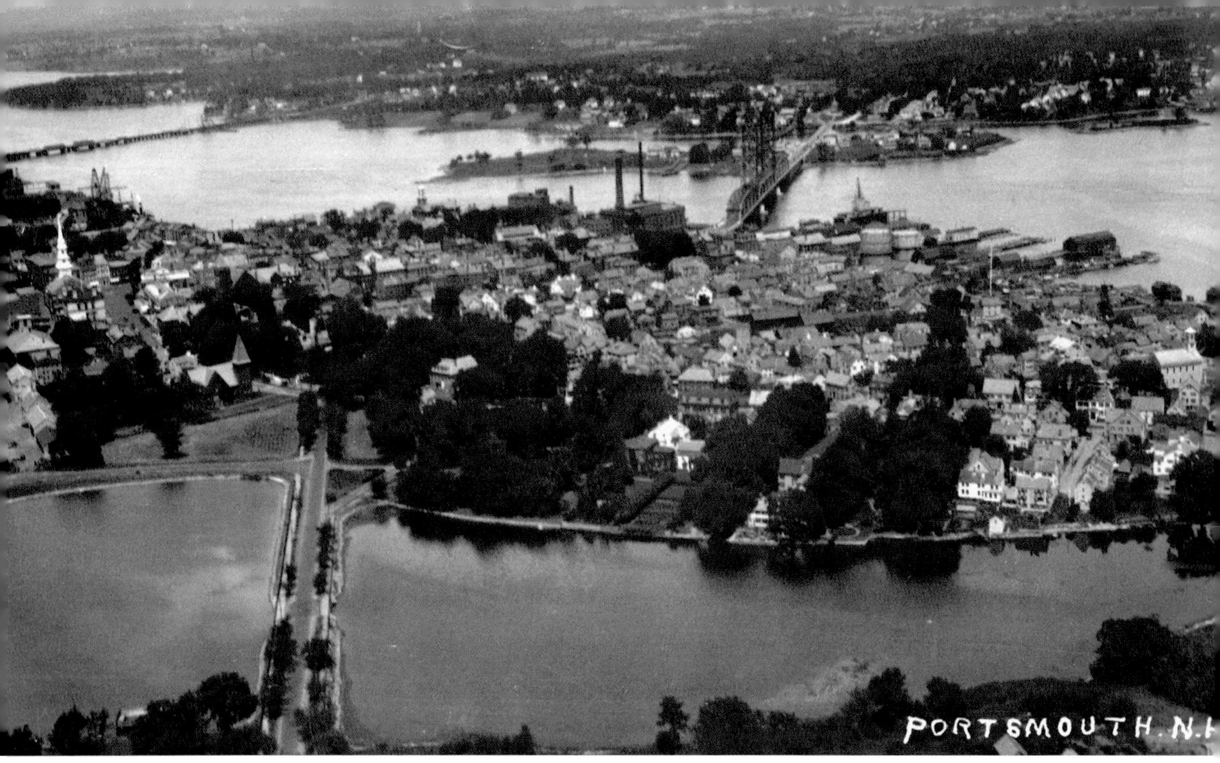

This aerial photograph of Portsmouth was taken *c.* 1925. The water in the foreground is South Mill Pond, and the background water is the Piscataqua River. On the river there are two bridges. The one on the right is the Memorial Bridge. On the left is the old railroad bridge that went from Freeman's Point to Kittery, Maine. Before the Memorial Bridge was built, Portsmouth Naval Shipyard workers who missed the ferry to Kittery had to walk to work via the railroad bridge, which was the long way around.

THEN & NOW®

PORTSMOUTH

William T. and Constance S. Warren

ARCADIA
PUBLISHING

ISBN 978-0-7385-0901-3

Published by Arcadia Publishing
Charleston, South Carolina

Printed in the United States of America

Library of Congress Catalog Card Number: 2001090585

For all general information contact Arcadia Publishing at:
Telephone 843-853-2070
Fax 843-853-0044
E-mail sales@arcadiapublishing.com
For customer service and orders:
Toll-Free 1-888-313-2665

Visit us on the Internet at www.arcadiapublishing.com

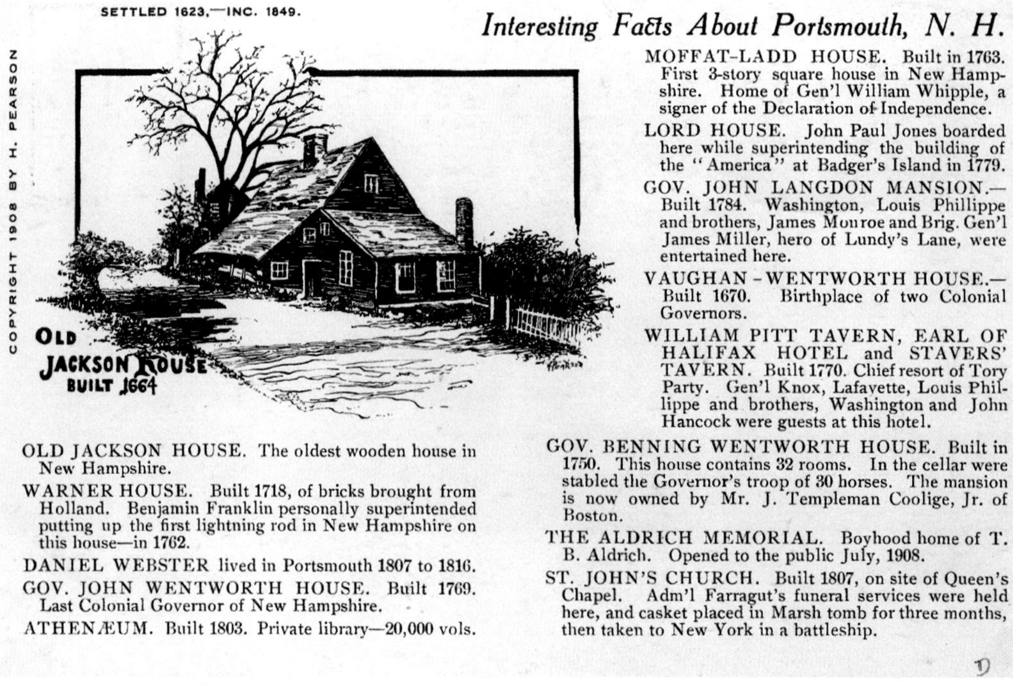
SETTLED 1623,—INC. 1849.

Interesting Facts About Portsmouth, N. H.

COPYRIGHT 1908 BY H. PEARSON

OLD JACKSON HOUSE BUILT 1664

MOFFAT-LADD HOUSE. Built in 1763. First 3-story square house in New Hampshire. Home of Gen'l William Whipple, a signer of the Declaration of Independence.

LORD HOUSE. John Paul Jones boarded here while superintending the building of the "America" at Badger's Island in 1779.

GOV. JOHN LANGDON MANSION.—Built 1784. Washington, Louis Phillippe and brothers, James Monroe and Brig. Gen'l James Miller, hero of Lundy's Lane, were entertained here.

VAUGHAN-WENTWORTH HOUSE.—Built 1670. Birthplace of two Colonial Governors.

WILLIAM PITT TAVERN, EARL OF HALIFAX HOTEL and STAVERS' TAVERN. Built 1770. Chief resort of Tory Party. Gen'l Knox, Lafayette, Louis Phillippe and brothers, Washington and John Hancock were guests at this hotel.

OLD JACKSON HOUSE. The oldest wooden house in New Hampshire.

WARNER HOUSE. Built 1718, of bricks brought from Holland. Benjamin Franklin personally superintended putting up the first lightning rod in New Hampshire on this house—in 1762.

DANIEL WEBSTER lived in Portsmouth 1807 to 1816.

GOV. JOHN WENTWORTH HOUSE. Built 1769. Last Colonial Governor of New Hampshire.

ATHENÆUM. Built 1803. Private library—20,000 vols.

GOV. BENNING WENTWORTH HOUSE. Built in 1750. This house contains 32 rooms. In the cellar were stabled the Governor's troop of 30 horses. The mansion is now owned by Mr. J. Templeman Coolige, Jr. of Boston.

THE ALDRICH MEMORIAL. Boyhood home of T. B. Aldrich. Opened to the public July, 1908.

ST. JOHN'S CHURCH. Built 1807, on site of Queen's Chapel. Adm'l Farragut's funeral services were held here, and casket placed in Marsh tomb for three months, then taken to New York in a battleship.

This postcard is entitled "Interesting Facts about Portsmouth" and was printed in 1908. Many of the houses listed on the card can be found in this book. The drawing of the old Jackson House illustrates the oldest house in Portsmouth.

Contents

ACKNOWLEDGMENTS

The authors thank their friend Ted Gray for his hours of assistance, helping us to identify many of the areas that are depicted in our photograph and picture postcard collection. His knowledge of Portsmouth, which he shared with us, was invaluable. With the help of maps (his and ours), we have found the locations of buildings that were taken down or burned down years ago.

We also want to thank the members of our family for their encouragement.

This postcard shows how Market Square is supposed to have looked when the old Colonial State House was in the square. As it was removed before photography was available, this is the only way to show why Portsmouth has such an open area in the heart of our town.

INTRODUCTION

Our book is a comparative pictorial study in urbanization, with old picture postcards and new photographs taken of the same scenes. To make some sense of our town, we need to consider why people came here to live. Portsmouth is, in literal terms, a town at the port's mouth. The first settlers came here because the geography was suited to their needs. There was a deep river (the Piscataqua River) and large estuarial area that was very suitable for sailing ships and small coastal boats (see the 1877 bird's-eye map, pages 90–91). There were trees that could be adapted to specialized uses in shipbuilding and repairs as well as for houses and fuel for heating and cooking. The forests were homes for animals used for food and clothing, and the ocean supplied valuable resources of fish and other sea life for self-sufficiency. Considered as exportable commodities, these primary products made the area rich in natural resources for early settlers from England, Ireland, Wales, and Scotland.

With the availability of natural resources, people came together for their common good: protection, socialization, and commerce. As they urbanized the seacoast, they tended to specialize. There were the "finders and minders," who brought the products to a common location. There were the "service providers," who arranged the goods for local people, for people who lived on nearby islands, and for shipment back to the United Kingdom. Lastly, there were the "urban managers," who provided necessities (government, organization, and protection) by managing goods and services for local citizens.

Portsmouth, like most early Colonial communities, is laid out in an export design. It had a suitable port where docks and warehouses could be erected on the river's edge. There were islands available for homesteads for fishermen and others. The streets of Portsmouth led from the waterfront to marketing areas in town and then twisted through the neighborhoods and into the interior areas of New Hampshire.

As we entered the industrial period of urban development in the 19th century, Portsmouth showed its signs of urban expansion. The town became an industrialized center. Importing and exporting were the important factors in Portsmouth's growth. A well-designed area was set aside as the central business district. Islington Street, leading away from the port and running parallel to the railroad, also became a commercial road. Residential homes slowly gave way to business: breweries and factories were producing a wide range of goods. On the river, there was increased boatbuilding, including the nation's first shipyard. With the inclusion of a government shipyard, the cross-river traffic increased.

The railroad from Boston came to Portsmouth. There were two stations, and a roundhouse was used to turn the engines around, since Portsmouth was the end of the line. As time went on, there were river crossings for the railroad. One crossed the Piscataqua River just upriver from Portsmouth, and the other crossed the Great Bay to Dover Point. Passenger trains were added, and the seacoast of New Hampshire became an accessible summer retreat for wealthy families from Boston and points farther south.

With commerce introduced to Portsmouth, the industrial base was in its infancy. Businesses joined together in a common-for-all good and formed the Portsmouth Board of Trade in 1868. This organization was the predecessor to the Portsmouth Chamber of Commerce.

In the latter part of the 19th century, Portsmouth, the major coastal town of New Hampshire, offered streetcar lines to the other seacoast areas of New Hampshire and (via ferry across the Piscataqua River) to coastal towns in Maine. The streetcars went to the resort town of Hampton Beach, crossing saltwater marshes along the way. There were stops at prominent centers (Rye Beach, Little Boar's Head, and Big Boar's Head) where summer homes and summer hotels were located. The streetcars, less expensive than the trains, made getting to the seacoast area affordable for a wide cross section of traveling visitors.

The route was clear. Visitors could take the train from Boston to Portsmouth and stay there at least one night. The next day, they might go to the seacoast of Maine or New Hampshire via the trolleys that ran from a starting point in Market Square, just in front of North Church. Or, they might go to the waterfront and take the ferry to the Isles of Shoals to stay in one of the hotels "10 miles out."

To examine Portsmouth's growth, we have provided our readers with maps at the end of the book. We offer an 1813 fire map that shows where the three great 19th-century fires practically destroyed our town. An 1850 town map shows urban development as the town grew along and away from the river. A *c.* 1870 downtown map shows the buildings and the property owners. An 1877 bird's-eye map is presented to show Portsmouth's growth as rendered in a three-dimensional drawing. We also include an 1888 ward zone map to show how our town was broken down into wards (for city management purposes). Finally, an 1890 map identifies the west end, which by that time had become the blue-collar workers' area of Portsmouth. From time to time throughout the text, we will refer to these maps.

From the waterfront to the outskirts of Portsmouth, the road development was forced to keep pace with urban growth. The three major roads leading out of Portsmouth were (and still are) Islington Street, Middle Street, and Miller Avenue. The importance of these thoroughfares is evident by their width as compared to other roads in Portsmouth. Islington Street, which became more commercial than residential, runs from the end of Congress Street to the Plains area and southwestward to Greenland, Stratham, Exeter, and points of interior New Hampshire. Middle Street, on the other hand, retained its residential flavor from just south of Haymarket Square to the town limits. It runs from the end of Congress Street to Miller Avenue and beyond. It continues until it becomes Lafayette Road (Route 1). Route 1 continues southward to the towns of Rye, North Hampton, Hampton, and Seabrook before crossing the state line into Massachusetts. Miller Avenue starts at the junction of Summer and Middle Streets and heads toward the seacoast. This was the route taken by the trolley line that serviced the resort hotels, which were prominent features on the New Hampshire coast.

Chapter 1

The Waterfront, Boston & Maine Railroad, and the Central Business District

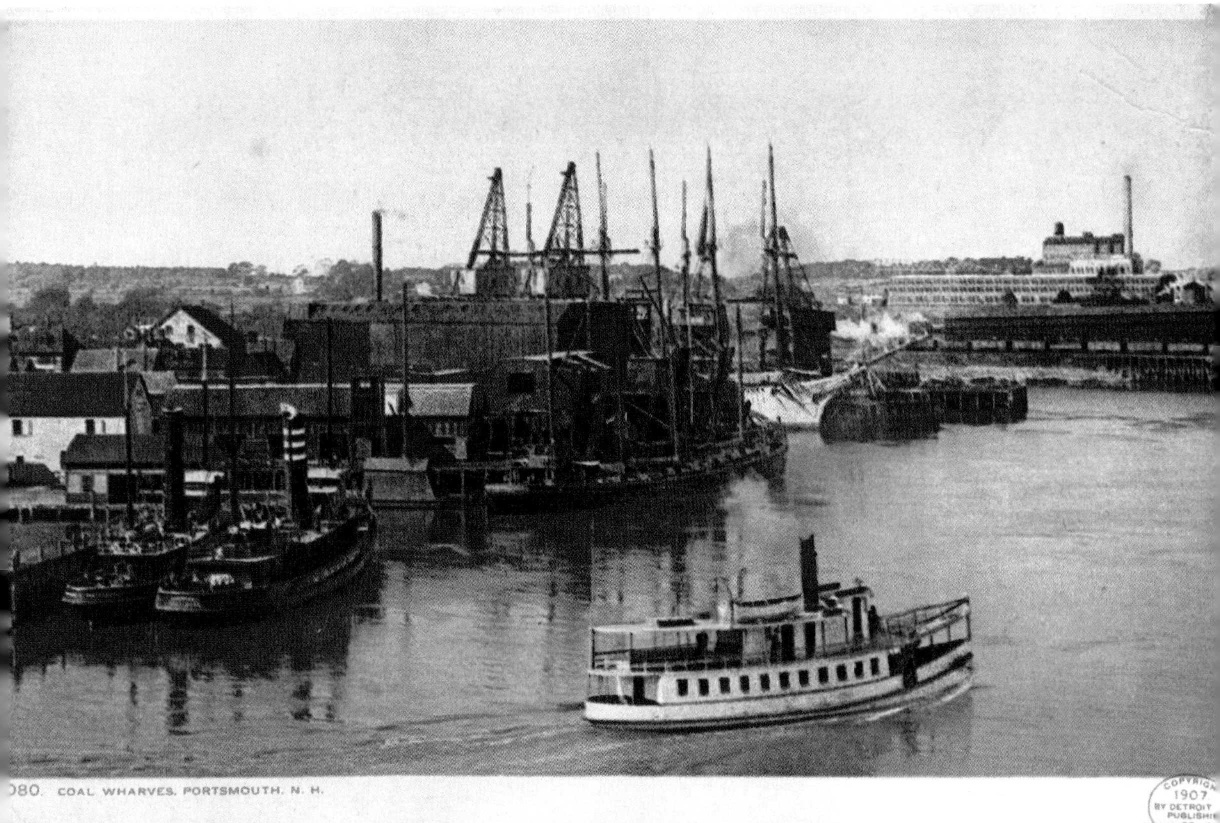

During all the years prior to the building of the Memorial Bridge, the wharves at the end of Daniel Street and along Water Street were the main shipping and receiving area for our seaborne commerce (see the 1877 bird's-eye map). In this *c.* 1907 postcard, the coal wharves are seen along with tugboats in the left foreground.

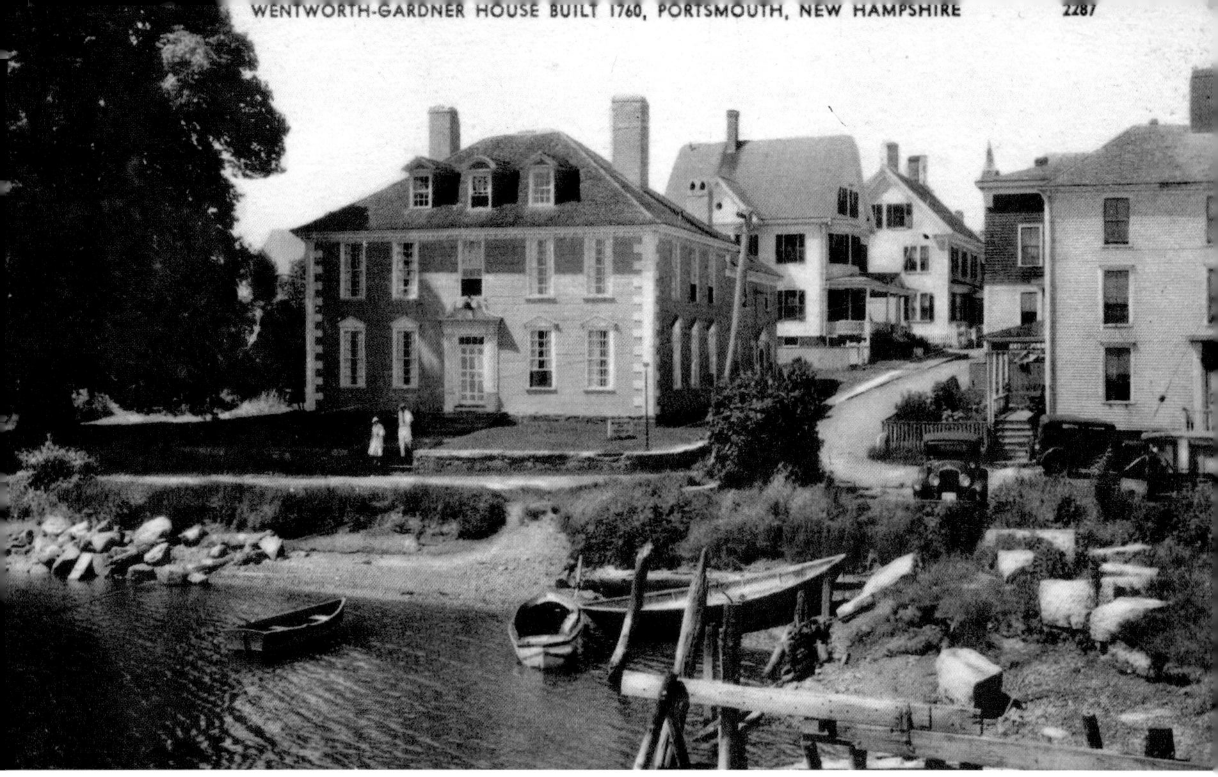

Our pictorial history starts at the waterfront. One of the many fine homes that have been saved for the enjoyment of all the people who come to Portsmouth is the Wentworth-Gardner House, located on the corner of Mechanic and Gardner Streets and built in 1760. Portsmouth, like many older American cities, has had to formulate policy regarding its older houses. Questions of renovation costs and building usage are a challenge to many New England communities. The city's historic district commission, board of adjustments, and planning board tackle these difficult questions and oversee the important work of saving our historic buildings, both public and private. While the intent of this book is to show the differences between our older city and what we have now, it is important to acknowledge that it is often a challenge to decide the best preservation methods where the older buildings are concerned. In the modern photograph, the Wentworth-Gardner House remains similar to the postcard. The waterfront has been altered to accommodate parking for visitors, and the river's edge has been changed to keep it in its present course without loss of land mass.

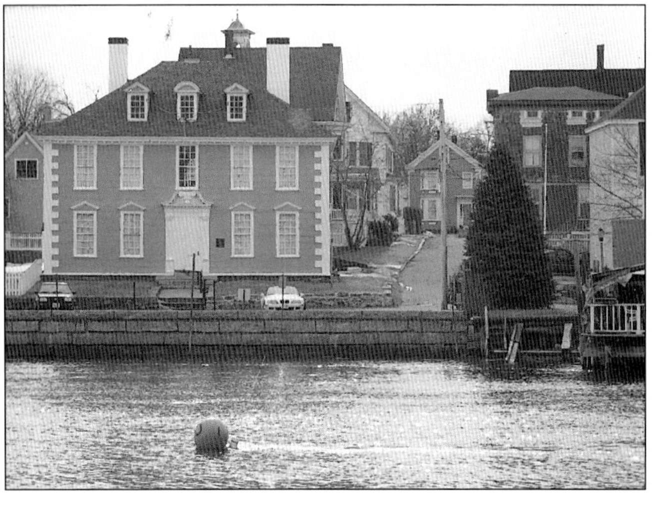

In our older photograph, we are looking down the river. The view is uninterrupted around that point of land. In the background on the left, buildings in the Portsmouth Naval Shipyard are visible. This contrasts with our modern view. The shoreline is recognizable by the steeple of St. John's Church and the general shape of the riverfront. Today, tugboats are tied up near Ceres Street, and there are no longer rowboats along the riverfront.

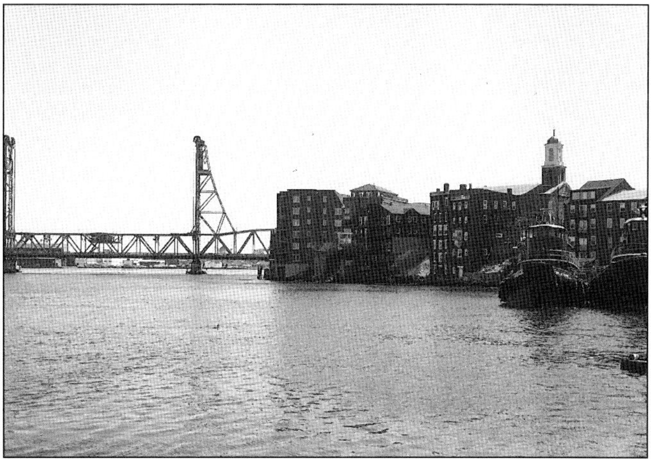

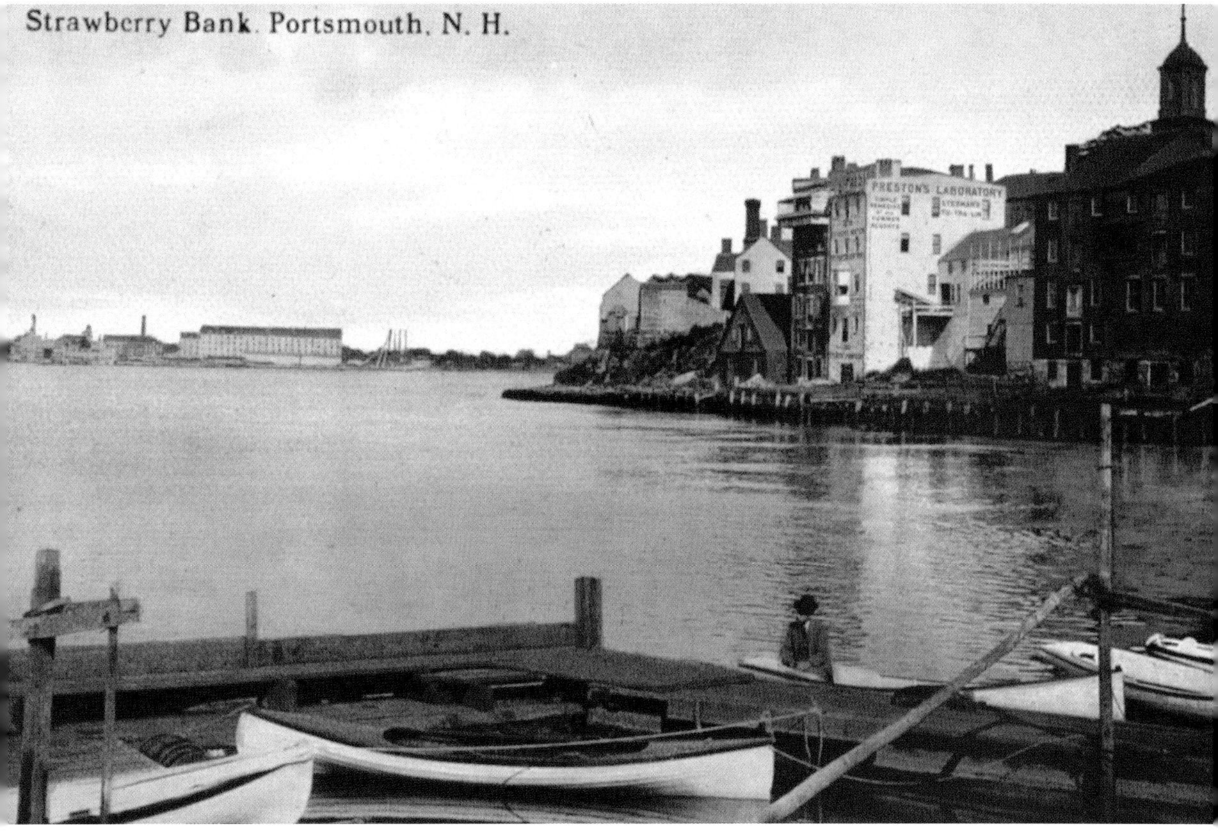

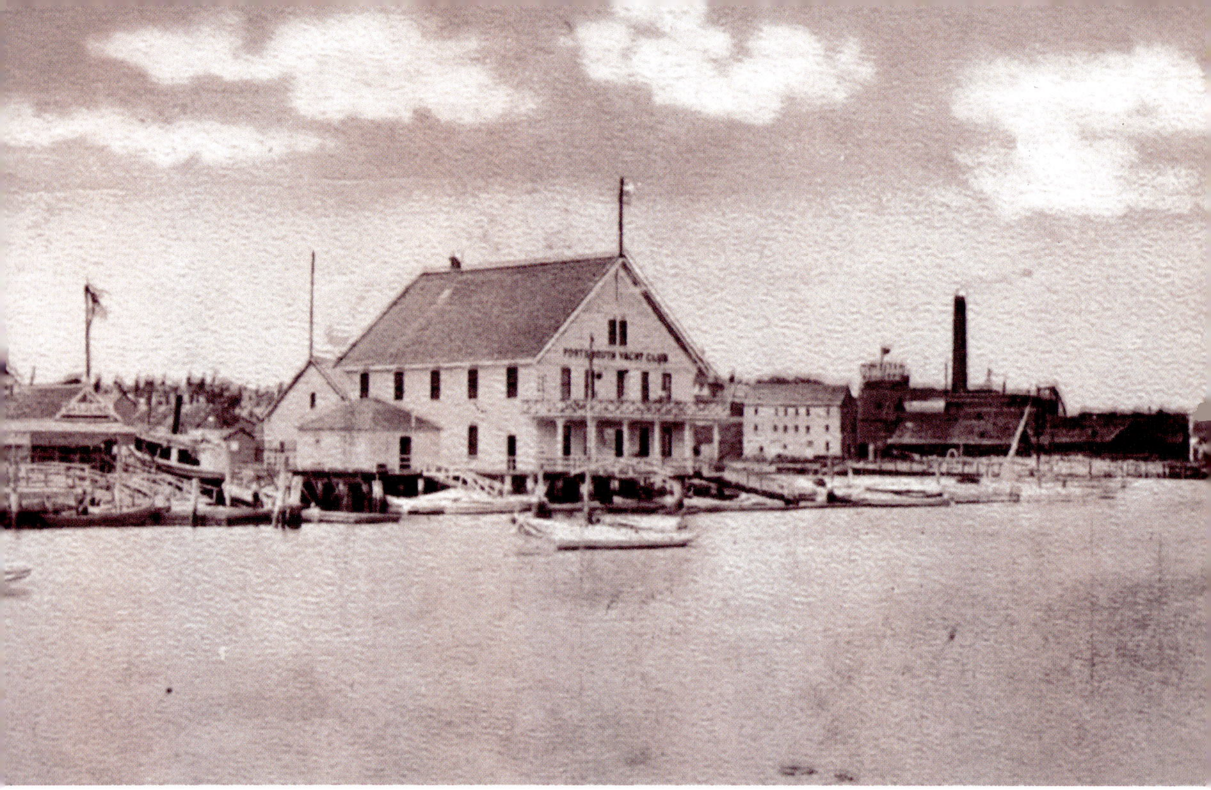

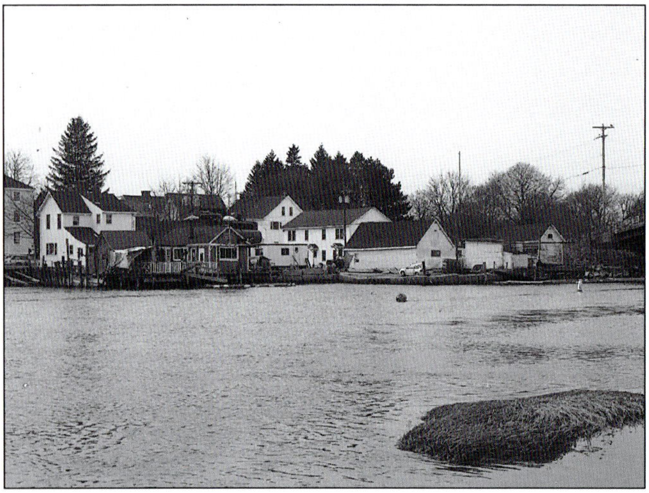

Around 1815, the citizens of Portsmouth built their yacht club on the shores of the Piscataqua River just in view from Pierce Island. It was a grand structure that stood for many years, but it burned to the ground in 1938. The Portsmouth Yacht Club's coming and demise are parts of the story of the waterfront. In the good years, the waterfront appealed to many people, and they in turn made investments to improve its quality. In the lean years, the waterfront lost its monetary support, fell upon hard times, and became seedy and undesirable. When the fire took the club, we were just coming out of the Great Depression, and the members of the club relocated to the island of New Castle.

A Portsmouth waterfront panorama is shown below in a 1904 postcard from the shores of Badger's Island. The signs of industry on the shore are evident in the tall smokestack to the left of St. John's Church. In today's premium-valued waterfront properties, industry has moved to less expensive locations. Older buildings have been saved, renovated, and recycled to serve modern uses. Now there are business offices, condominiums, restaurants, and other clean, nonpolluting businesses along the shoreline.

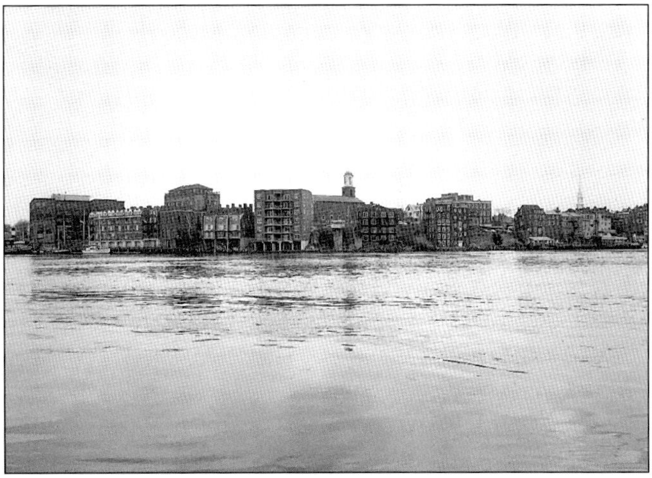

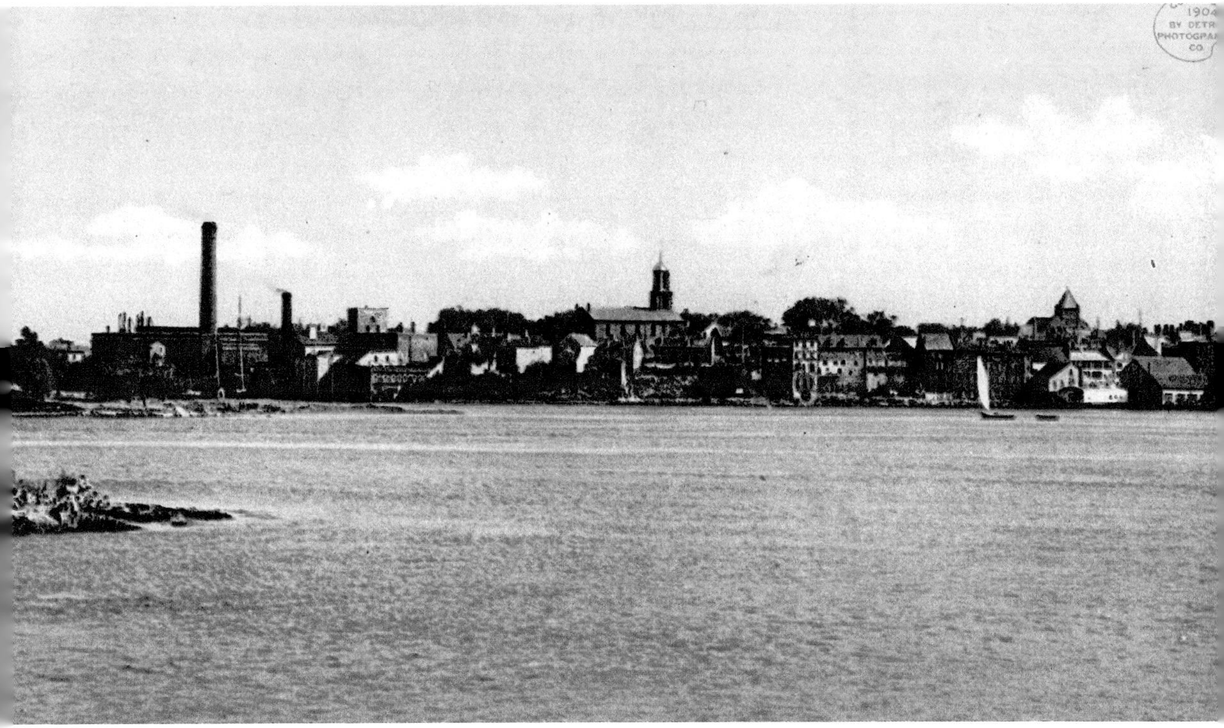

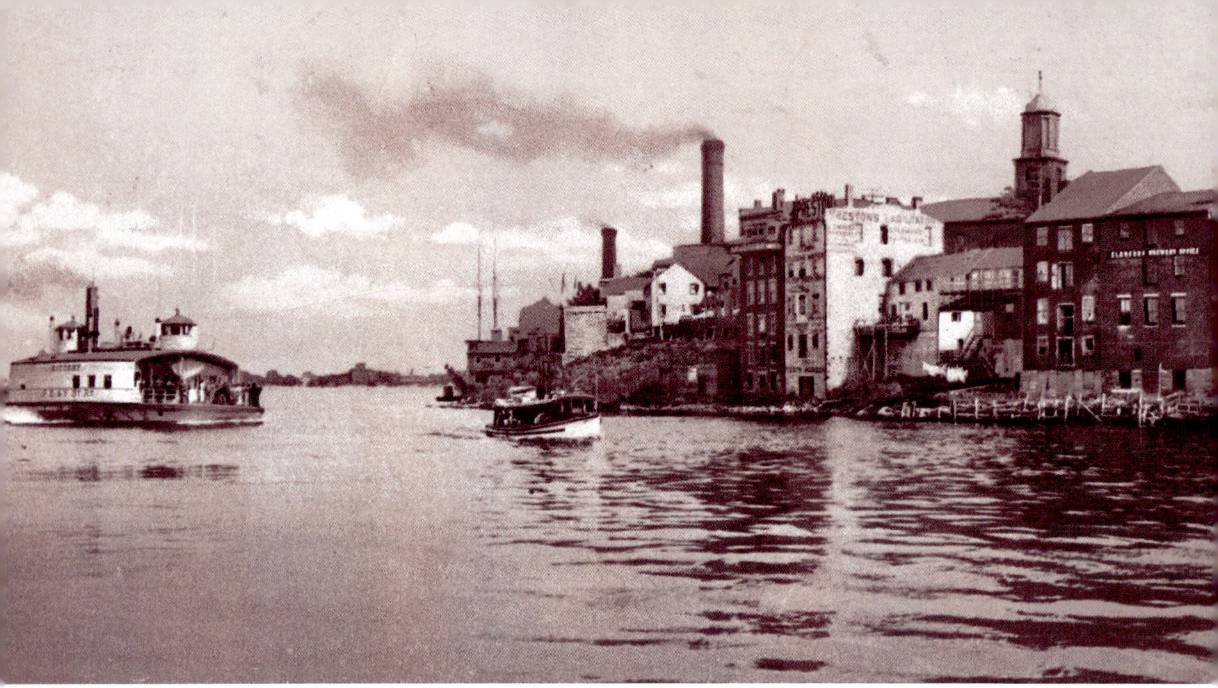

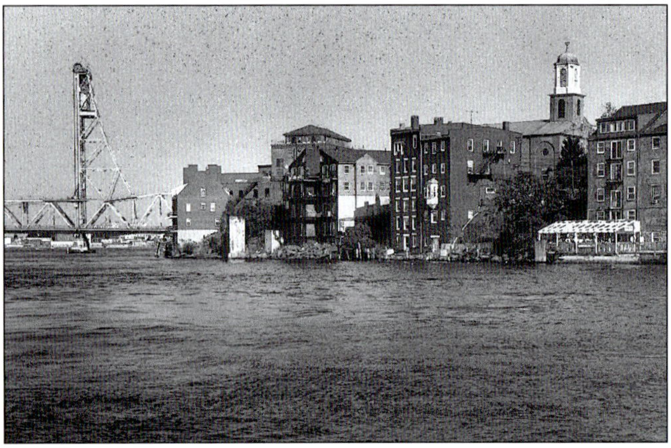

Again, we take a close-up view of the old waterfront scene. Here we see more of the contrast of yesterday's Portsmouth with the present. The Kittery ferry from Badger's Island is plowing its way toward the steamboat wharf at Market Street in Portsmouth. The easiest way across the river was by ferry. Ferryboats still move in and out of a docking area, shown in the modern photograph to the right. The ferries, however, do not not simply cross the river; they go to and from the Isles of Shoals, which are 10 miles off the mainland. The Memorial Bridge, on the left, carries traffic to and from Badger's Island and Kittery.

Below is a close-up of the Kittery ferry as it leaves its berth on Badger's Island. The ferry carried businesspeople, visitors, horses and buggies, streetcars, and workers to and from the numerous boatyards, including the Portsmouth Naval Shipyard. Shipyard workers who missed the morning ferry from the Portsmouth side of the river had to get to work by walking to the railroad bridge (which crossed the river at Freeman's Point), hiking across the trestle bridge, and finally walking to the entrance of the shipyard.

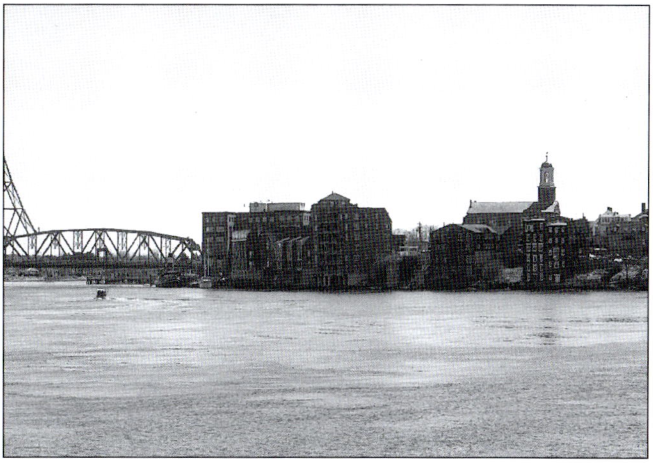

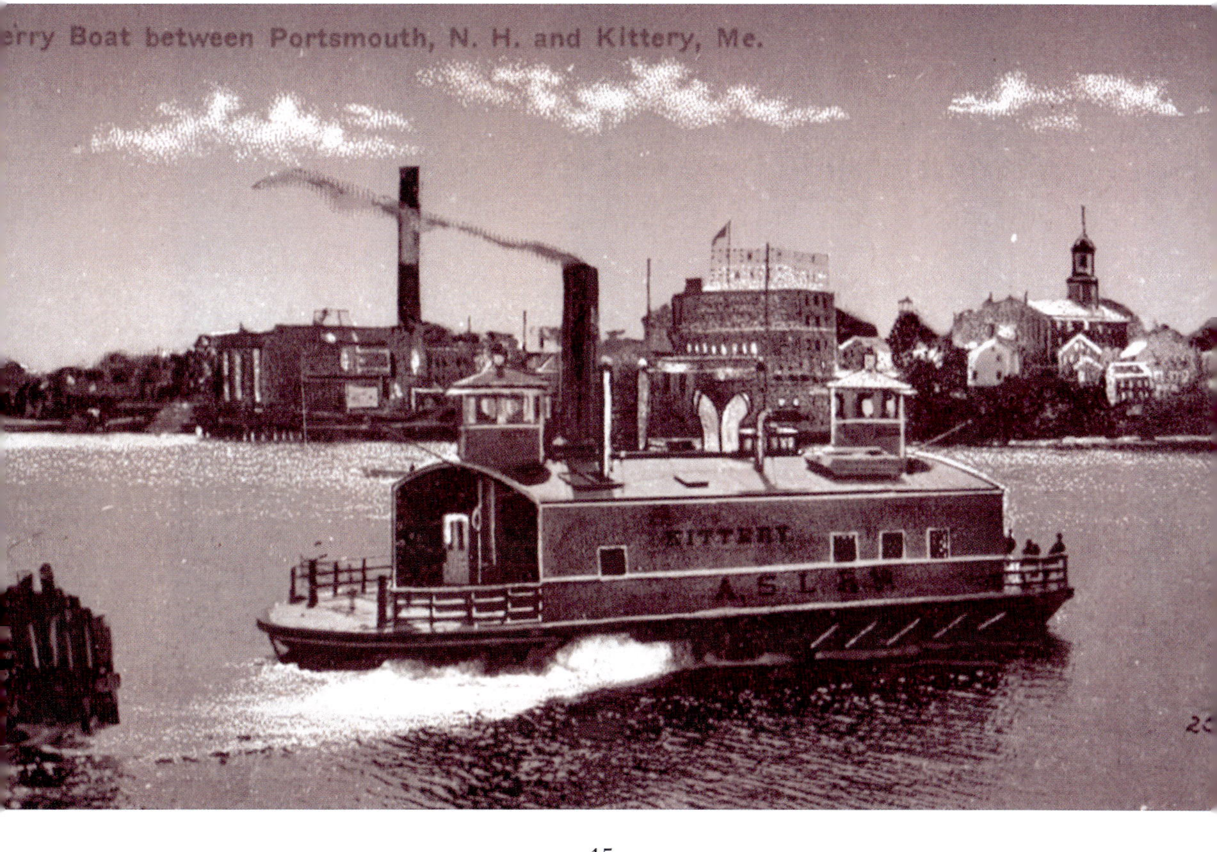

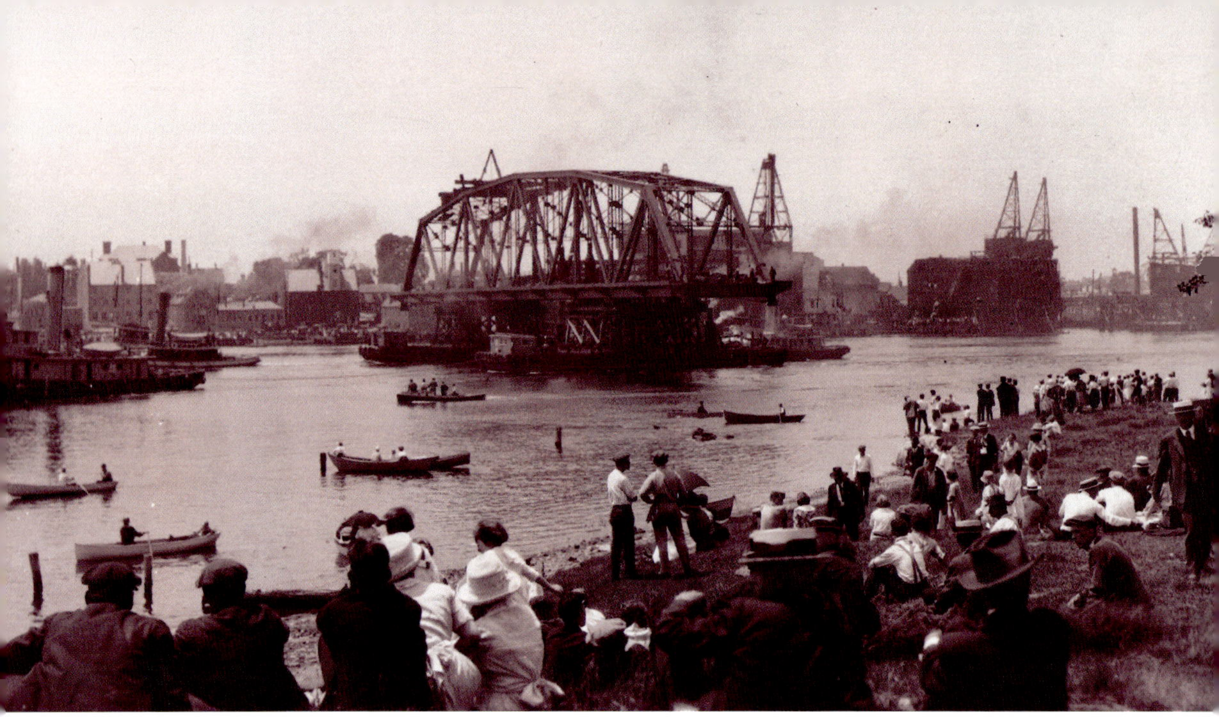

In the years that followed World War I, the Piscataqua River crossing was changed from ferries to a steel and concrete bridge. In these two photographs from 1922–1923, the fantastic spectacle of the building of the bridge can be seen. The sections of the bridge were built on land, loaded onto barges when completed, and (with the help of tugboats) pushed onto concrete abutments when they were cured and ready for the weight of the sections. It was a major construction adventure, and citizens from both sides of the river went out to watch. When it was finished, Maine and New Hampshire were joined at Kittery and Portsmouth. The bridge was dedicated with a plaque that stated, "A memorial to the sailors and soldiers of New Hampshire who participated in the World War 1917–1919."

Since the Memorial Bridge was built, there have been two more bridges that span the Piscataqua River: the Sarah Long Bridge (carrying Route 1) and the Interstate 95 bridge. However, the Memorial Bridge remains the major crossing for Kittery and Portsmouth traffic as well as for workers at the Portsmouth Naval Shipyard who live in New Hampshire but must go through Maine to get to the yard.

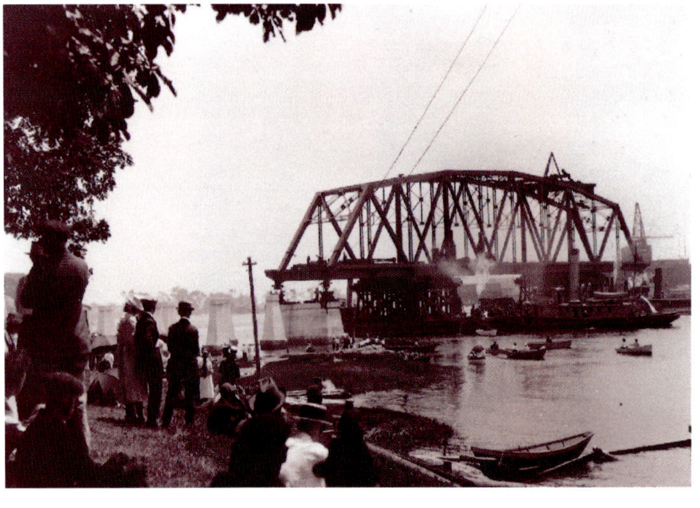

Portsmouth was the end of the line for Boston & Maine trains for many years. The 1877 bird's-eye map (pages 90–91) shows the railroad tracks coming into Portsmouth from points south. At North Mill Pond, a steam engine is drawn with its cars headed toward its destination. Just to the left front of the engine is the Portsmouth roundhouse. Here the engines were turned around and rejoined to the cars before they headed back to Boston.

This photograph shows a Boston & Maine steam engine, No. 907, sitting on the tracks in Portsmouth in 1926. To the left of the engine are the grave markers in North Burying Grounds. A tender and boxcar are in tow, and there are probably passenger cars too, as the engine is where it ought to be if it is backed up to the passenger station.

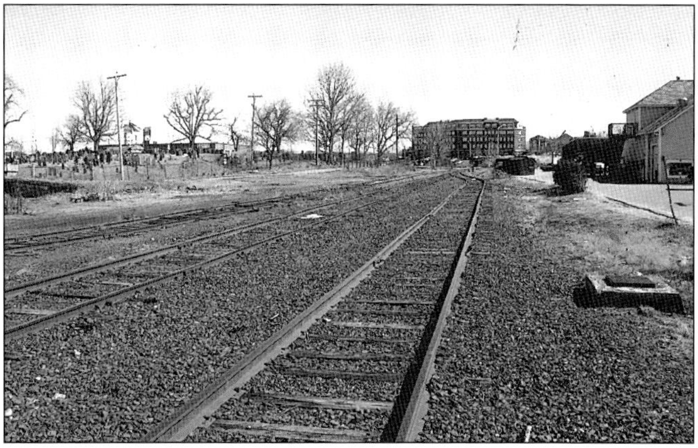

Some of the tracks are still where this train was. All but one track ends before the location of the old passenger station.

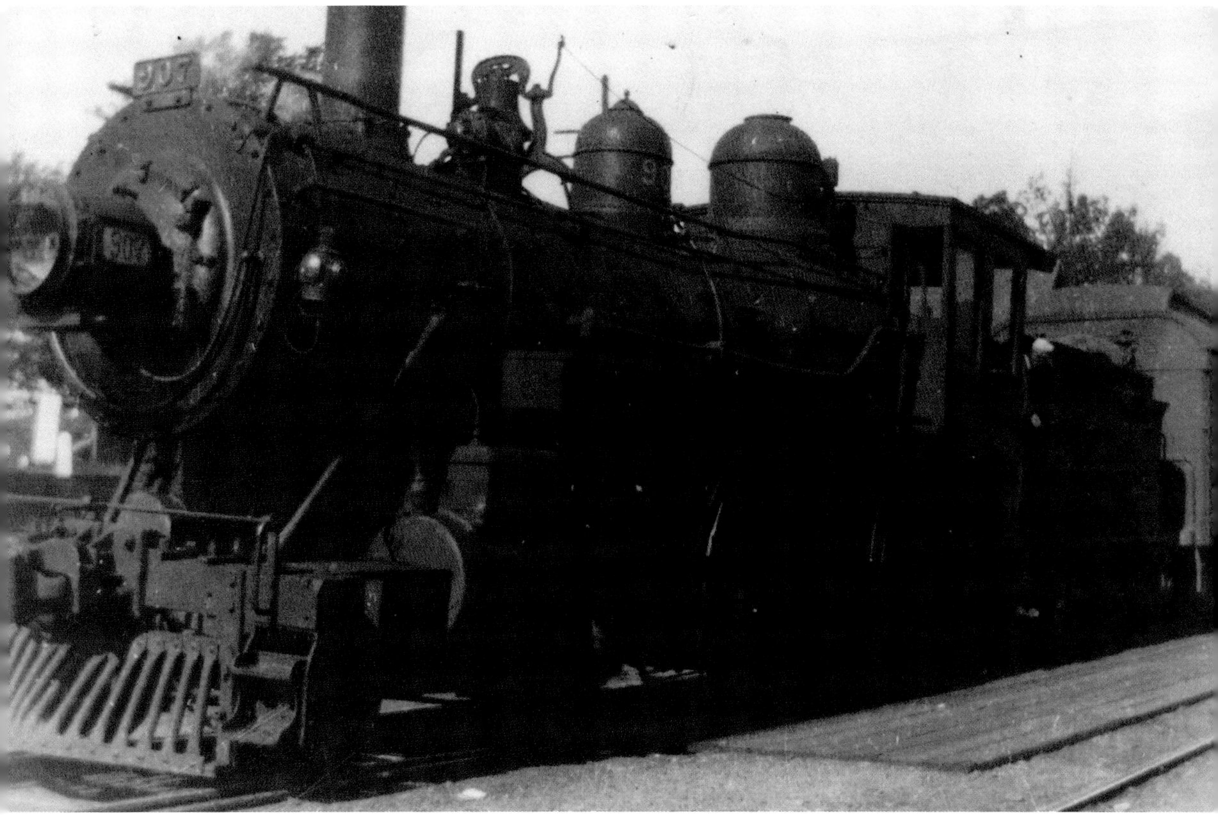

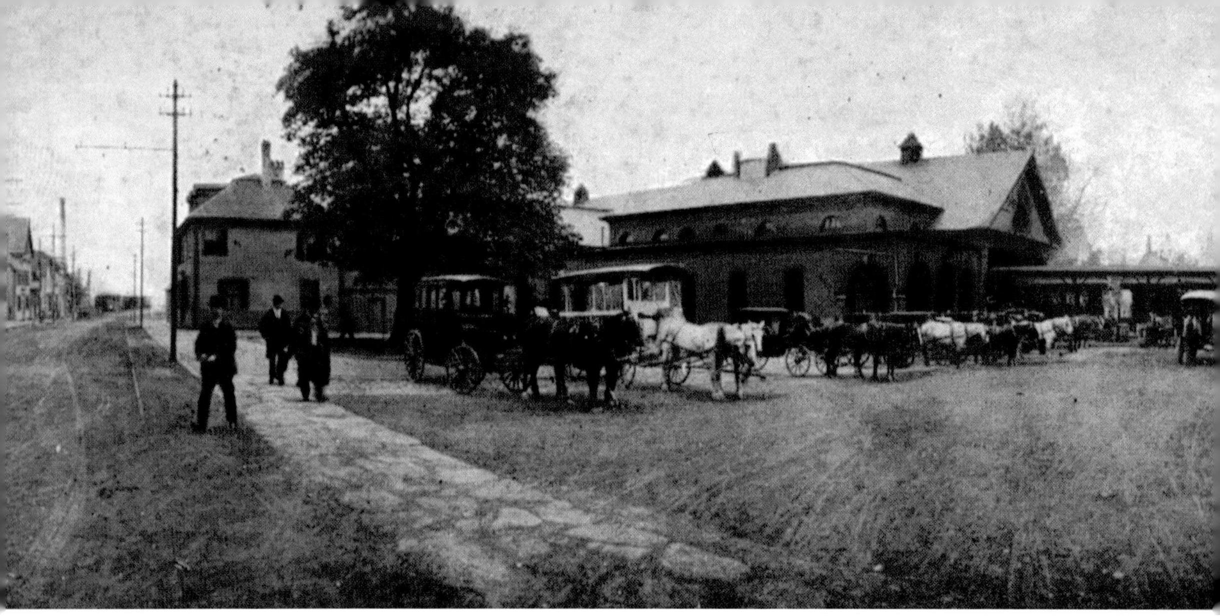

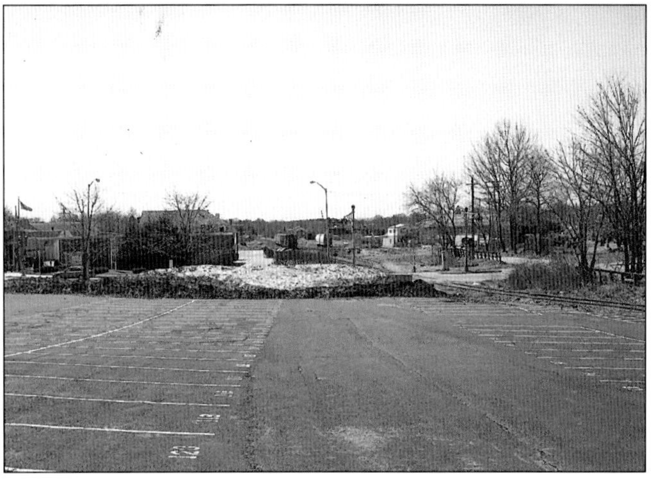

The passenger station was located off Deer Street, just before Vaughn Street. This photograph was taken *c.* 1890. The horses, buggies, and drivers await passengers from a train that has pulled up into the covered platform and station. This station and the freight station were torn down years ago. Today's photograph shows a parking lot where the old station stood. The curvature of a single track is off to the right. Occasionally, there is a freight train or a couple of cars sitting on the rails, as is seen in the new photograph.

Market Square is seen *c.* 1858 through the lens of Portsmouth's first landscape photographer, A. Gregory. We can date a lot of the early photographs because we know when the photographers were in our town. Gregory's photograph, taken from around Fleet Street, shows some amazing details in Market Square that no longer exist today.

The current photograph shows the Sheafe Block (building on left) as having only two floors above the ground floor, but the old photograph shows three. The cupola is no longer visible, as it was removed from the school building. The Pearce Block (center) and North Church are still part of the Market Square streetscape.

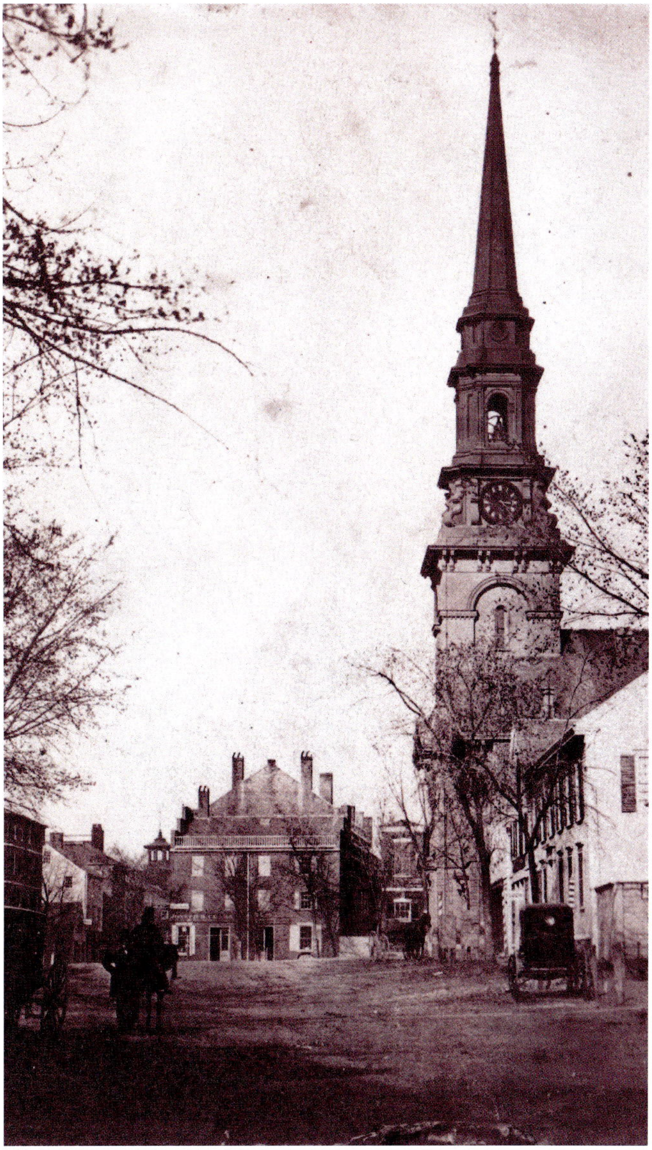

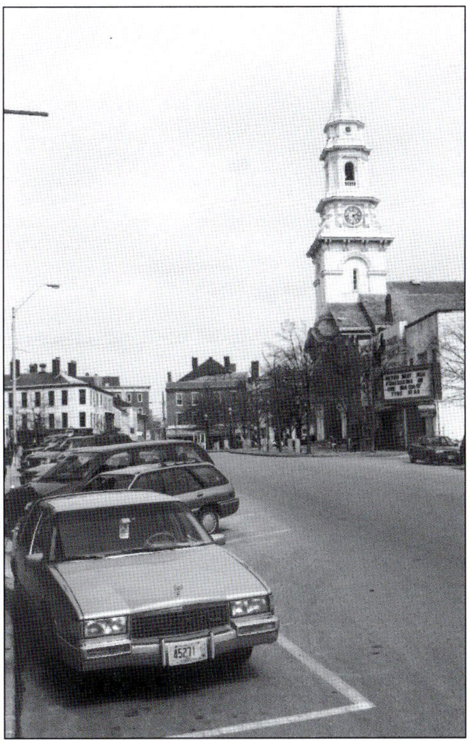

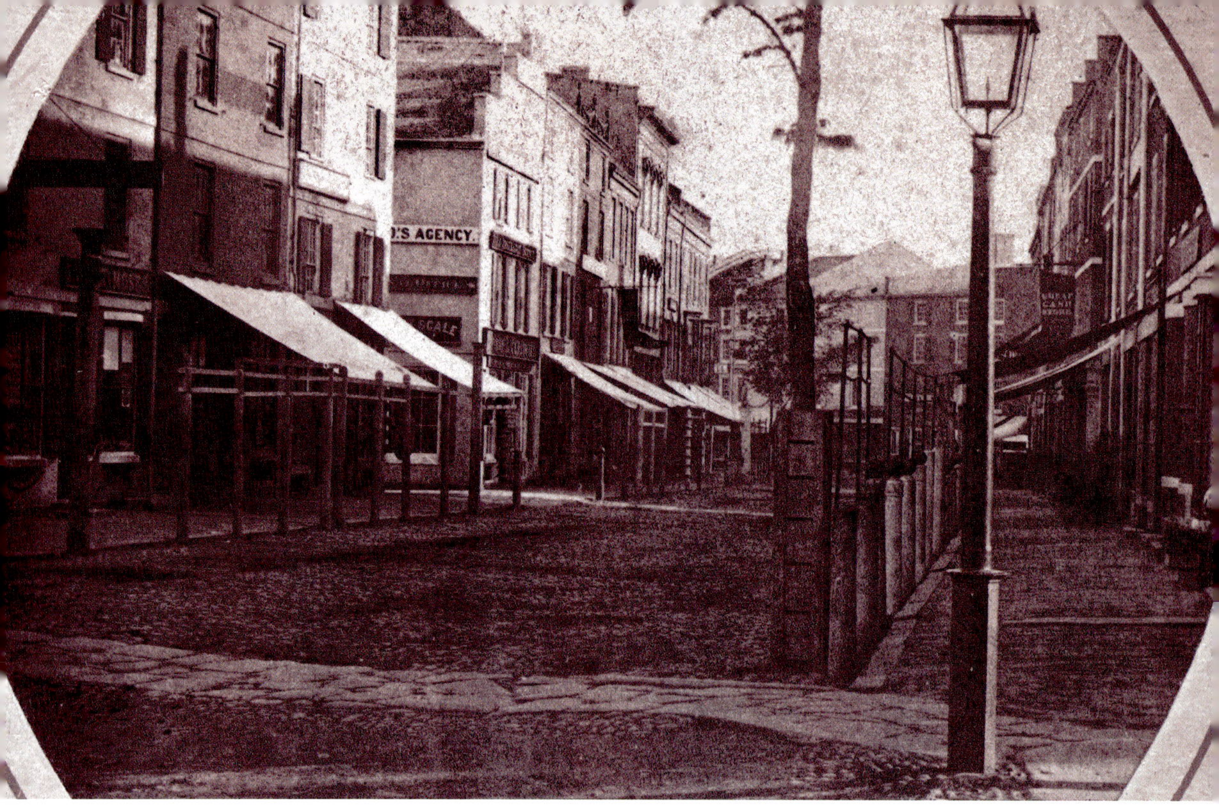

From the center of Market Square, we turn our attention to some of the buildings on the west side of Market Street. This stereo-photograph was taken by Carl Meinerth *c.* 1860. He was the photographer who followed A. Gregory as a Portsmouth landscape photographer. All of his Portsmouth photographs were taken between 1860 and 1863 before he moved to Newburyport, Massachusetts.

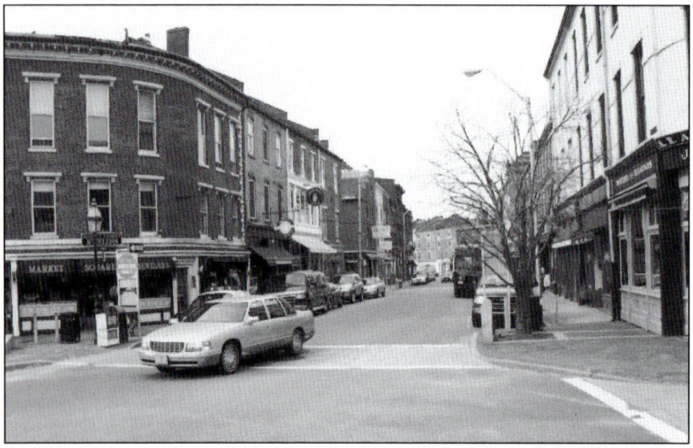

Market Street was the first center of local commerce. The street leads from the waterfront into Market Square (see the 1877 bird's-eye map). The cross-street walking areas are paved in stone. When looking at Market Street, one should also look at the 1813 fire map, because this was one of the areas completely destroyed in the first great fire (1802). That fire consumed the buildings at the corner of Market and Bow Streets, both sides of Market Street, both sides of Penhallow Street, and some of the buildings in Market Square and some on Court Street (now Pleasant Street). Market Street is still part of the shopping mecca of Portsmouth. The buildings have been preserved, remodeled for today's uses, and are representative of 19th-century brick architecture.

Standing in front of North Church, looking toward the east, one of the Davis Brothers' photographers took this picture of the Sheafe Block *c.* 1865. The Sheafe Block was built in 1807. It is one of two buildings that have a rounded front that faces into Market Square. The street-level section of the building has almost always been a store. The upper floors were converted from three stories to two stories in the latter part of the 19th century. The streets are Market, on the left and Daniel, on the right.

From *c.* 1760 to 1836, Market Street was the address of the New Hampshire State and Court House (see the 1813 fire map). While that old building was removed long ago, the square remains open in the heart of our town.

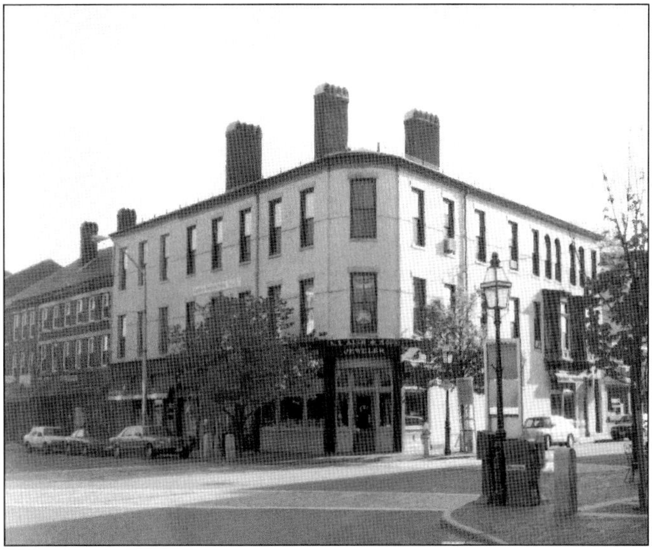

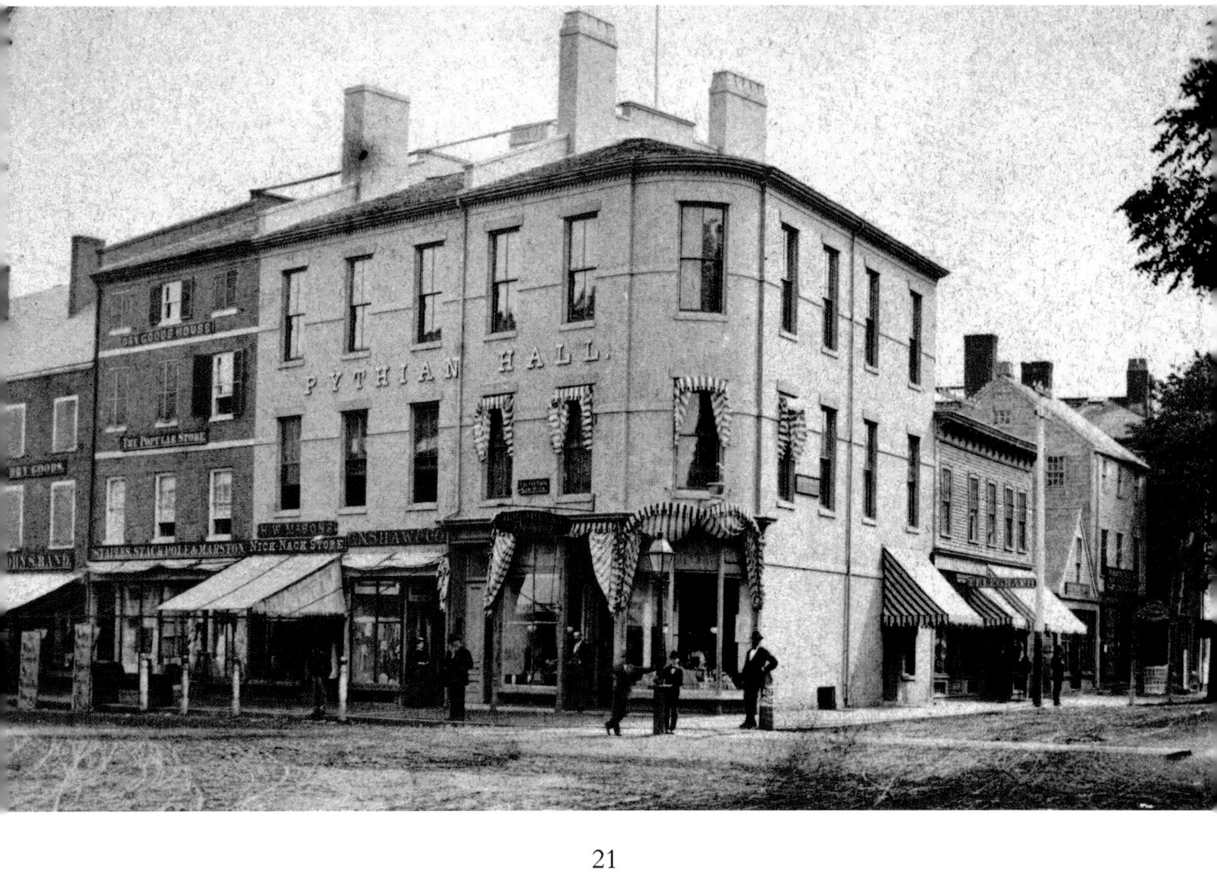

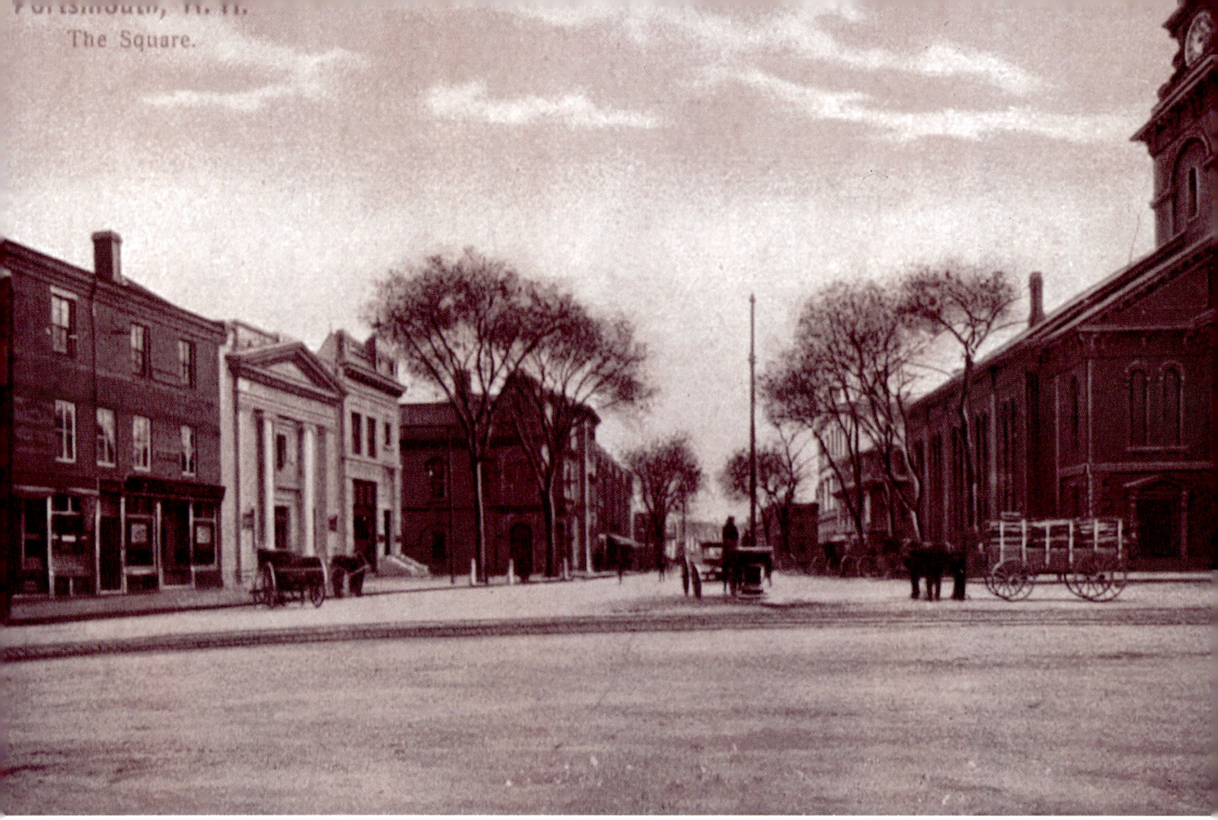

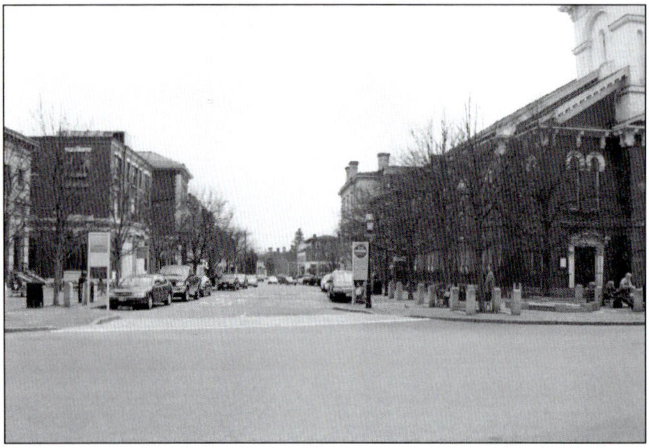

In this view looking down Pleasant Street toward State Street, Pleasant is hardly recognizable. Were it not for North Church, one would think it was some other street in town. At this end of Pleasant Street on the left was the financial zone of the city. In the old photograph, *c.* 1904, horses and buggies were the main transportation, and in the center of the entrance to Pleasant Street there was a fountain for the animals. In front of the fountain (just barely visible in the old photograph) is the curved arc of the Portsmouth trolley tracks. They were single tracks at this point, but just a few yards to the left, the tracks were double, as in front of North Church, where the trolley lines started to all destinations.

Looking toward Market Square from Daniel Street *c.* 1900, we see the Pearce Block on the immediate left. In the center left is North Church. In front of the church are two trolleys. The trolleys went from the center of Portsmouth to points north, via one of the ferries, to York, Maine, and to points south, including Hampton Beach and coastal stops along the way.

The Pearce Block has always had a store on the side that runs along Daniel Street. Today, just as in the old photograph, there is an advertising sign on the side of the building.

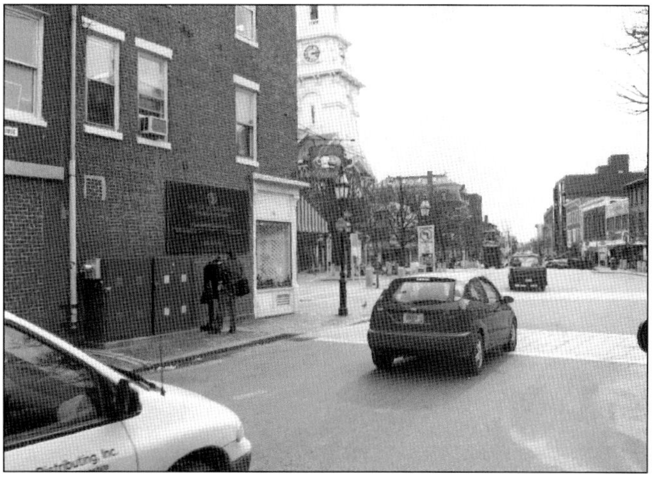

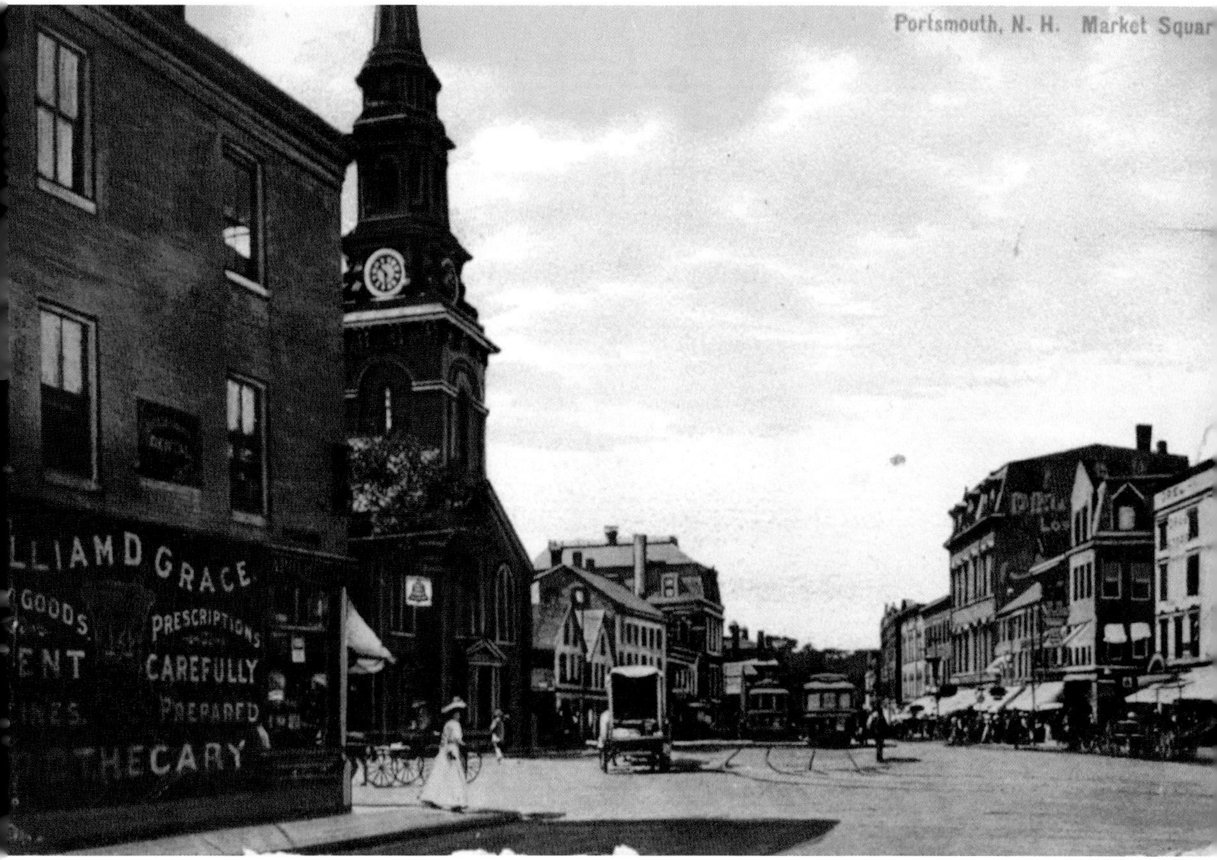

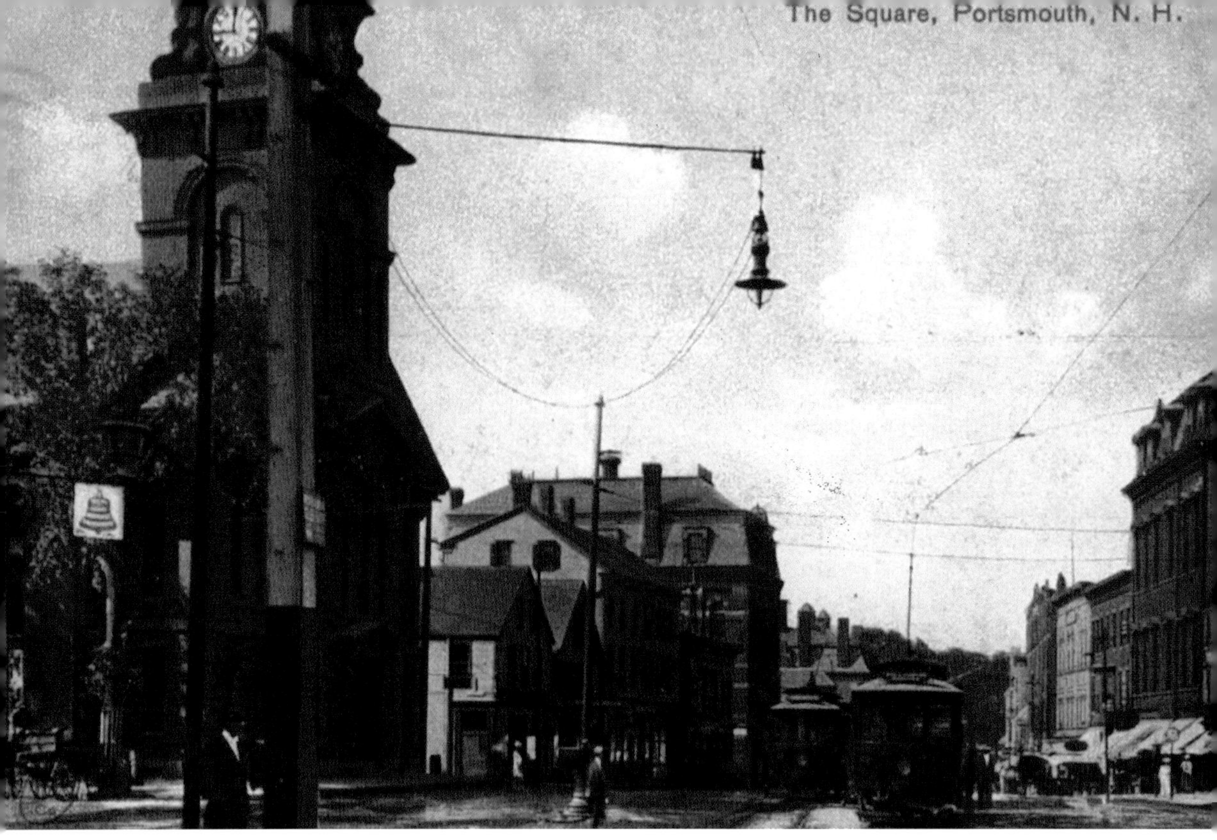

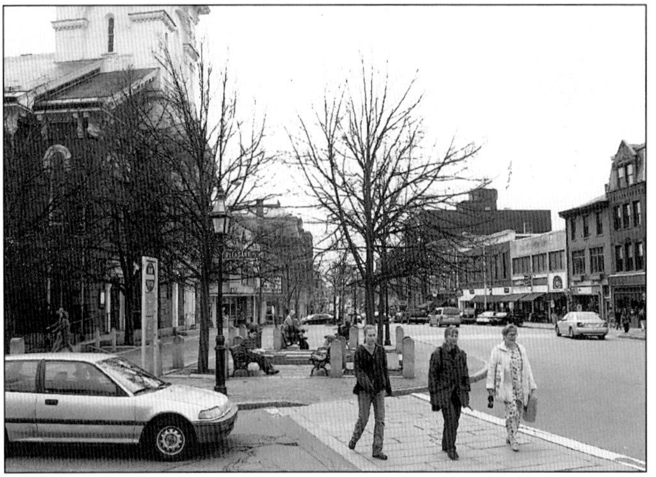

Taking a closer look at the square in front of North Church, we can clearly see the trolleys. Meeting friends in Market Square has been a long-standing tradition for people in Portsmouth, or visitors to the city. There were two trolley companies that picked up travelers in the square. One was the Portsmouth Electric Railroad, which was established in 1899 and had an estimated 20 miles of track mainly around the greater Portsmouth area. The other was the Portsmouth, Kittery, Dover, and York Street Railway. They claimed over 40 miles of track in addition to the trip on one of the ferries to the other side of the Piscataqua River.

Near where there were trolleys and tracks, there is now a brick paved area to sit, relax, and enjoy the square. With crosswalks that offers the pedestrian the right-of-way, the square is still the place to be when visiting downtown Portsmouth.

North Church, *c.* 1900, is the landmark most people associate with Portsmouth. From local folks to visiting national politicians, this is the backdrop where they want to be seen. If one looks at the 1813 fire map (pages 84–85), North Church is identified as the Meeting House.

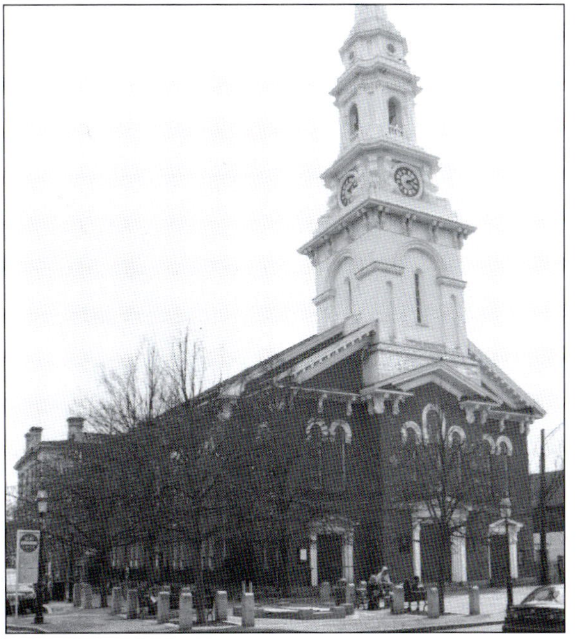

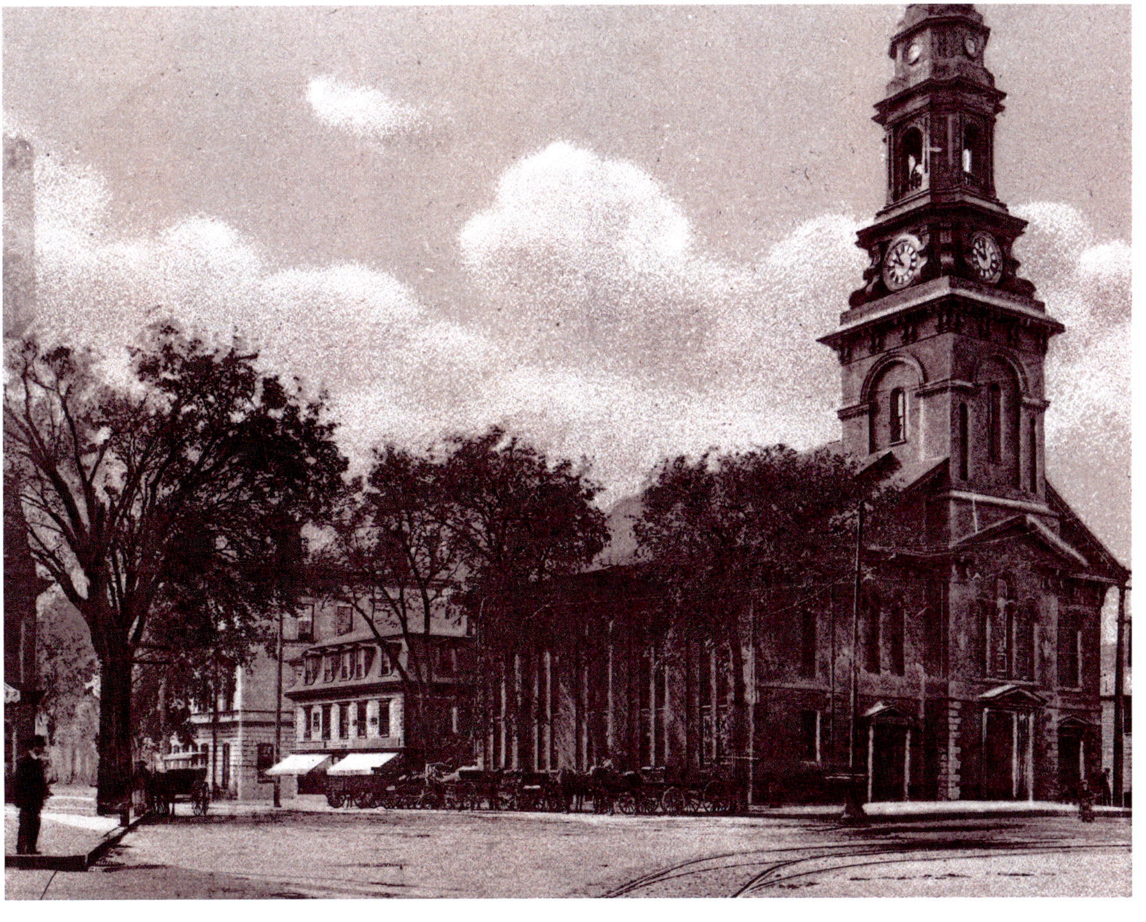

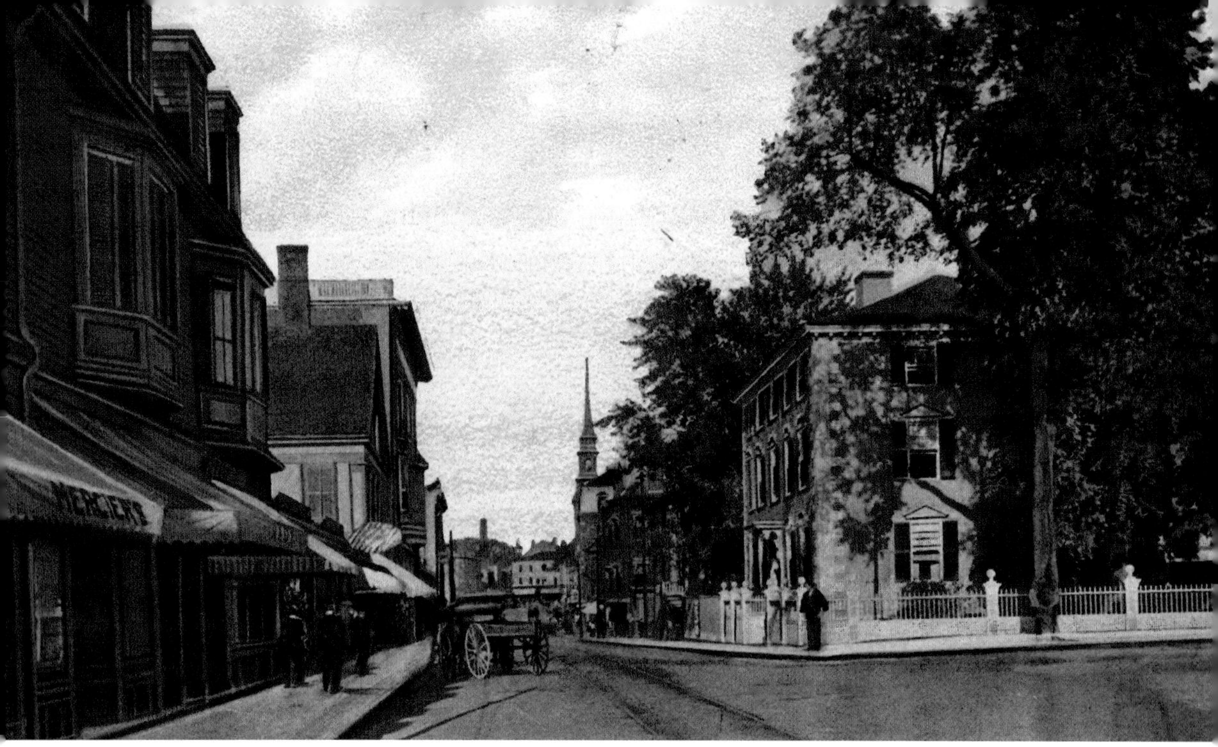

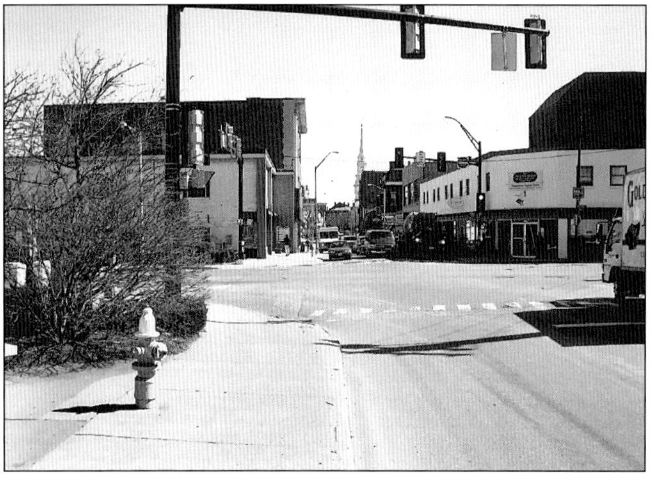

In this *c.* 1910 photo postcard (taken from in front of the Portsmouth Public Library and looking back up Congress Street), most of the buildings are not identifiable, but the steeple of North Church marks Market Square. In the old photograph, there are trolley tracks; this line went to the end of Islington Street, an area called the Plains, which was supposed to be a city of its own but always remained a part of Portsmouth.

The wood-framed buildings in the left foreground of the old photograph were taken down to make room for Maplewood Avenue, creating a four-way intersection. In comparing the two images, only the multistoried building on the left and the steeple of the church give clues to the location.

Some streets become even more obscured by the modernization that has taken place in Portsmouth. State Street, shown from the intersection with Pleasant Street, would be difficult to identify had the photographer, Carl Meinerth, not labeled the photograph, which he took in 1860. What was once a tree-lined street is now another concrete, brick, and macadam streetscape with wires and telephone poles. The old charm of a country town has been removed in favor of the business environment of a small modern city.

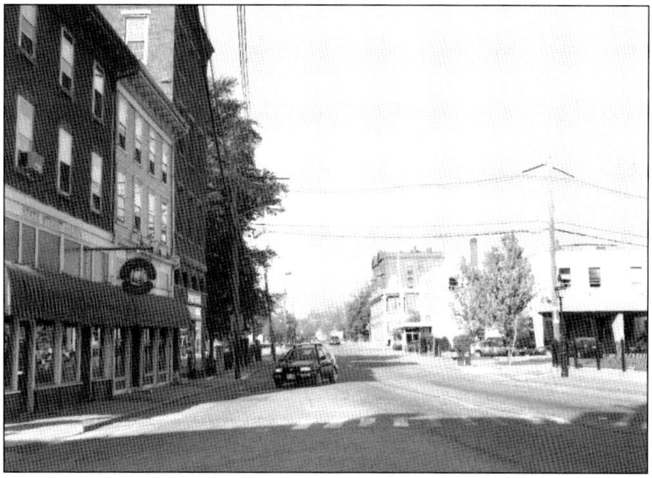

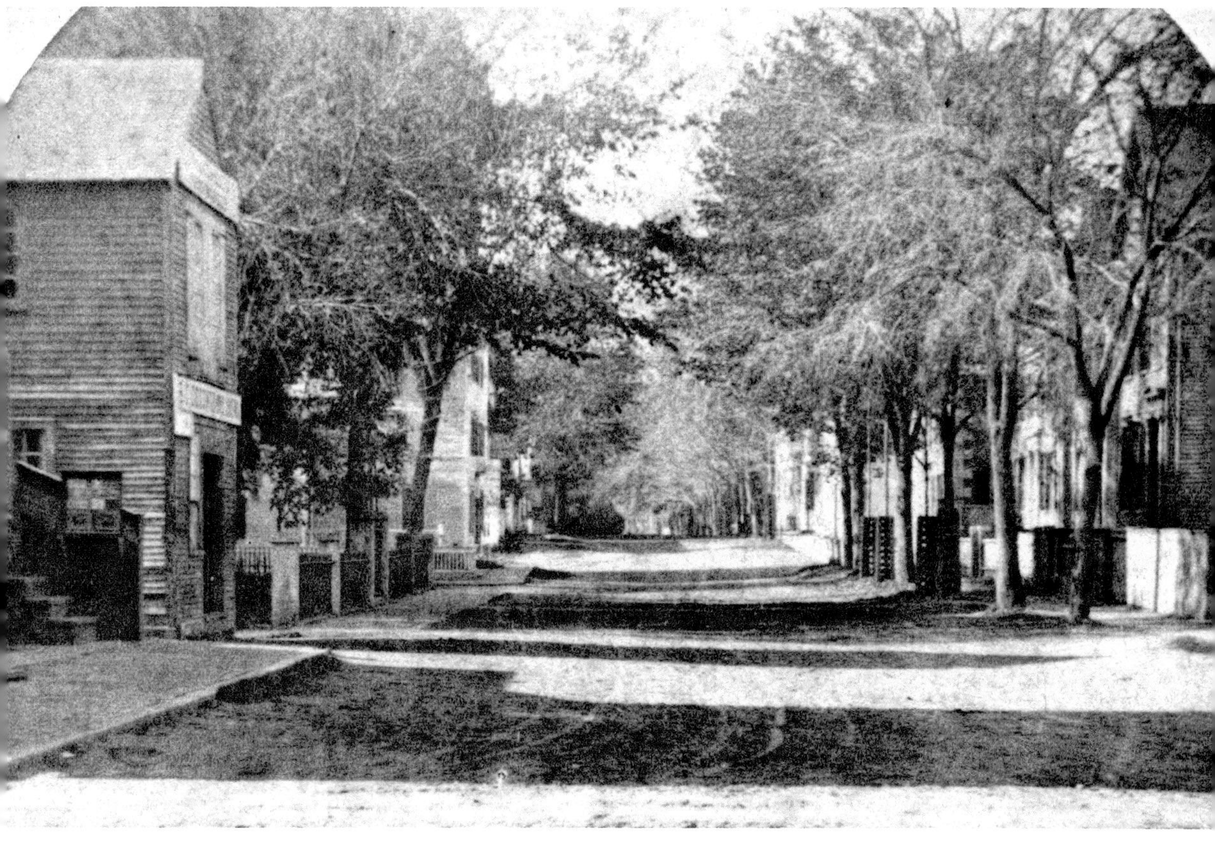

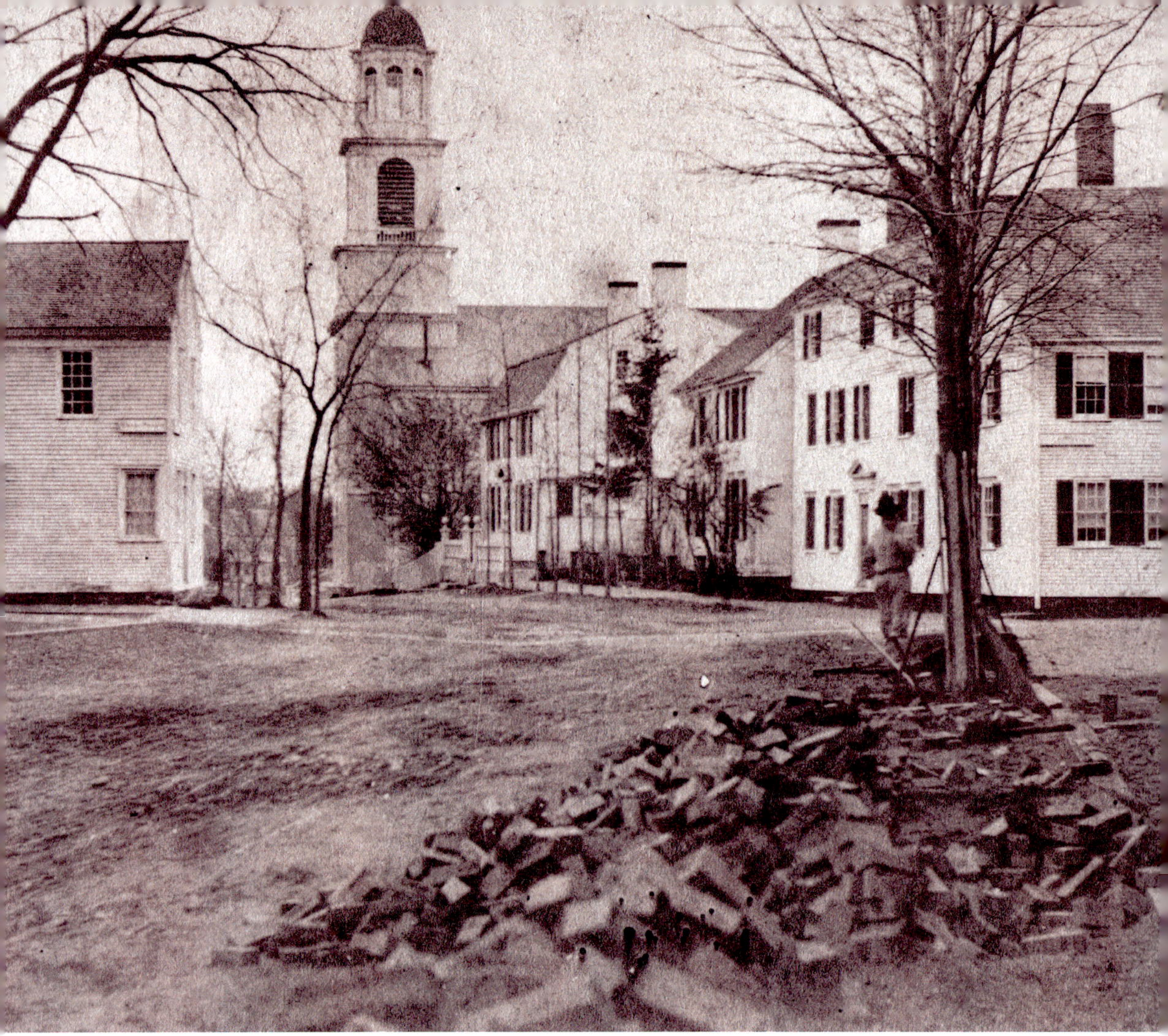

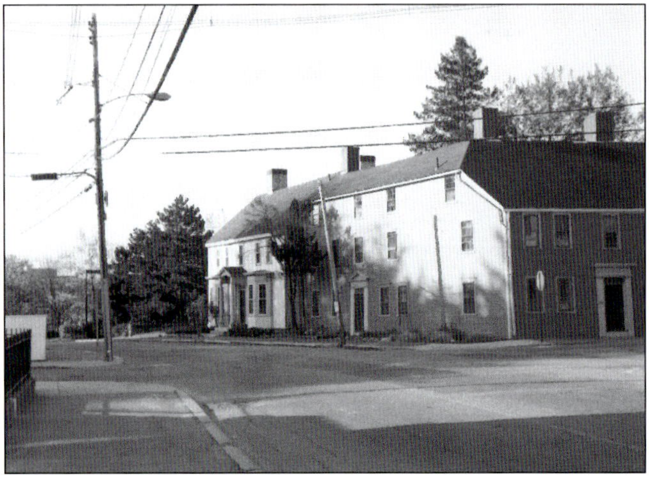

Another street that has changed greatly over the past 140 years is Pleasant Street. Carl Meinerth took this photograph *c.* 1860 when the city was laying bricks for its sidewalks. The view shows the buildings on Court Street and the first Universalist church, on the corner of Pleasant Street and Junkins Avenue. The first house on the corner (right) was destroyed by the fire of 1813 (see pages 84–85). The current building on the corner replaced Daniel Webster's second residence in Portsmouth. Had the second corner building not been in the photograph, finding its location would have been difficult.

The line of brick buildings facing Market Square on Congress Street is shown below *c.* 1890. Today's photograph is almost the same as the earlier one. The building with the arched fanlight over the door was originally used by an insurance company. It is now the Portsmouth Athenaeum, a nonprofit membership library and museum incorporated in 1817. The members have access to an extensive collection of books, periodicals, maps, and newspapers. The Portsmouth Athenaeum also holds public meetings and informative history talks. It opens its doors to the public every week.

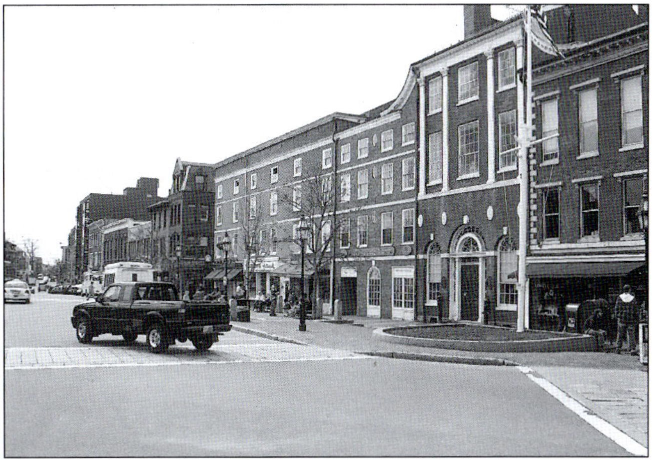

While the sidewalk has been widened and space has been provided with benches for people to rest and wait for public transportation, the buildings have all undergone renovations to keep the outside appearances the same while making the inside suitable for today's uses.

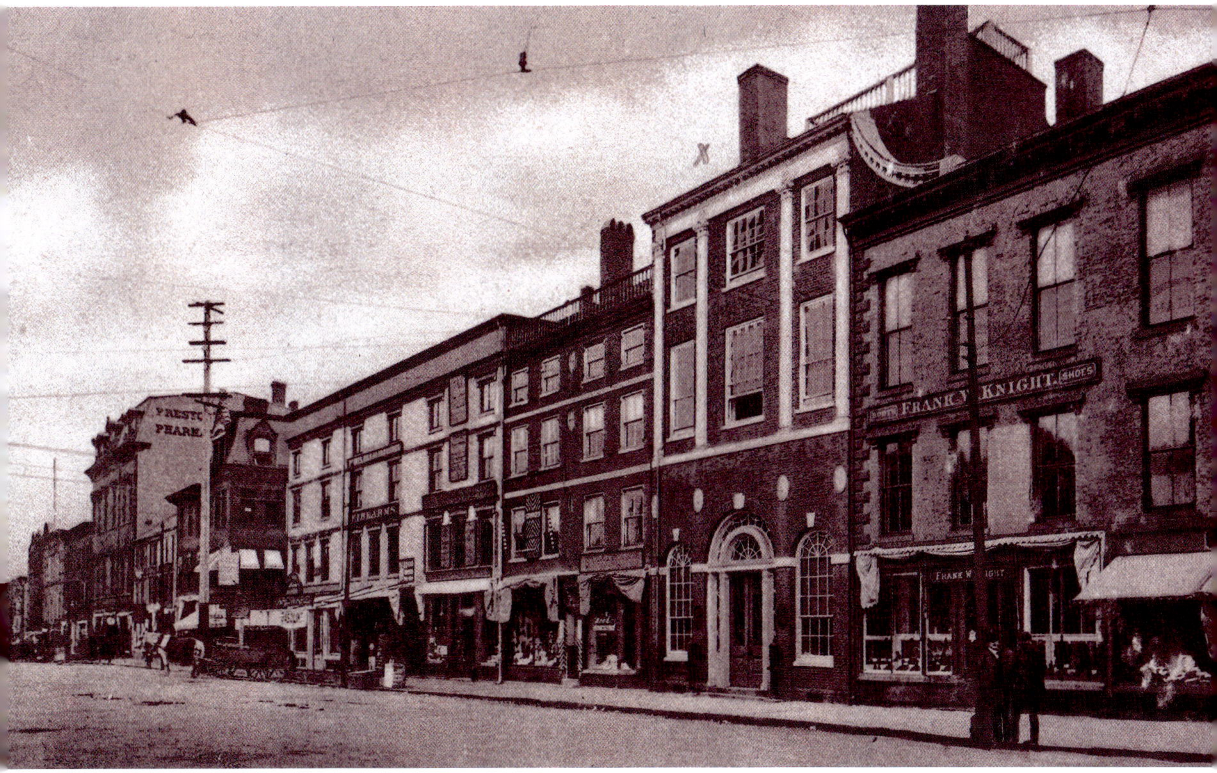

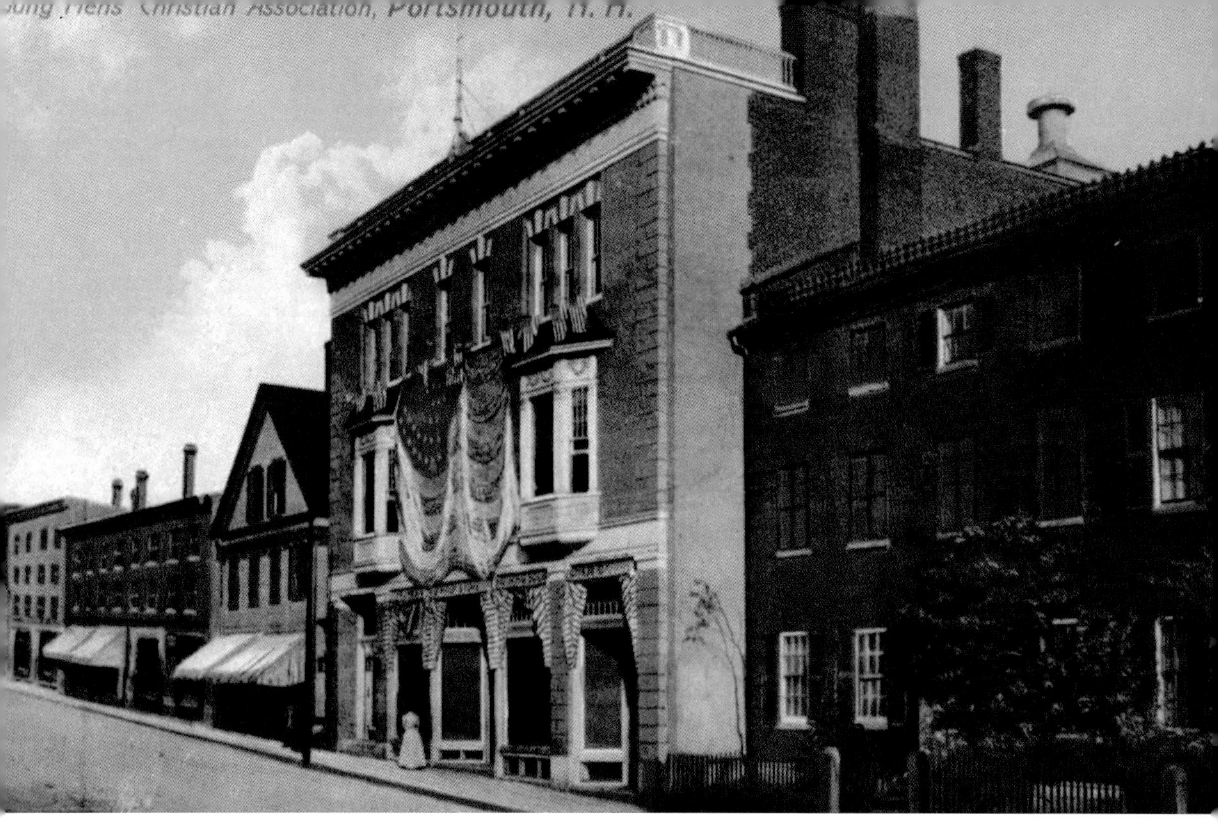

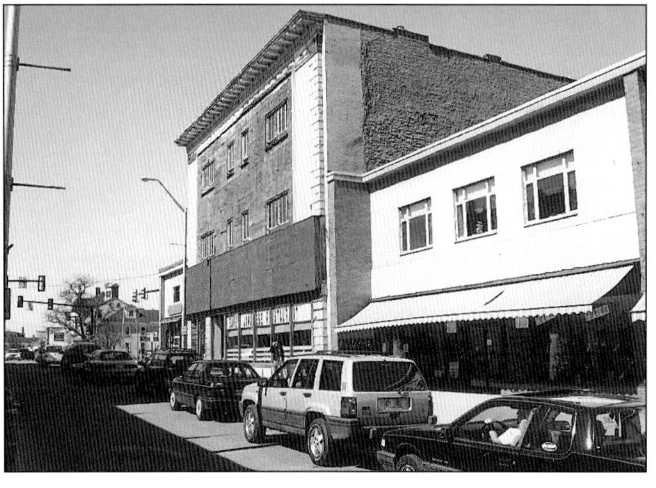

A sign of the modernization is clearly shown in some of the central business district buildings. Where the Young Men's Christian Association (YMCA) was once housed, we now have a Japanese restaurant. The stark front of this building is a reminder that we cannot always keep the look of our older downtown businesses. Beyond the YMCA, all the buildings were taken down. While there is another shop before the road on the other side of the YMCA, the tie to the past is gone.

Going from one end of the central business district to almost the other, we find on Daniel Street the first Portsmouth High School. When it was built in 1858, many citizens found it hard to believe that a town the size of Portsmouth could afford such a large schoolhouse as this new building on the corner of Chapel and Daniel Streets. This school building was the first one erected with more than two rooms. For the next 50 years, this was the high school. In the 20th century, however, the school population outgrew the building. A new school was built on the other side of the library. The city offices, which had been in rooms in one of the buildings on Pleasant Street near the square, moved into the old high school.

From 1908 until just a few years ago, this was the city hall, but the city also outgrew the building. Today, it is privately owned and has been renovated as an office building.

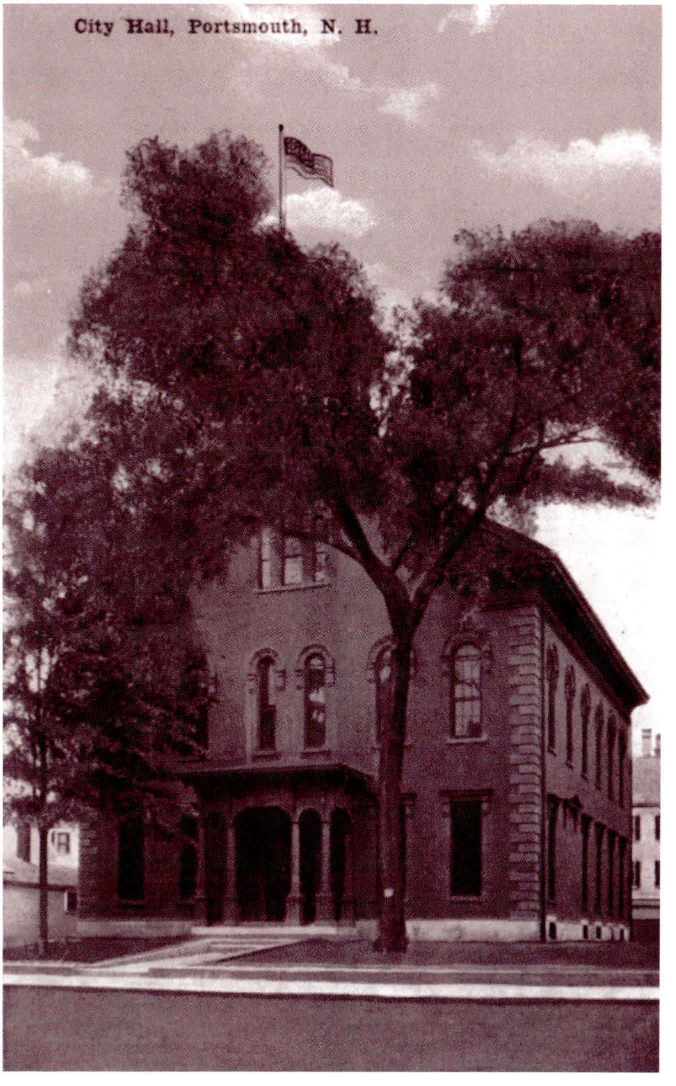

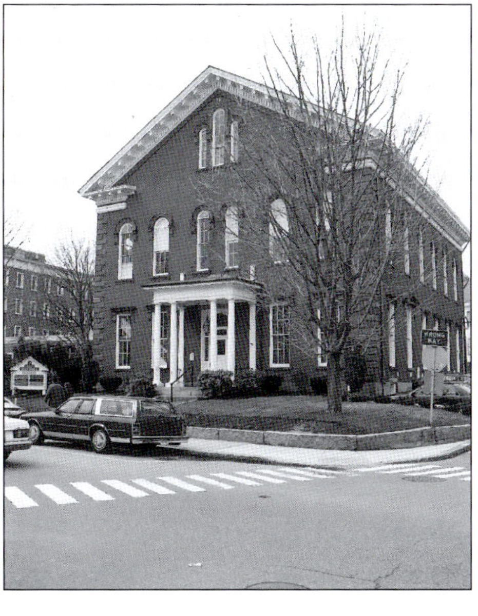

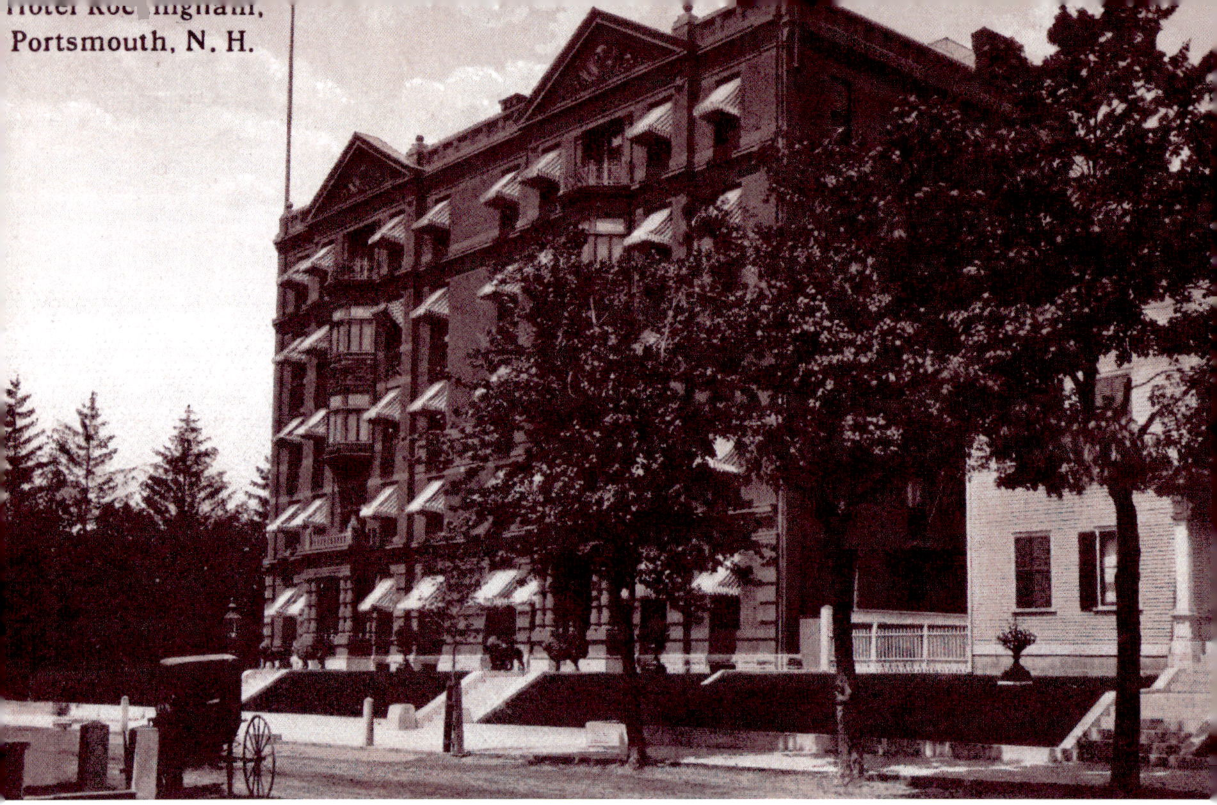

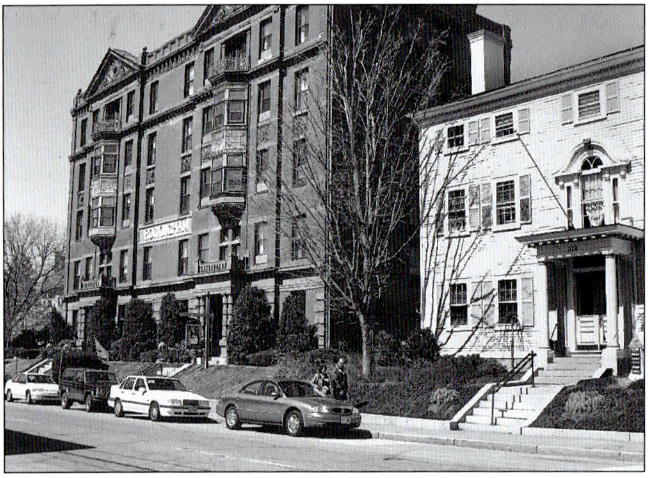

While some buildings lose their original appearances, others retain practically all of their features. A great example of this is the Rockingham Hotel, remodeled and extended in 1888 by Frank Jones, a local entrepreneur and businessman. Before Jones remodeled the building, it was the residence of Woodbury Langdon, the elder brother of Gov. John Langdon. The Rockingham Hotel ran as a hotel for nearly 100 years before becoming condominiums on the upper floors and the Library Restaurant on the ground floor. Except for the awnings, foundation shrubs, some ornaments, and a few trees, the building looks the same today as it did in years past. This postcard photograph was taken *c.* 1910.

Visitors who come to Portsmouth are often amazed at the diversity of our religious intensity that helped define who Portsmouth people are. Some churches, such as our downtown St. John's Episcopal Church, drew more people to its dedication than the entire population of Portsmouth. North Church, pictured here, has been the downtown landmark for most of our history.

Chapter 2
Churches, Schools, Public Buildings, and Monuments

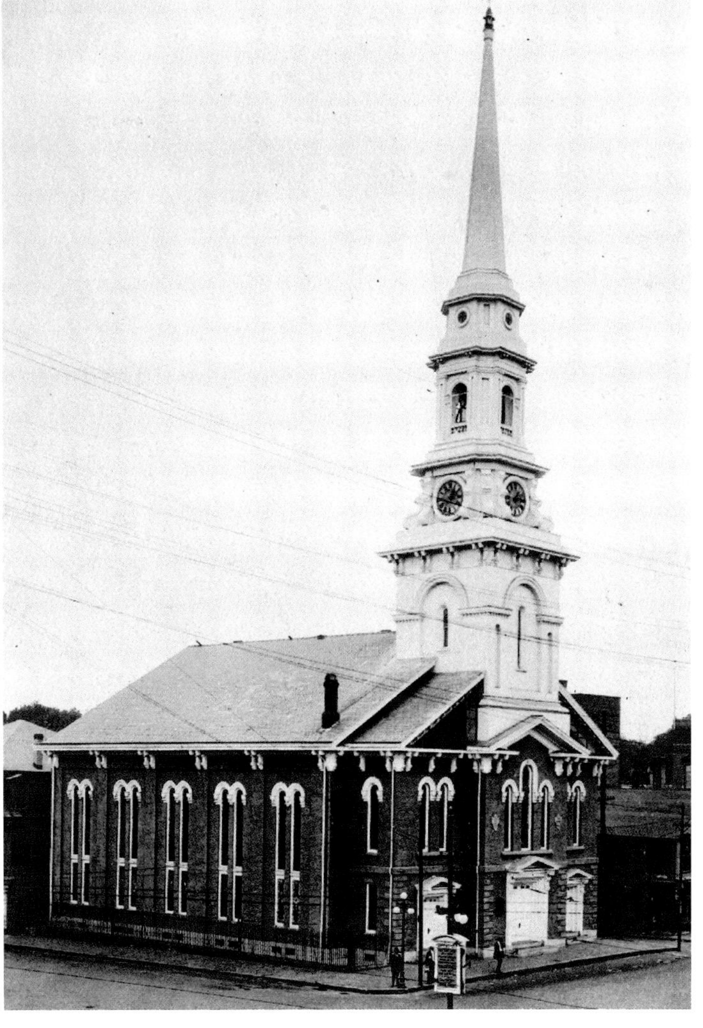

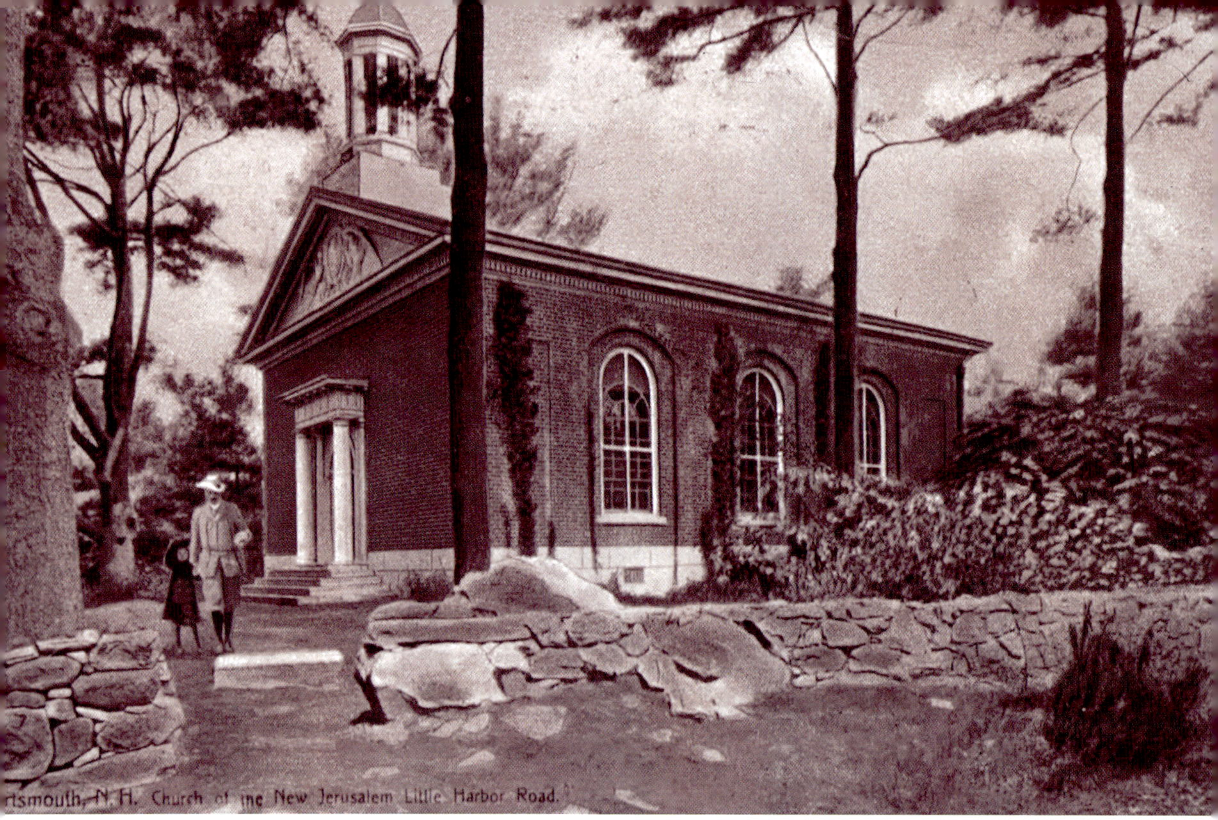

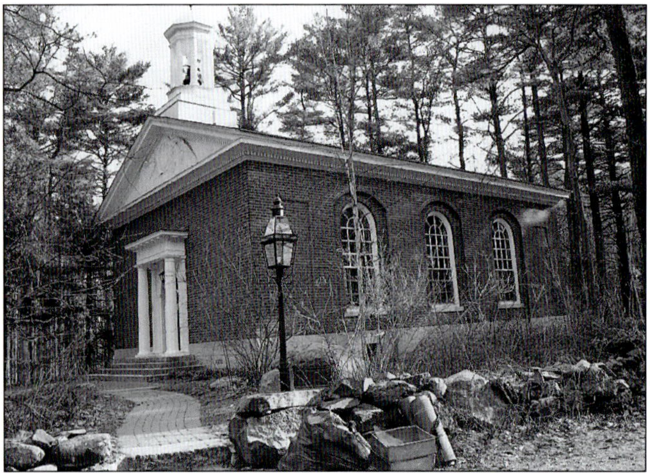

One church that is known to only a few local residents is the chapel on Little Harbor Road. Arthur A. Carey, a summer resident from Boston, built the chapel in 1902. The chapel is nondenominational and was built along the Carey property line for use by families who lived along Little Harbor Road. It continues to hold summer services with visiting guest ministers. Carey left an endowment for the chapel's future. Little Harbor Road is off Sagamore Road, just past the large cemetery.

The second Universalist church was built on the location of the first at the corner of Pleasant Street and Junkins Avenue. The first church was made of wood and burned to ground in 1896. The second church was brick, finished in 1897, and dedicated that same year. In 1947, that building was also destroyed by fire. The block of land was sold, and the site is now occupied by a parking lot, which hosts a popular farmers' market on Saturdays in warmer weather. On the 1877 bird's-eye map (pages 90–91), Junkins Avenue has not yet been built. Find Pleasant Street, starting at Market Square, and then follow it to the first church near a grassy, wooded area.

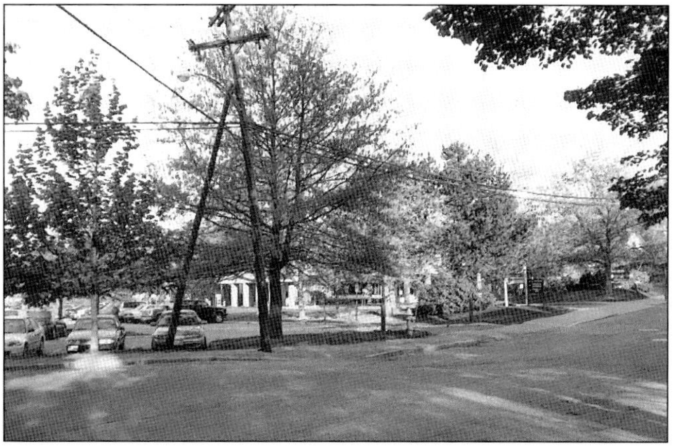

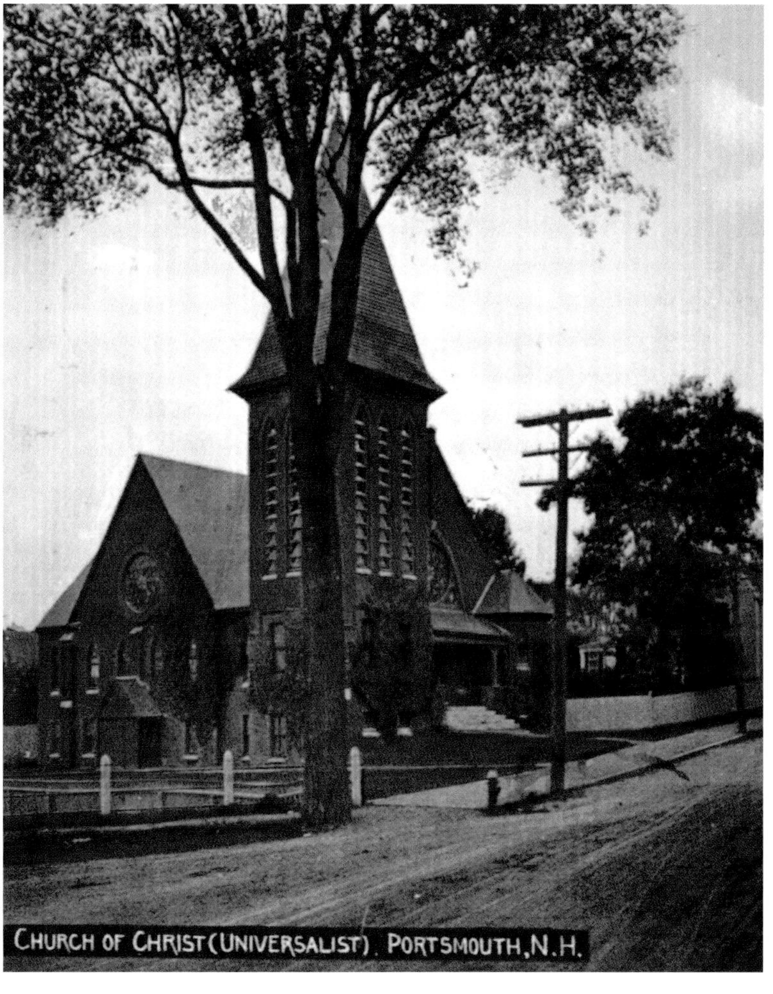

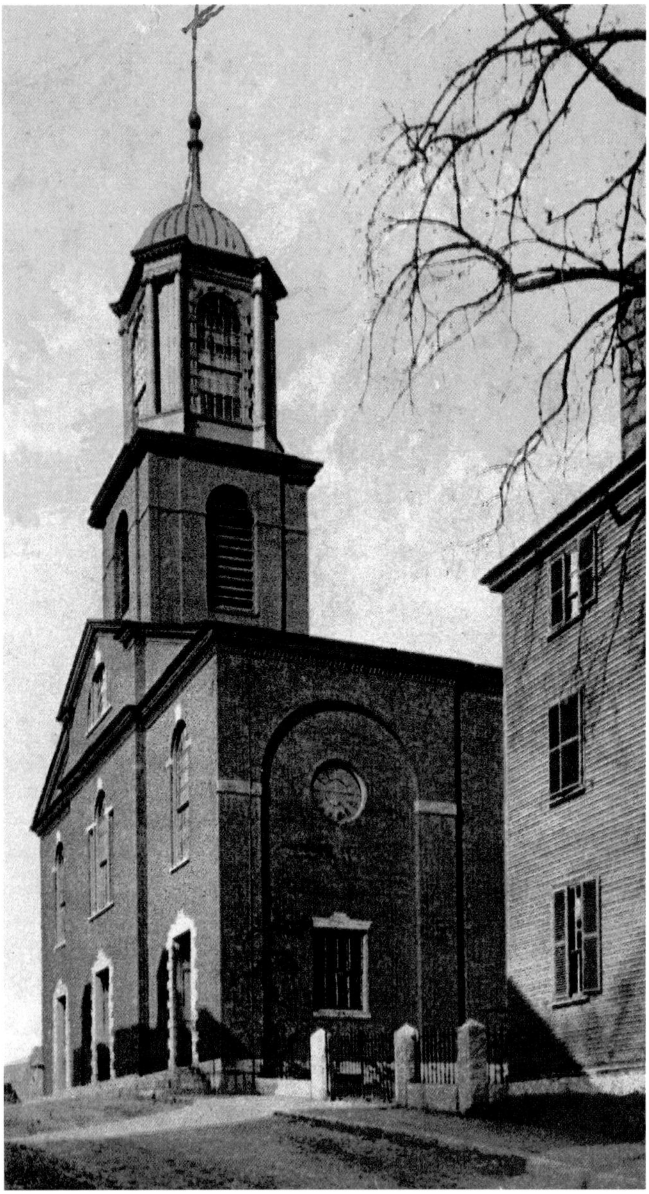

St. John's Episcopal Church is on Chapel Street. The street is named for the Queen's Chapel that was the first church. It was destroyed by fire in 1806 (see pages 84–85). St. John's was built in 1807. The church is a tourist attraction because it holds the "Vinegar Bible," published in 1717, and the Brattle Organ, which is one of the oldest in the country. The church bell was liberated from the French at Louisburg in the mid-18th century and was later recast by Paul Revere. Today's St. John's looks like it has in years past, with the exception that a brick parish hall has replaced the wooden building in the old photograph, *c.* 1907.

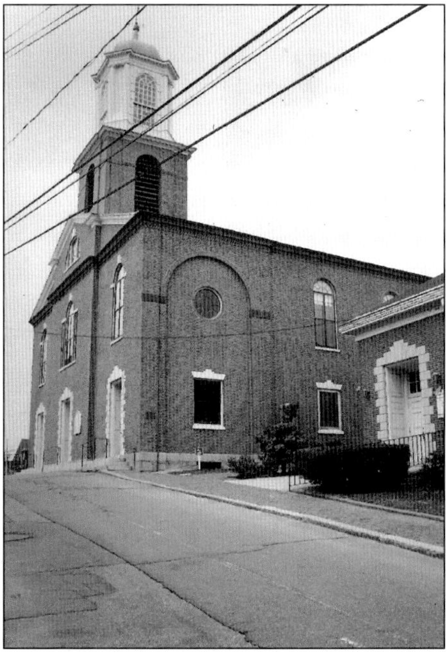

Below, a 1920s automobile is parked next to the Unitarian Universalist Church, also known as South Church. This church, located on State Street, is the only Greek Revival public building that survives. It was built in 1826 during Dr. Nathan Parker's ministry. At that time, there were two Congregational parishes: North Church and South Church. The communicants of South Church, by the persuasions of Dr. Parker, became Unitarian rather than Congregational.

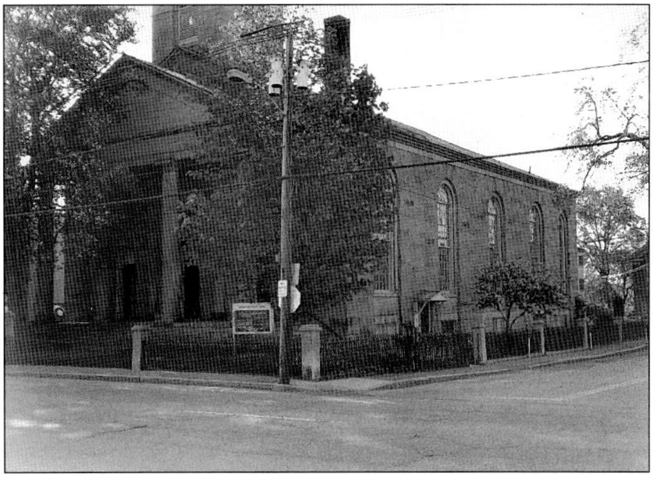

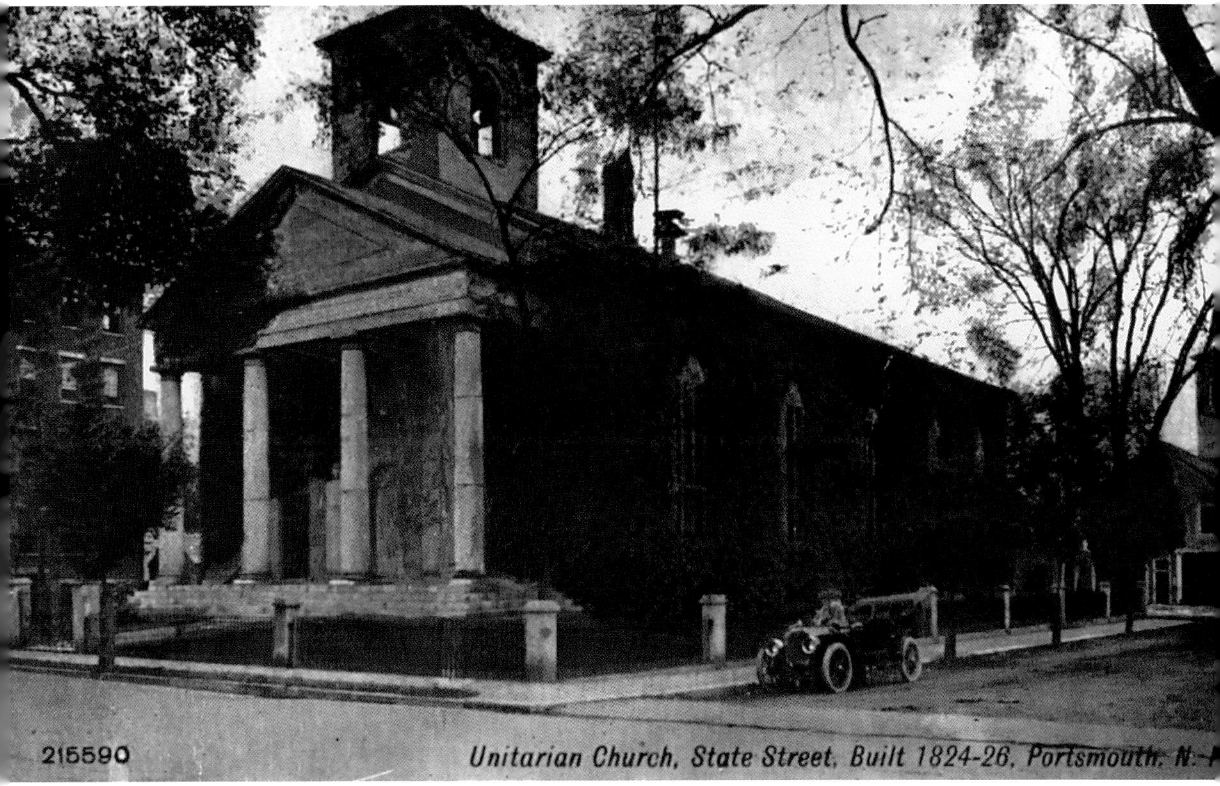

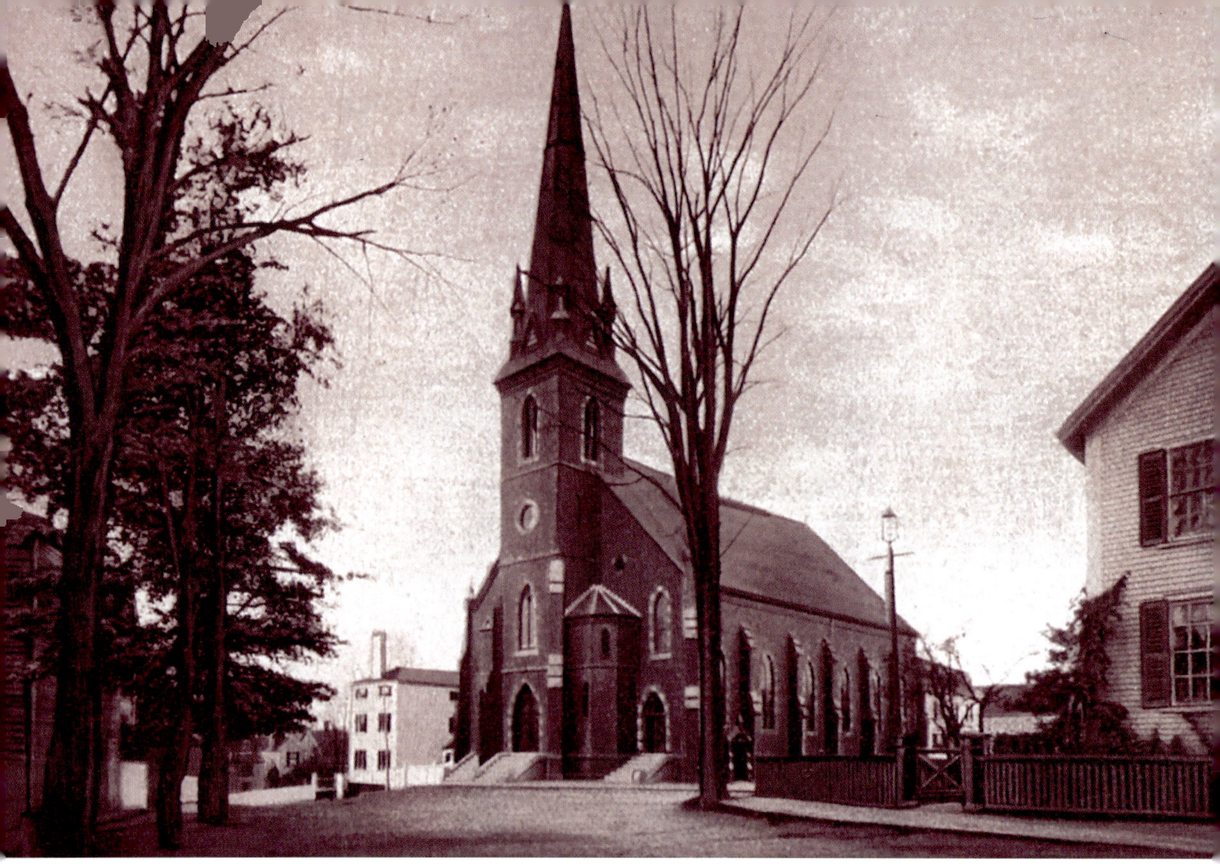

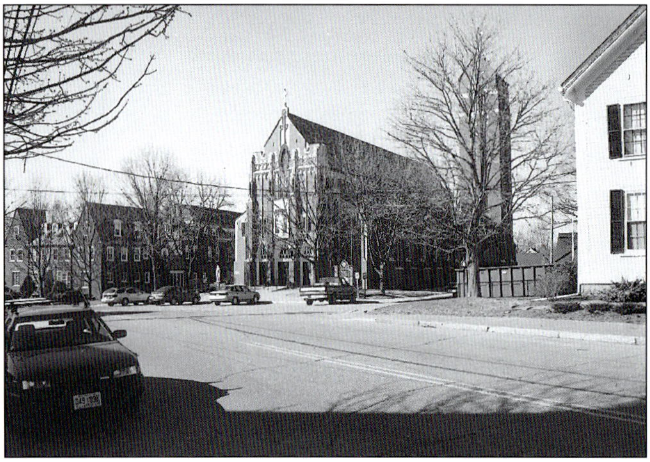

The second Catholic church, pictured here *c.* 1900, was erected in 1872. The first church building was built in 1852 but was destroyed in a fire 19 years later. The second church was initially named St. Mary's Catholic Church, but when it was dedicated, it was renamed as the Immaculate Conception Catholic Church. The building was brick, and the steeple faced onto Summer Street. This church was taken down in 1933–1934 when the communicants outgrew its seating capacity. The third church is set back from the street, and the steeple now faces Chatham Street. The stained-glass windows and pews (from the second church) were installed in the new church.

Christ Episcopal Church was one of the most beautiful churches in Portsmouth. Built in 1880–1883, it was dedicated on July 3, 1883. It was constructed of native stone taken from Leach's or Murphy's Island in the back-channel waters running between the Piscataqua River and Little Harbor. This church gained national prominence when it was selected as one of the places nondenominational services would be held for delegates from Russia and Japan during the peace treaty negotiations of 1905, which took place at the Portsmouth Naval Shipyard. Christ Church was located on Madison Street at the end of Austin Street. In 1963, it was destroyed by fire. As the neighborhood had changed, the congregation did not rebuild on Madison Street; instead, they built a new brick church on Lafayette Road.

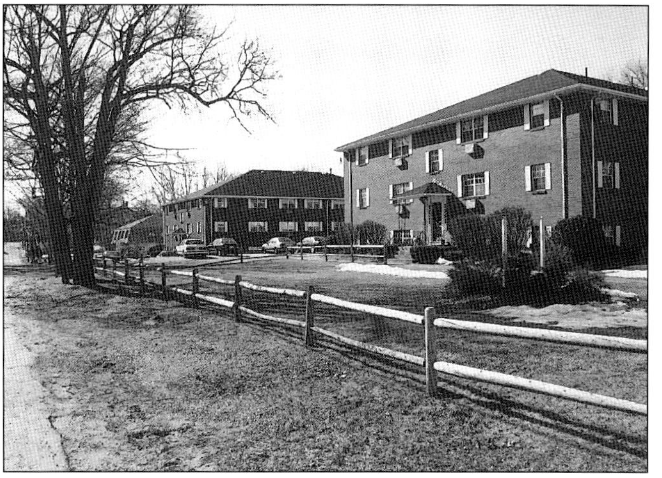

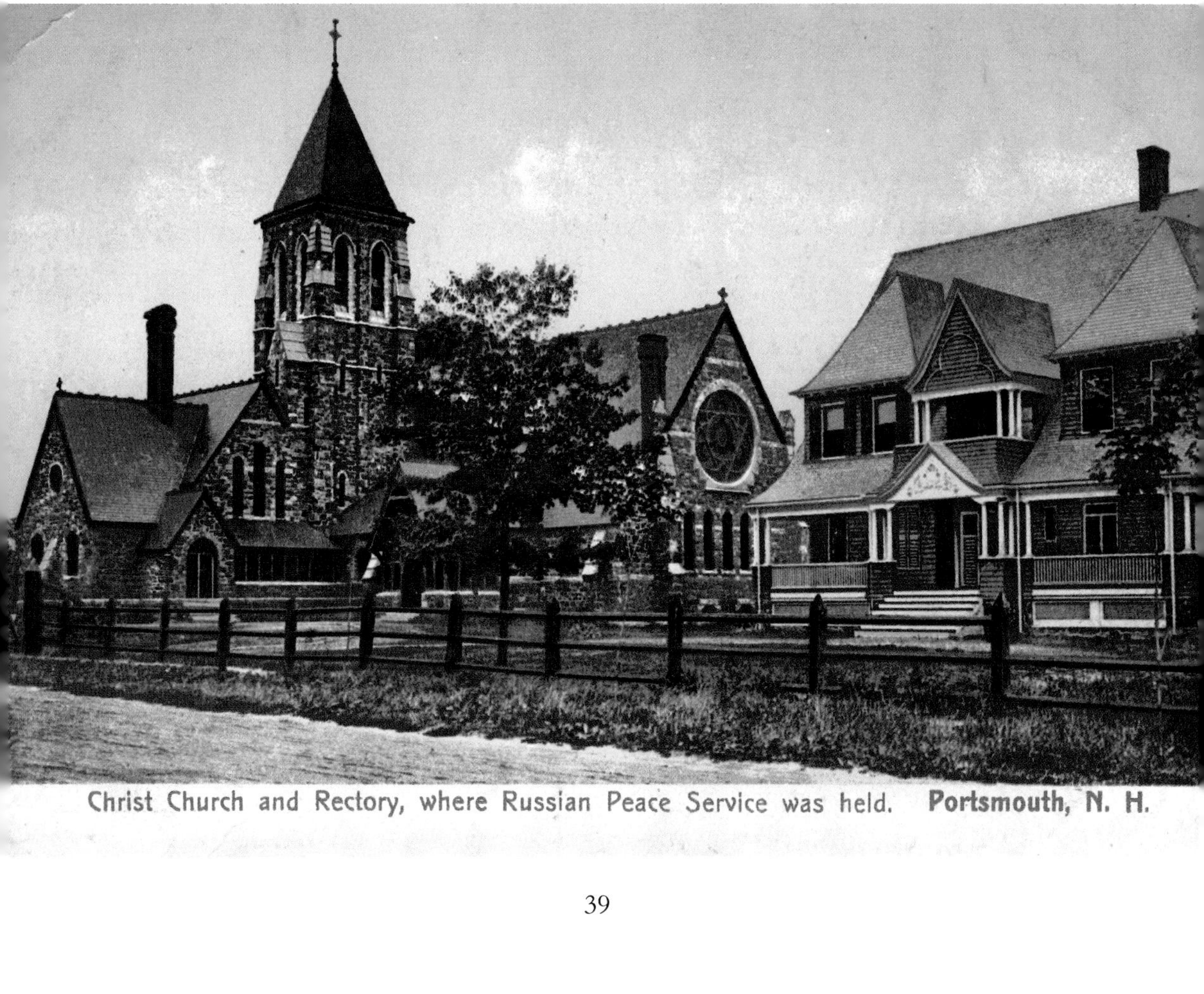

Christ Church and Rectory, where Russian Peace Service was held. Portsmouth, N. H.

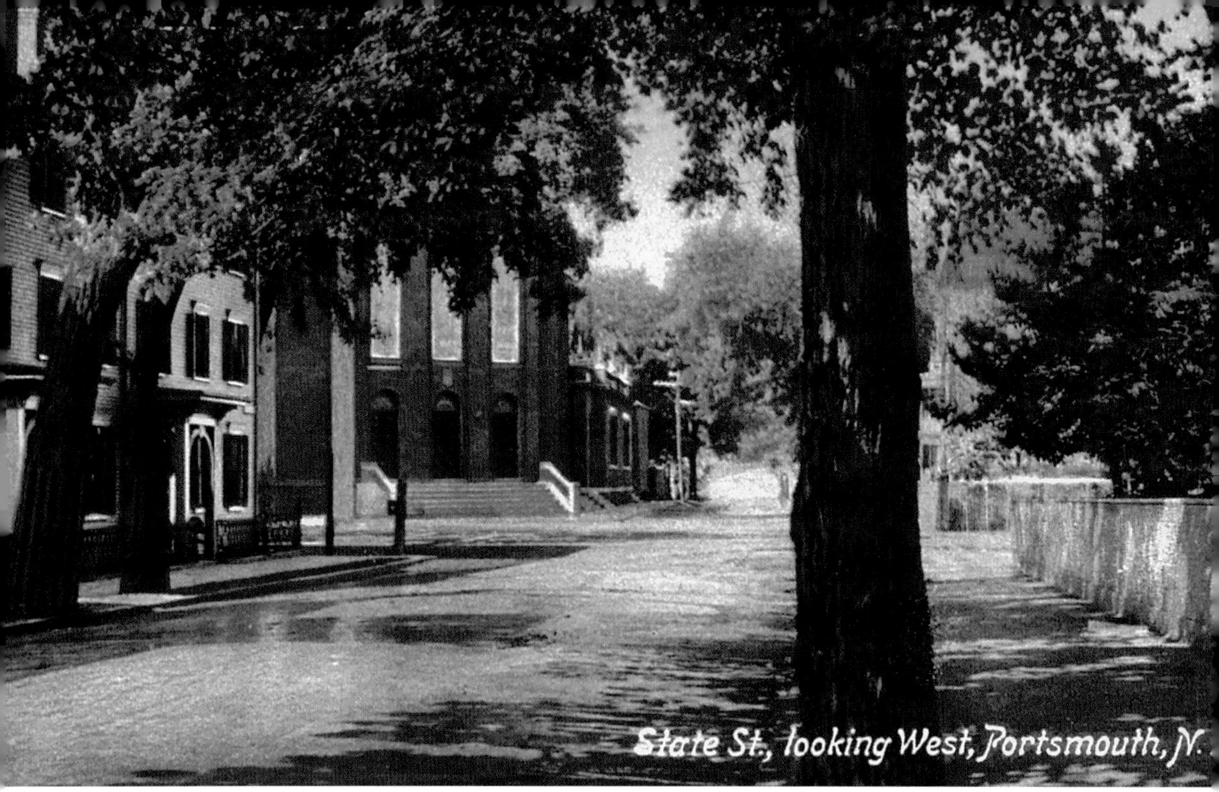

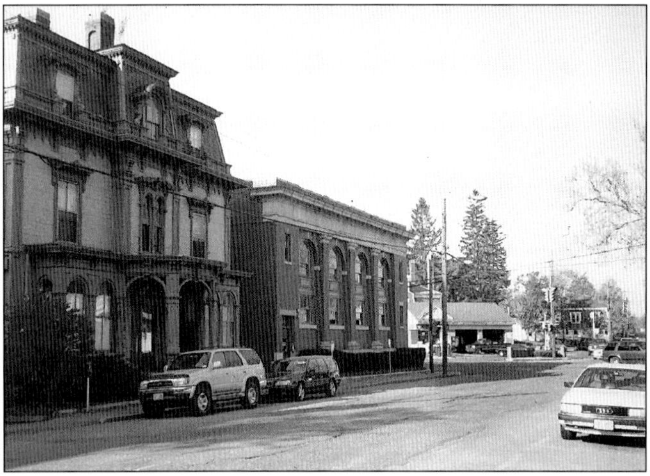

Shown from a point approximately in front of the John Paul Jones House, the corner of State and Middle Streets used to be the site of a Baptist church. In the old photograph, *c.* 1920, the church is the last building on the left. Only the ground floor of the church can be seen, as the foliage of the trees obscures the rest. The first church was built in 1828. It was followed by another church, built on the same location in 1852. It remained on this corner until the 1950s, when it was taken down and replaced with a filling station. The Baptist church is on Middle Street at Haymarket Square. Today, State Street is just barely recognizable, as most of the buildings and trees have been removed or replaced. (Postcard courtesy of Frederick Gray Jr.)

Portsmouth High School, *c.* 1908, was relocated from its place on the corner of Chapel and Daniel Streets to this new building on Islington Street, opposite Bridge Street and immediately to the west of the Portsmouth Public Library. The new building was much larger than the previous one and served the city for about 50 years. As with the previous school, however, the population in Portsmouth continued to grow, and this building once again became obsolete. The new high school was built farther away from downtown, and this high school was remodeled and renamed the Farragut Apartments. It is still in use today as a home for many of Portsmouth's senior citizens.

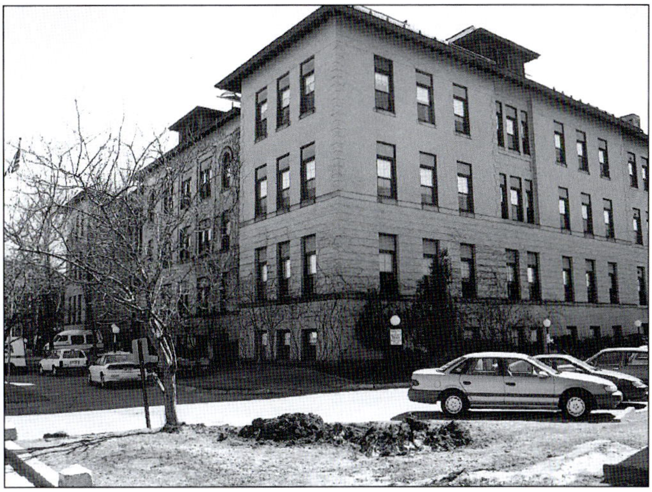

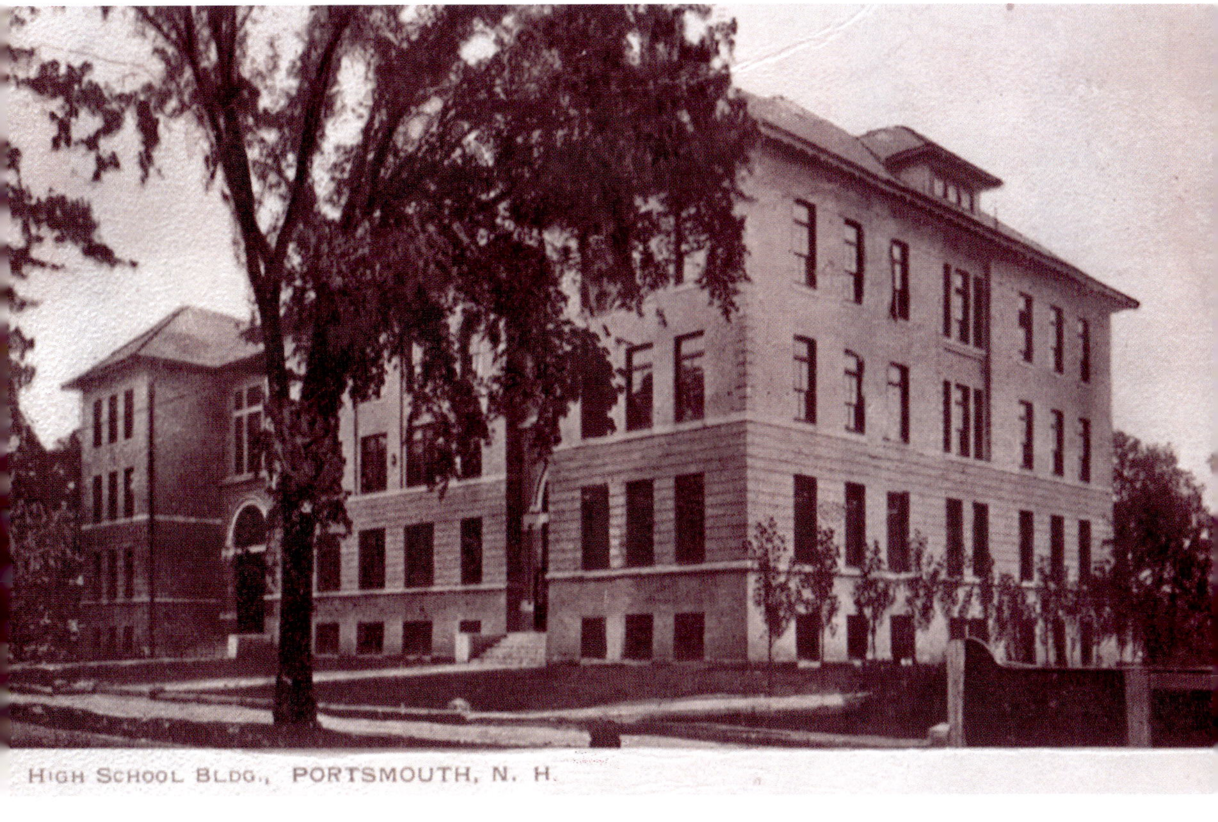

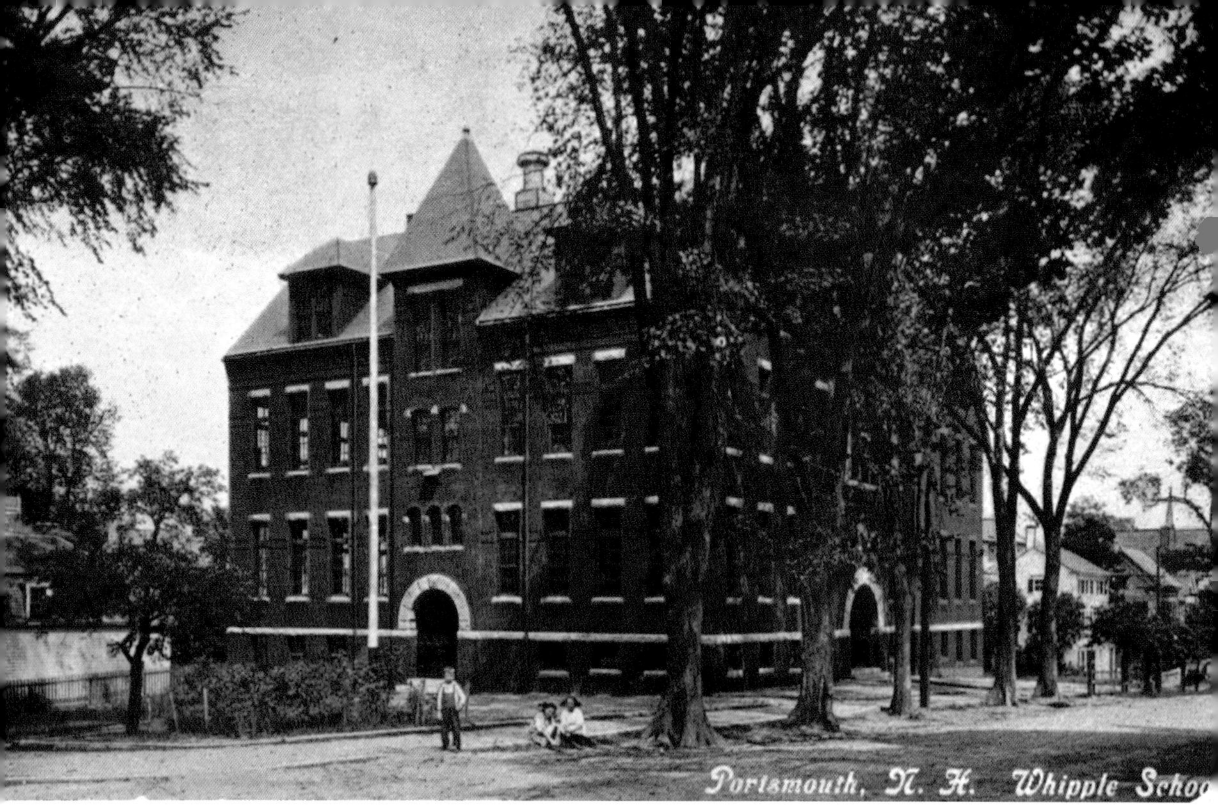

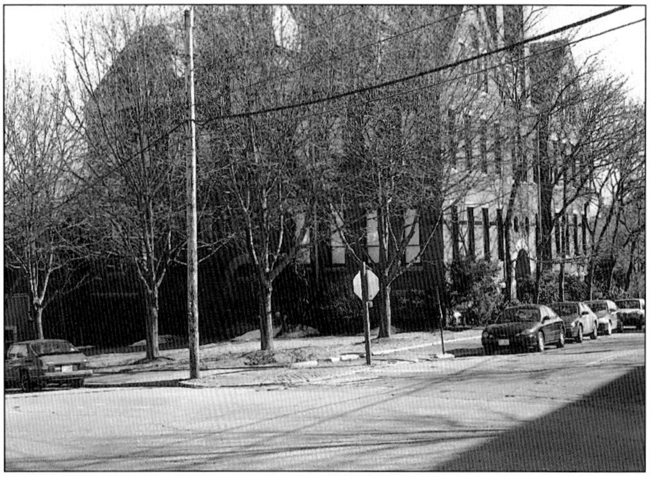

The Whipple School, *c.* 1900, is located on the corner of State and Summer Streets. The school was erected in 1887 as a school for seventh- and eighth-grade students. It was named for William Whipple, a Portsmouth resident and one of the signers of the Declaration of Independence. When the population of the city outgrew the capacity of this school, the building became another one of our recycled renovated buildings. Now the Whipple School is Whipple House and contains a number of condominiums.

Around the corner from the Immaculate Conception Church, on Austin Street, the Catholic community built a parochial school for their children's education in 1887. The building was drastically renovated in 1904 (the approximate date of the older photograph). When the renovations were completed, the school was reopened, with classrooms and teaching sisters available for 500 grade school children. The outside of the building looks the same today as it did almost 100 years ago. To provide a space for children to play, the street is blocked off to traffic on Austin Street during school hours.

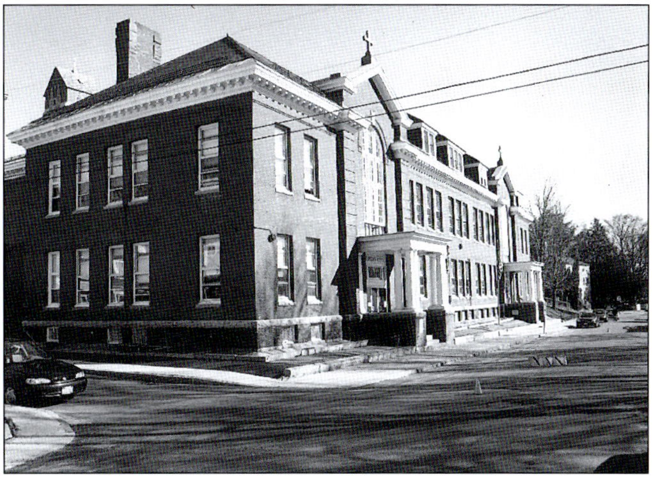

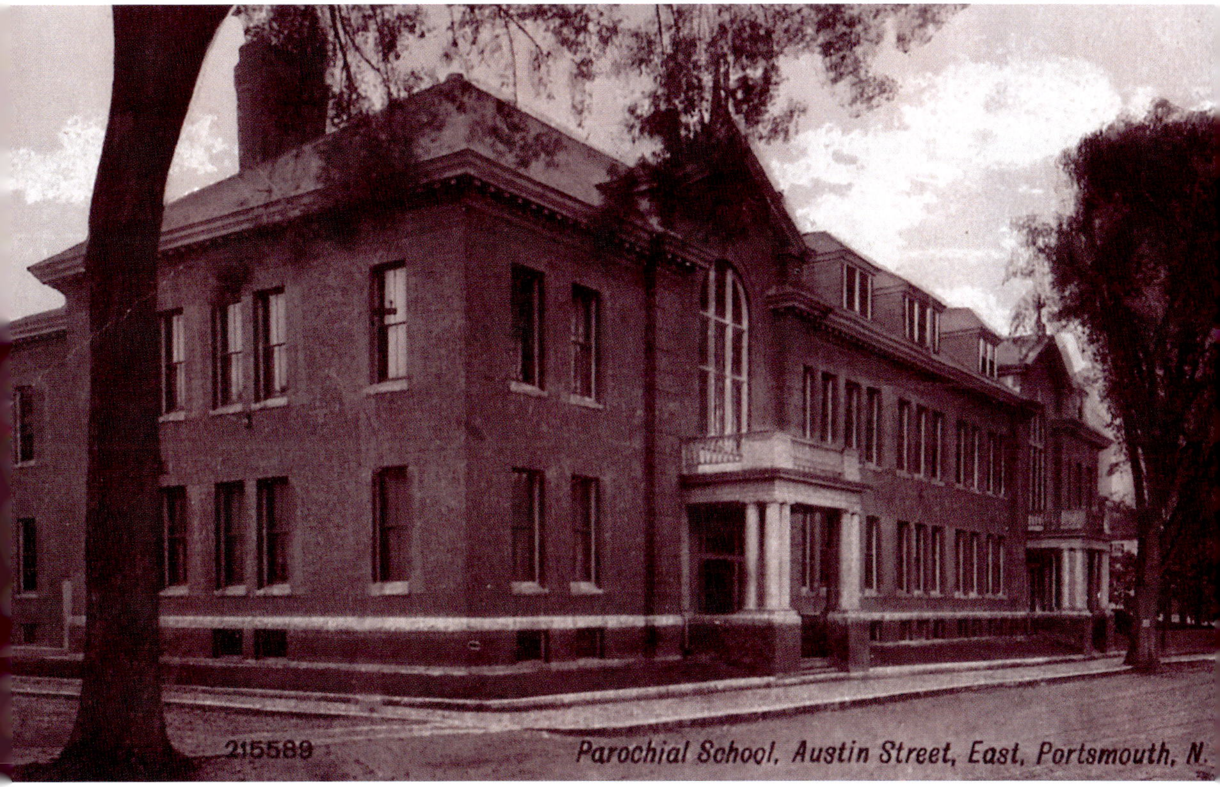

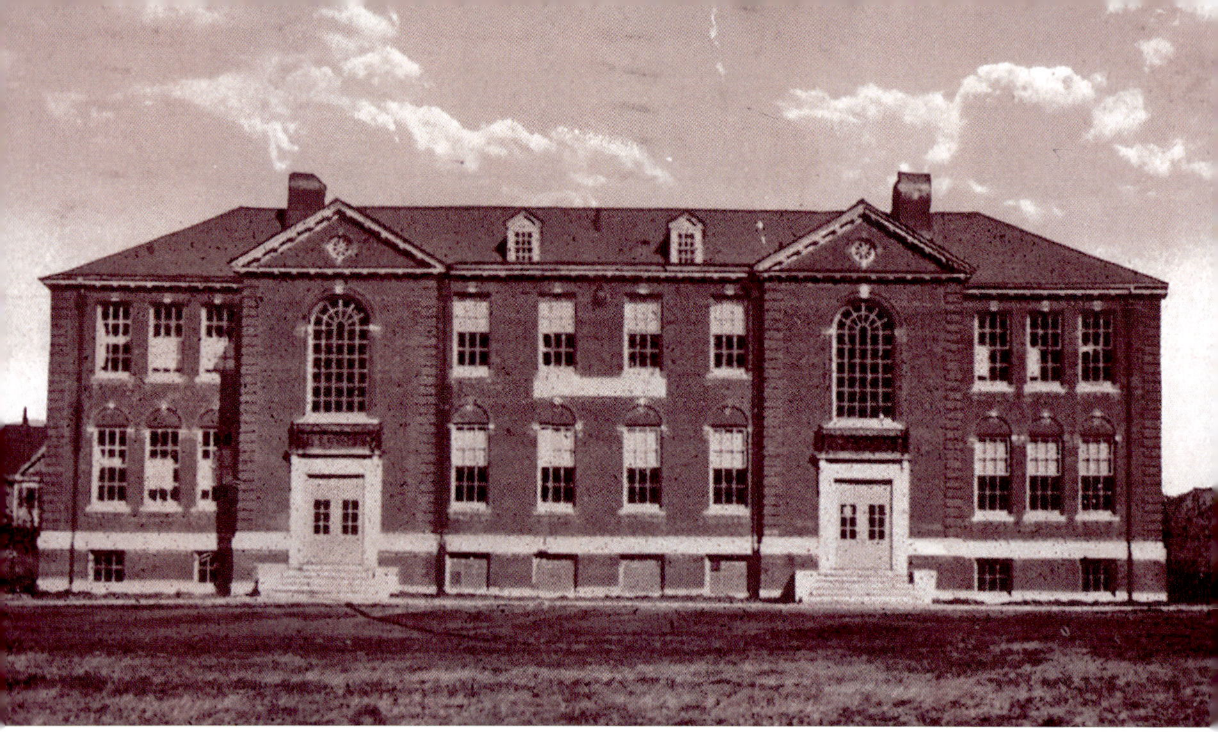

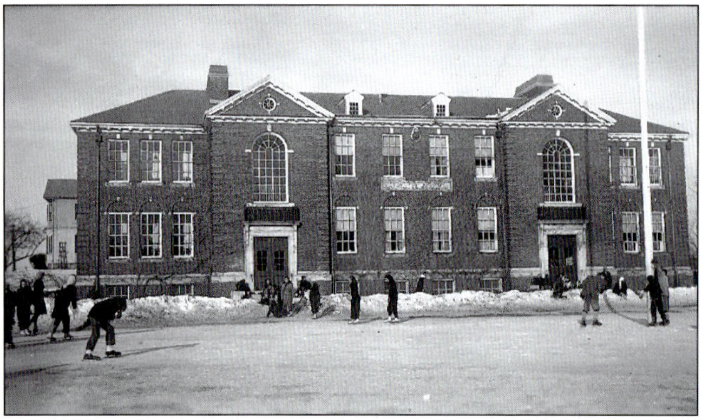

The Lafayette School, *c*. 1920, was erected in 1910–1911 to provide much needed additional classroom space. It was built on a parcel of land donated to the city by Thomas A. Ward. The school faces South Street with Middle Street off to the right as viewed in the photograph. Built of brick, it was an interpretation of 19th-century architectural style. The photograph to the left shows the building in the winter of 1947, with children skating on ice made by neighbors. The exterior of the building looks the same today.

Portsmouth Junior High School was built in 1932 to accommodate the increasing number of grade school children who needed a facility to bridge the gap between grade school and high school. Located on Parrott Avenue, it overlooks South Mill Pond and faces the former Portsmouth Hospital buildings. It is now called the Portsmouth Middle School and provides educational space for students in the sixth, seventh, and eighth grades.

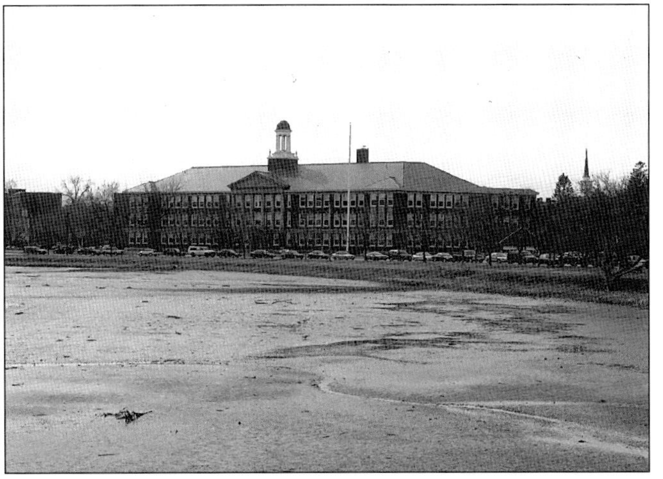

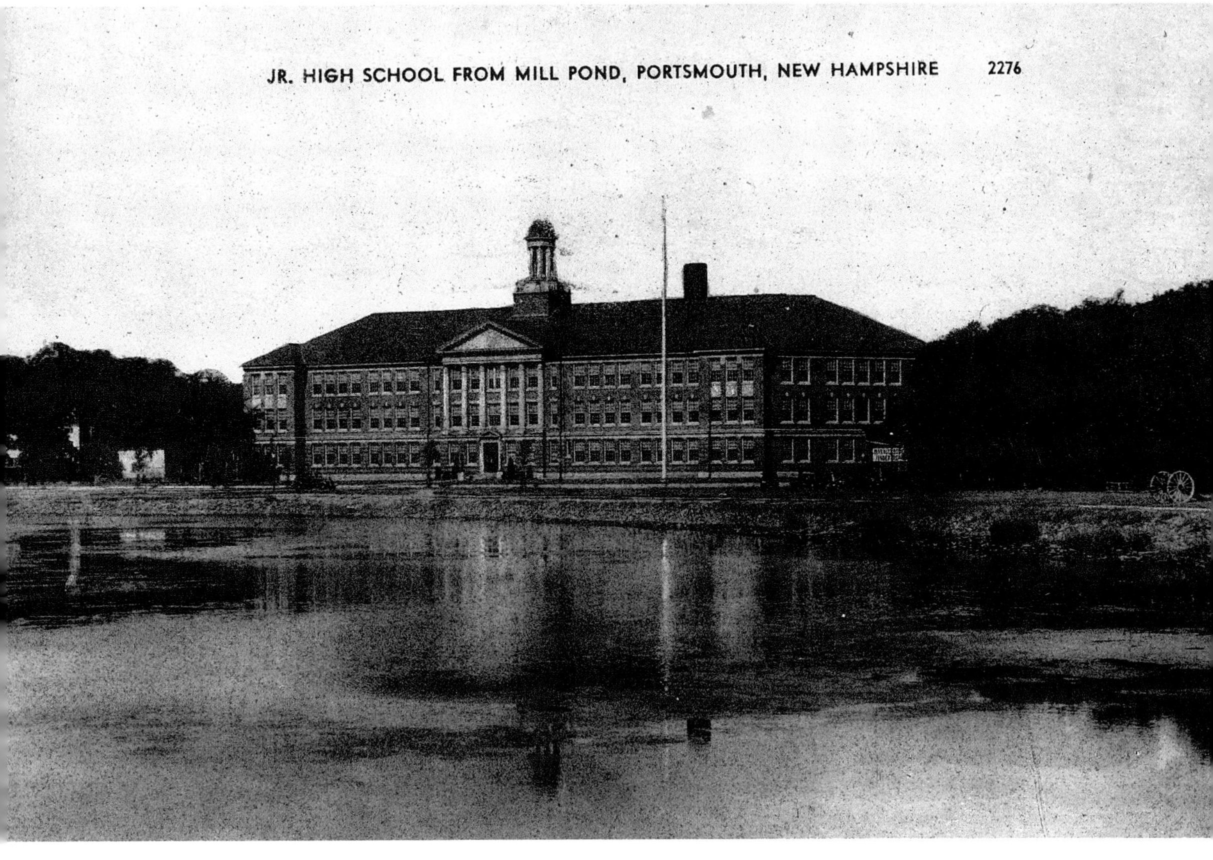

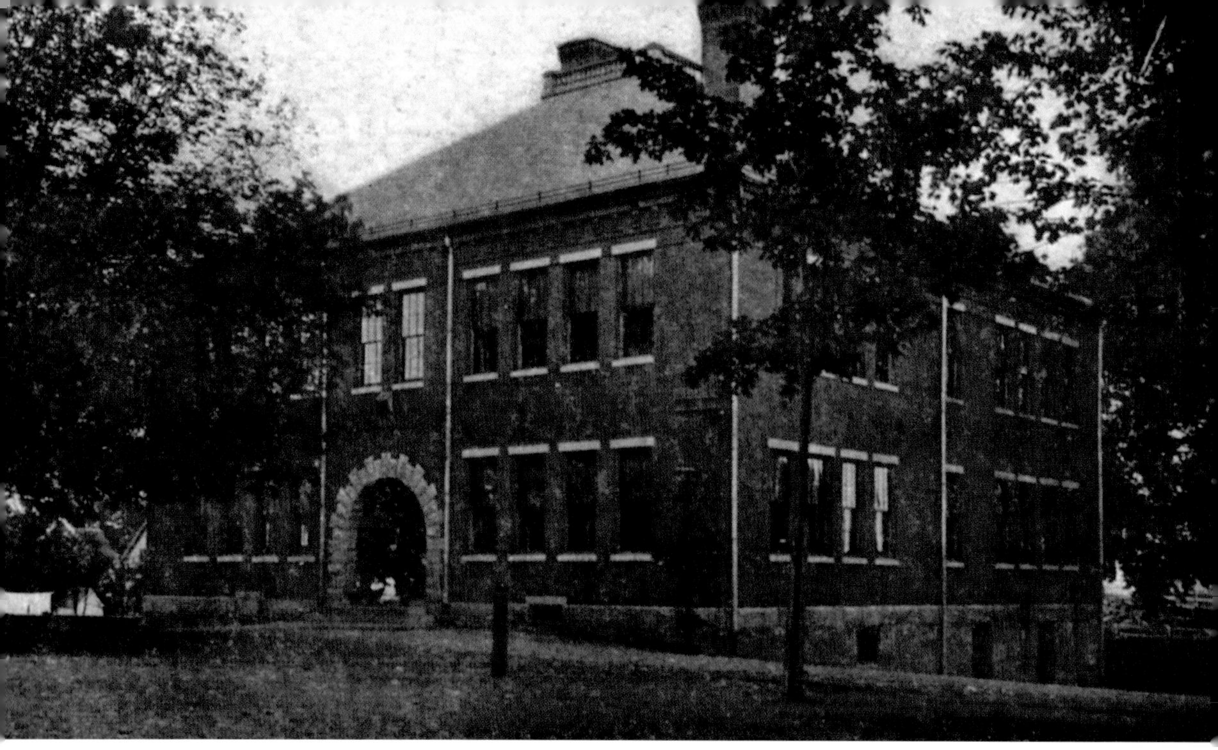

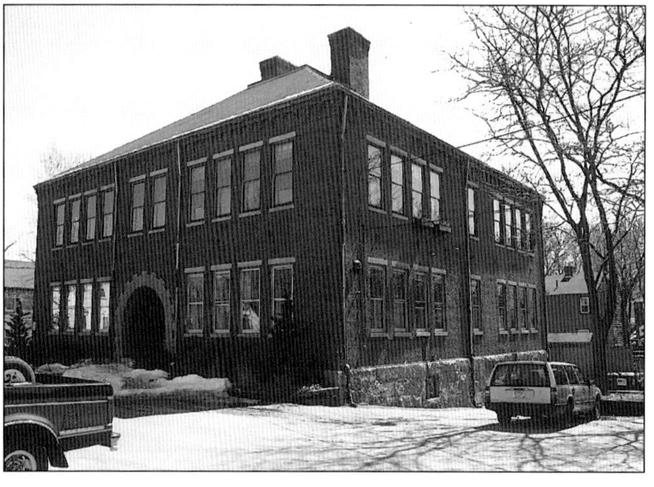

The Haven School, *c.* 1900, was built in 1846. It is located on School Street near the corner of South Street. In the building's early years, it was a magnificent schoolhouse, seemingly far too big for the population of school-aged children that would be educated here. Yet this school, like the others built during the 19th century and the early 20th century, was made obsolete by the expansion of our population. The Haven School is another very good example of the city's success in saving older buildings by renovation. Today this building houses much needed apartments.

The Cottage Hospital is seen here from the Parrott Avenue side of South Mill Pond *c.* 1910. Junkins Avenue spans South Mill Pond to provide easy access to the hospital from downtown and other parts of the city. When compared to the new photograph of the same hospital area, all the expansions can be easily identified. As the need for more hospital beds was called for, the hospital became a hospital complex. The first major addition was the erection of a nurses' home to the left of the older building. In the 1950s, the entire complex was enlarged again. Finally, the needs for modern healthcare for Portsmouth citizens were greater than the existing hospital could accommodate. In the 1980s, the hospital complex became the City of Portsmouth Municipal Complex, with the police department, jail, city hall, and other city-related services taking over the buildings. The hospital was relocated to 333 Borthwick Avenue.

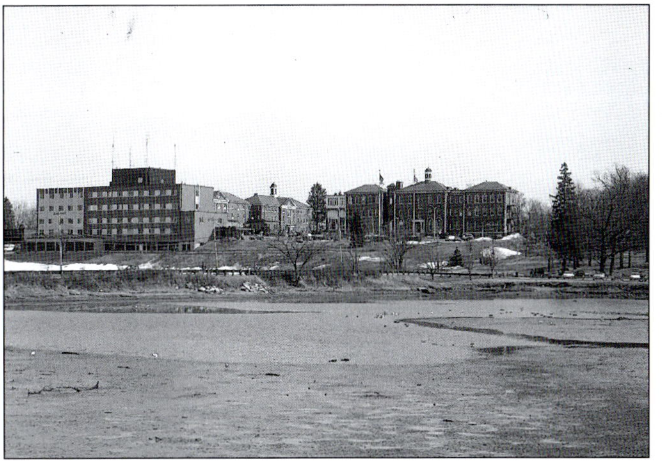

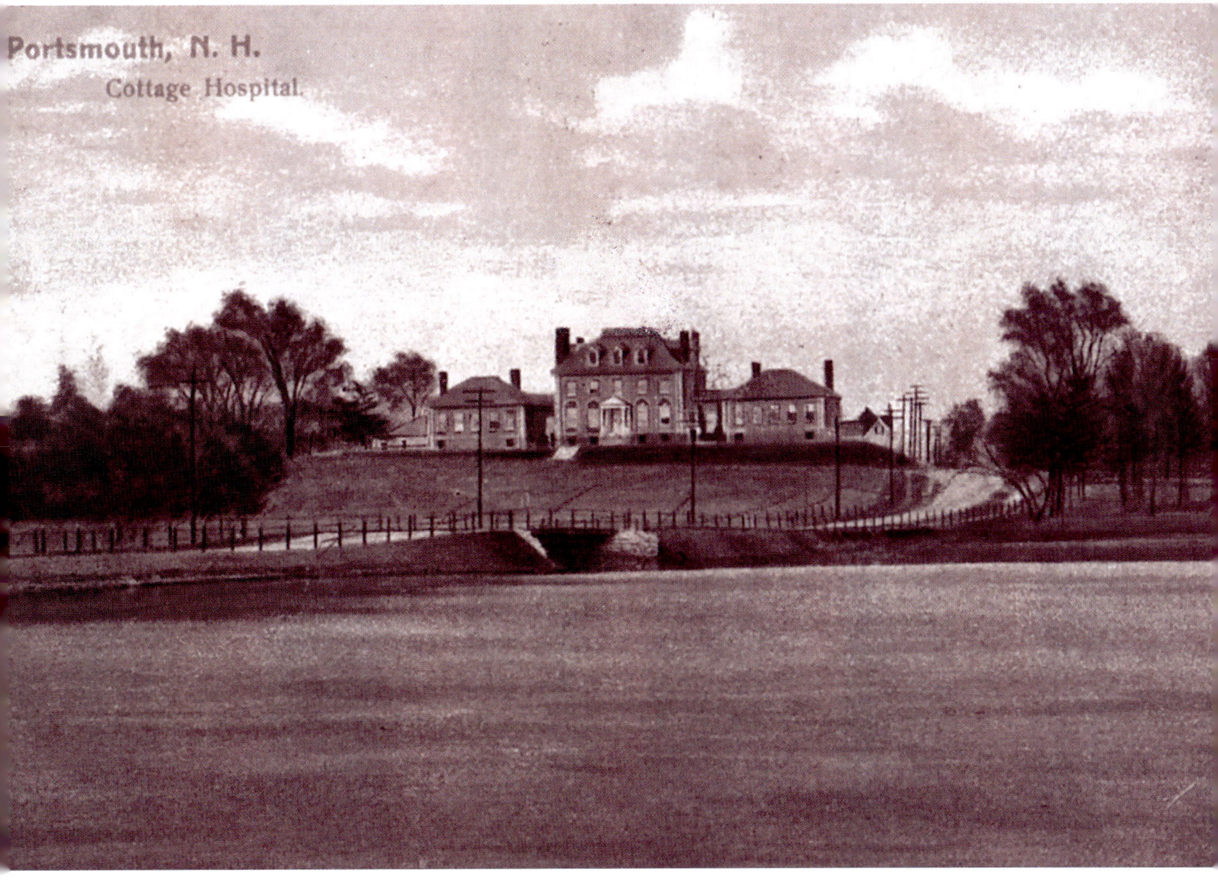

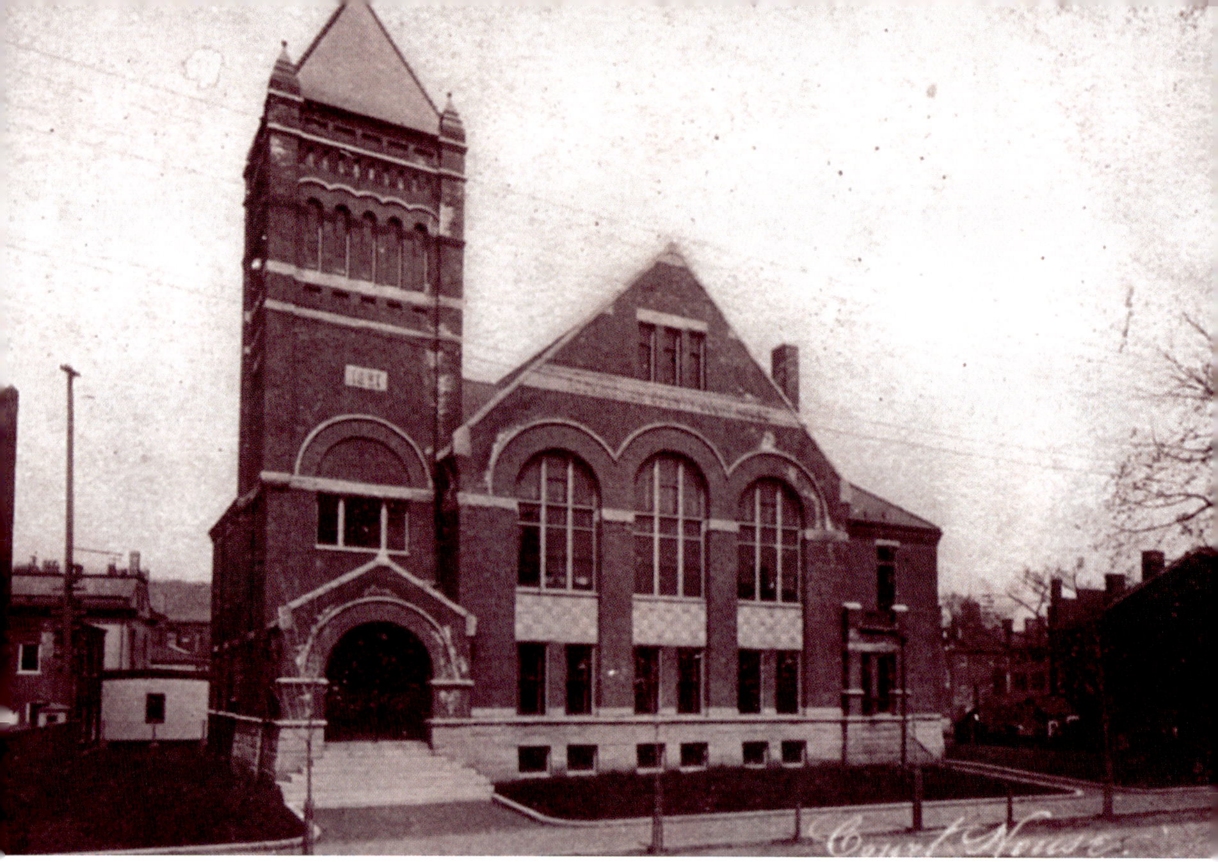

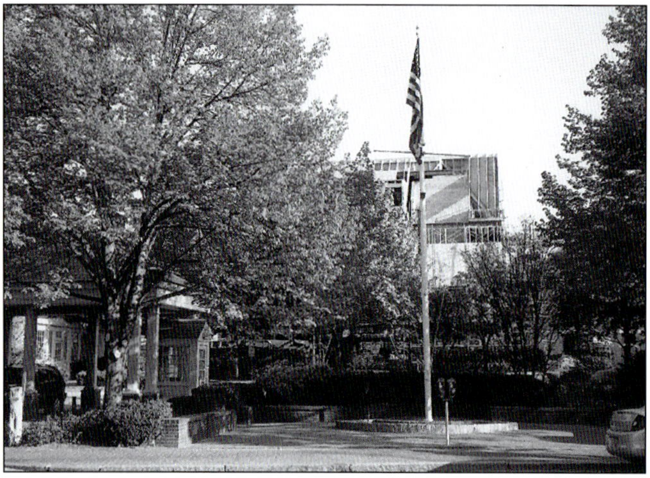

The courthouse in Portsmouth, a grand brick building on State Street, was erected in 1891. The building was one of the sites chosen by the governor to greet the envoys from Russia and Japan. Portsmouth had been chosen as the location for talks between the two nations that resulted in the Russian-Japan Peace Treaty in 1905. Until the 1960s, the court was in Portsmouth; then, a new building was built on the Exeter-Hampton Road, and the court was relocated. This building was torn down. Today, a bank parking lot occupies the site. Looking through the parking lot on the right side of the photograph, we see the old police station and jail.

The new county jail and jailer's residence, on Penhallow Street, is shown below *c.* 1930. Ivy-covered brick with awnings on some of the windows let this structure meld into the Portsmouth central business district. It was built in 1891. Until the late 1980s, when the jail and police station were relocated to the municipal complex on Junkins Avenue, this remained the city lockup and police station. The building's proximity to Market Square is easy to note, as the steeple and spire of North Church are visible in both photographs. After the city vacated the premises, the building was sold, renovated, and recycled as office space for private business.

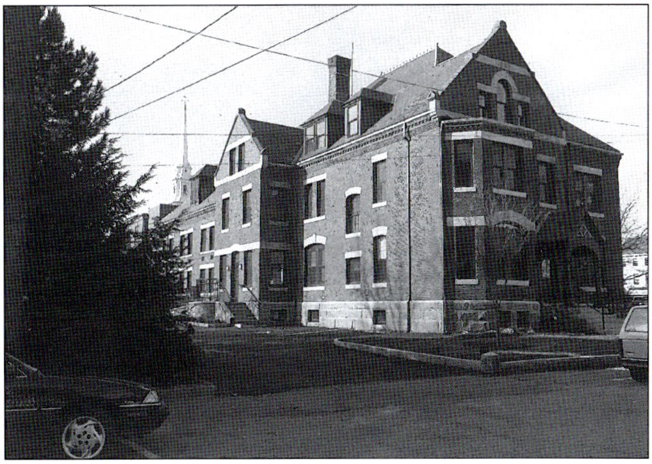

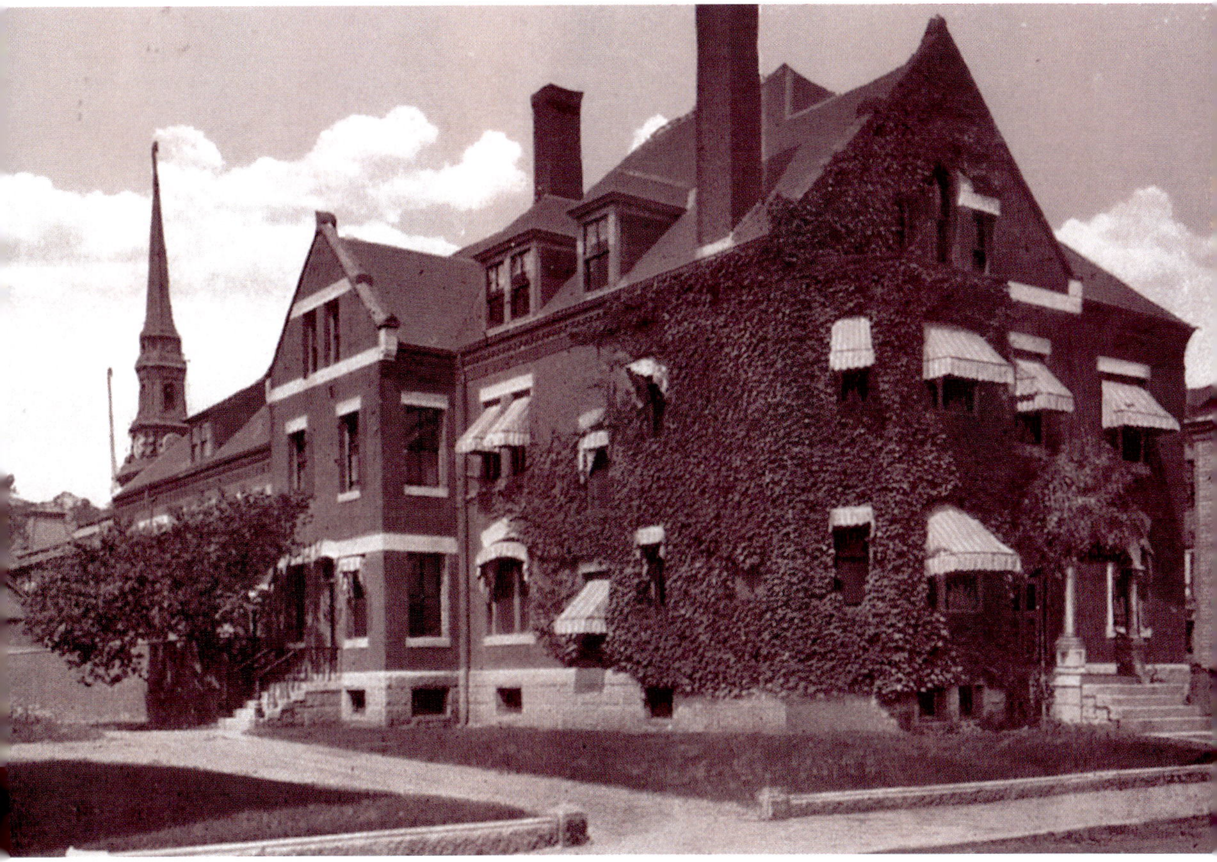

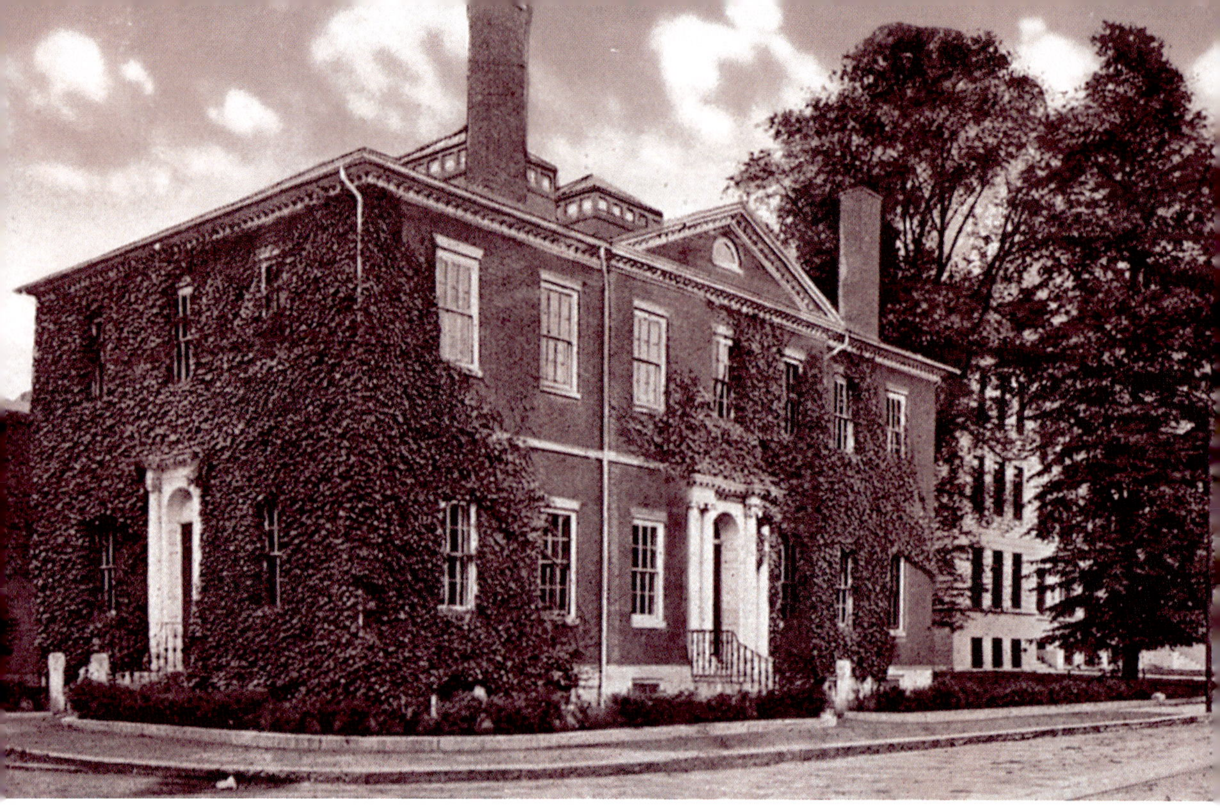

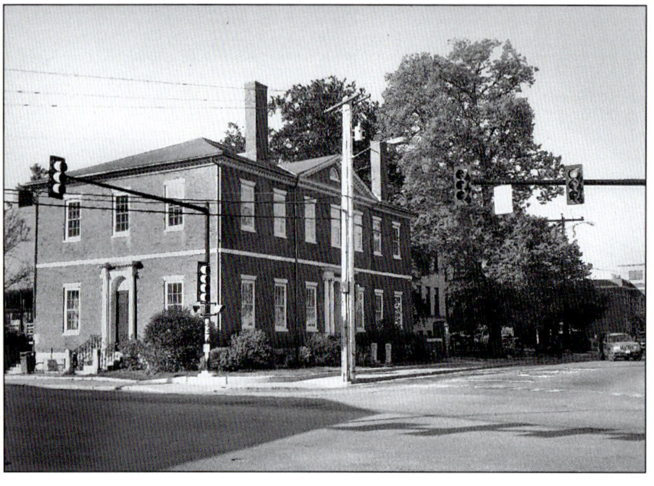

In 1809, Portsmouth Academy was built on the corner of Islington and Middle Streets. Between 1810 and 1812, a library annex was built. Later in the 19th century, the city first leased the building and then purchased land and building with plans of turning it into a library. The building was totally remodeled early in the 20th century. For the past 100 years, it has remained the Portsmouth Public Library. The need for more library space has been on the minds of the city councilors for a number of years, but to date there have been no permanent solutions. Here we have another old building that is in need of saving to enable it to join the other "museum of old buildings" that Portsmouth is known for.

Around 1907, the courthouse and post office, on the corner of Pleasant and State Streets, was one of the city's finest buildings. It was built in the mid-19th century (1857–1860) in the Italianate style typical of federal buildings during that time. Today, the building remains almost as it was when it was built. Only an addition to the right has altered its appearance.

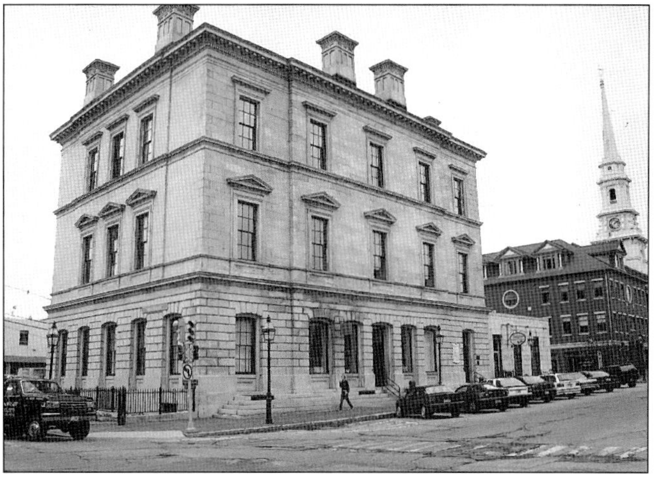

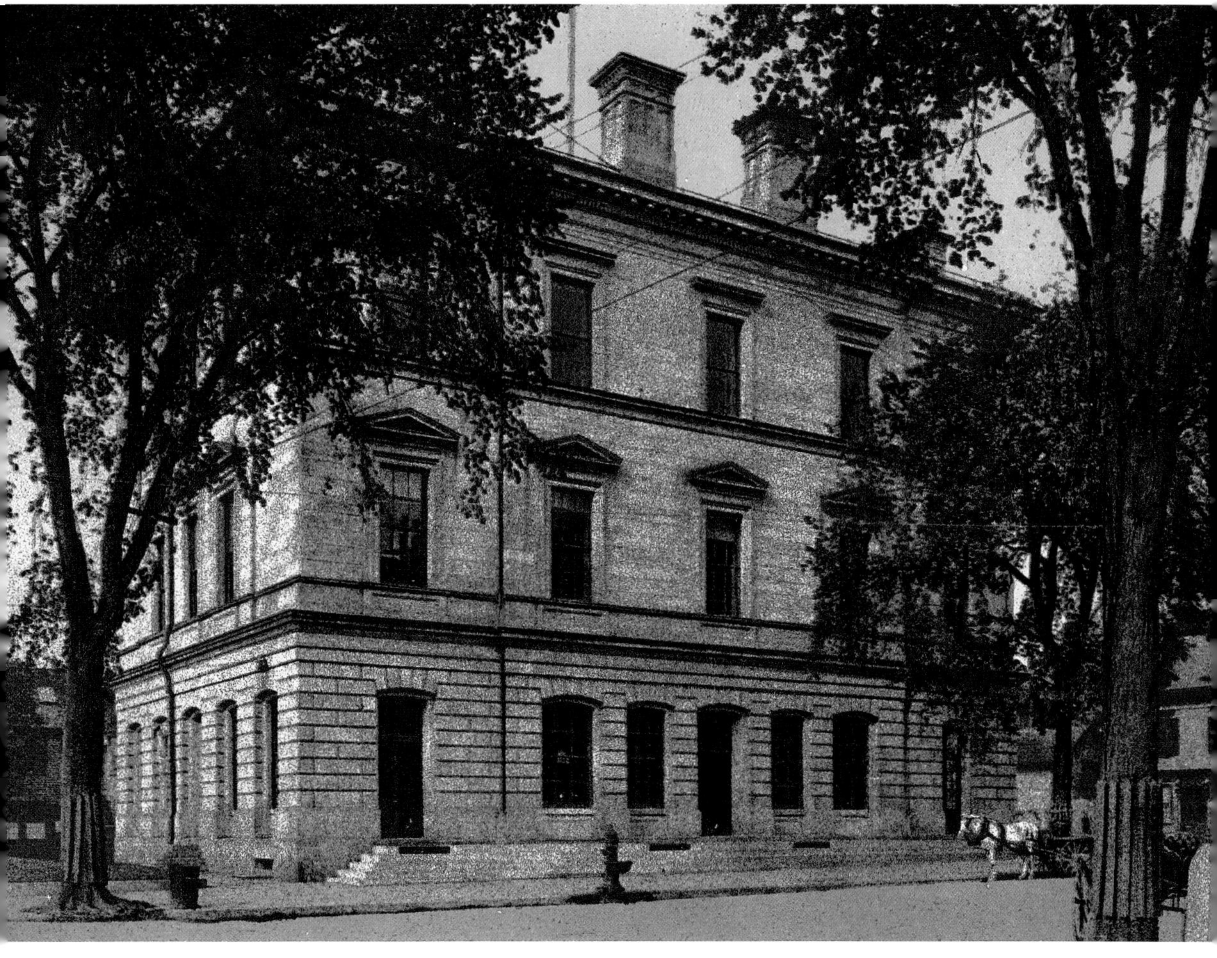

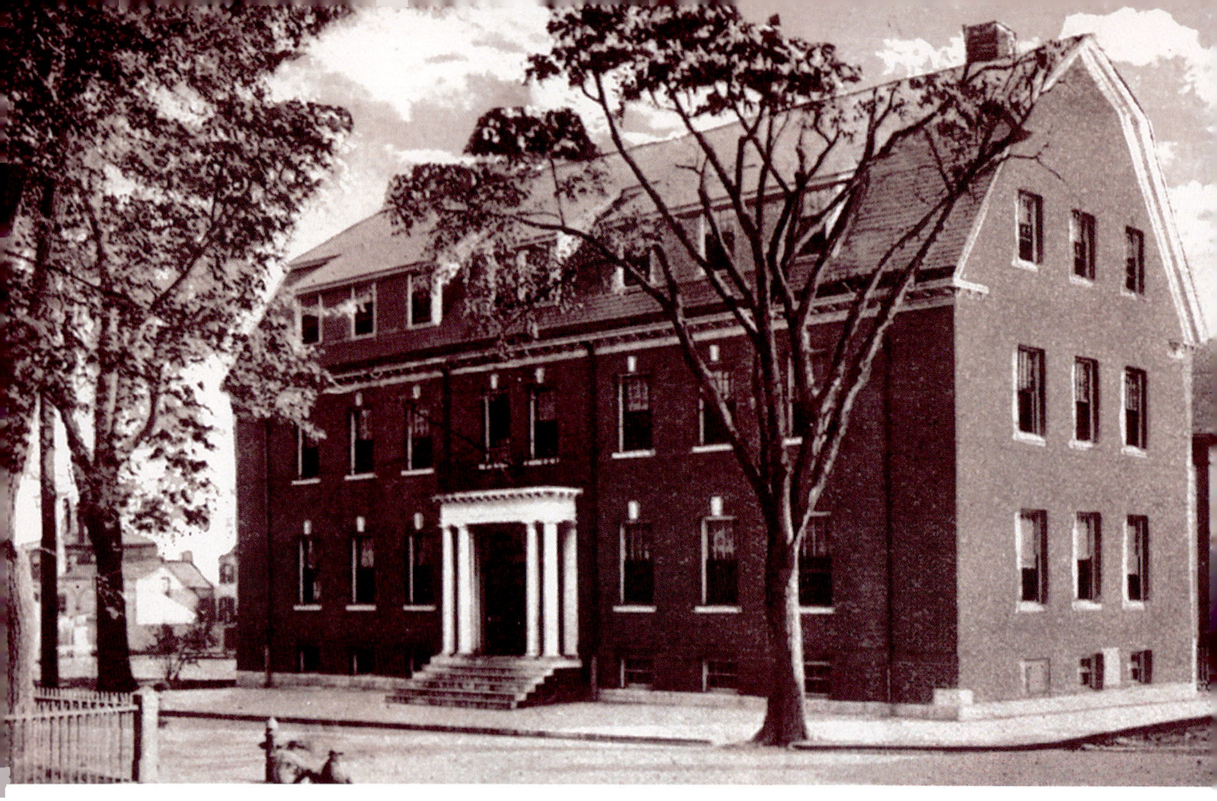

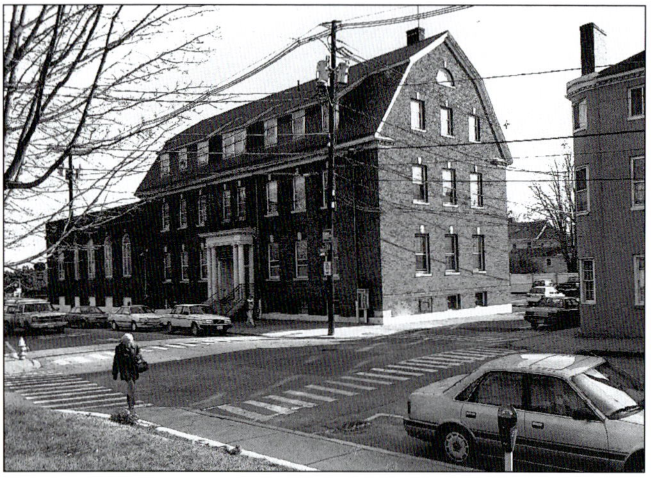

On the corner opposite the old high school on Daniel Street, the Army and Navy Association building was erected in 1917. It was built as an off-base site for army and navy personnel from the Portsmouth Naval Shipyard. Its chief benefactor was a local personality, William Lowell Hill, who was a career sailor, a Congressional Medal of Honor recipient, and was attached to our navy base for 30 years as his official place of duty. Hill chaired the committee that raised the funds needed for the building. In 1940, the building was turned over to the Salvation Army. Today, it is the Connie Bean Center. Various community activities are held here. At the river end of the building, an annex has been added.

Goodwin Park, located on Islington Street, was dedicated "in honor of the men of Portsmouth who gave their services on the land and on the sea in the war that preserved the Union of States." Grateful citizens erected it in 1888. Three of four sides of the monument are labeled Antietam, Fredricksburg, and Gettysburg for the three great battles of the Civil War. The fourth side is labeled for the *Kearsarge,* the ship built in Portsmouth that fought with the Confederate frigate *Alabama* on June 19, 1864, off the coast of Cherbourg, France. In the last few years, the park has been renovated by the city with a few small changes. The statue has been lowered by the removal of a pedestal piece, and instead of a brick walk, we have a concrete path with benches. In the background, the steeple of the Immaculate Conception Catholic Church can be seen as a square structure instead of the old spire.

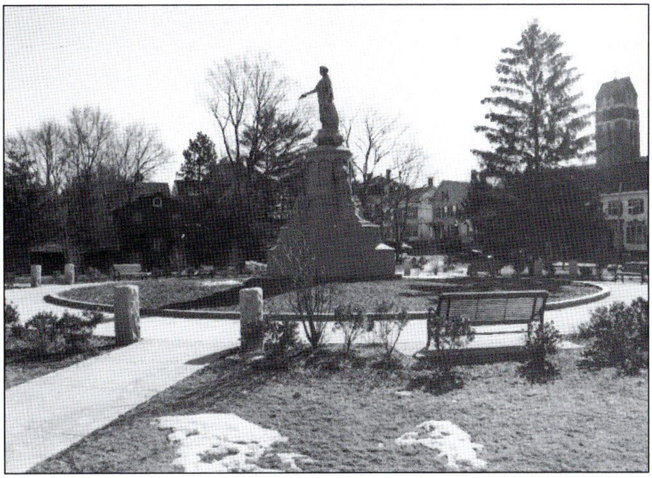

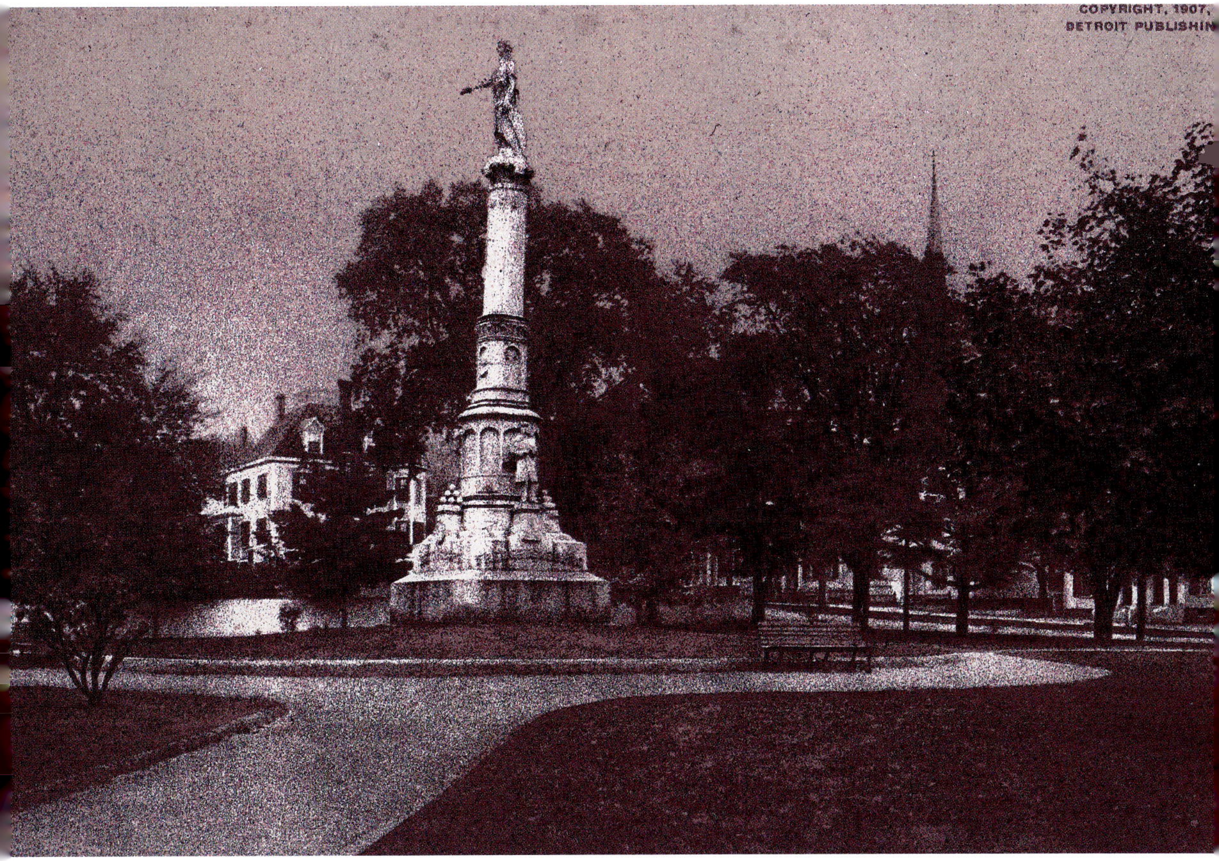

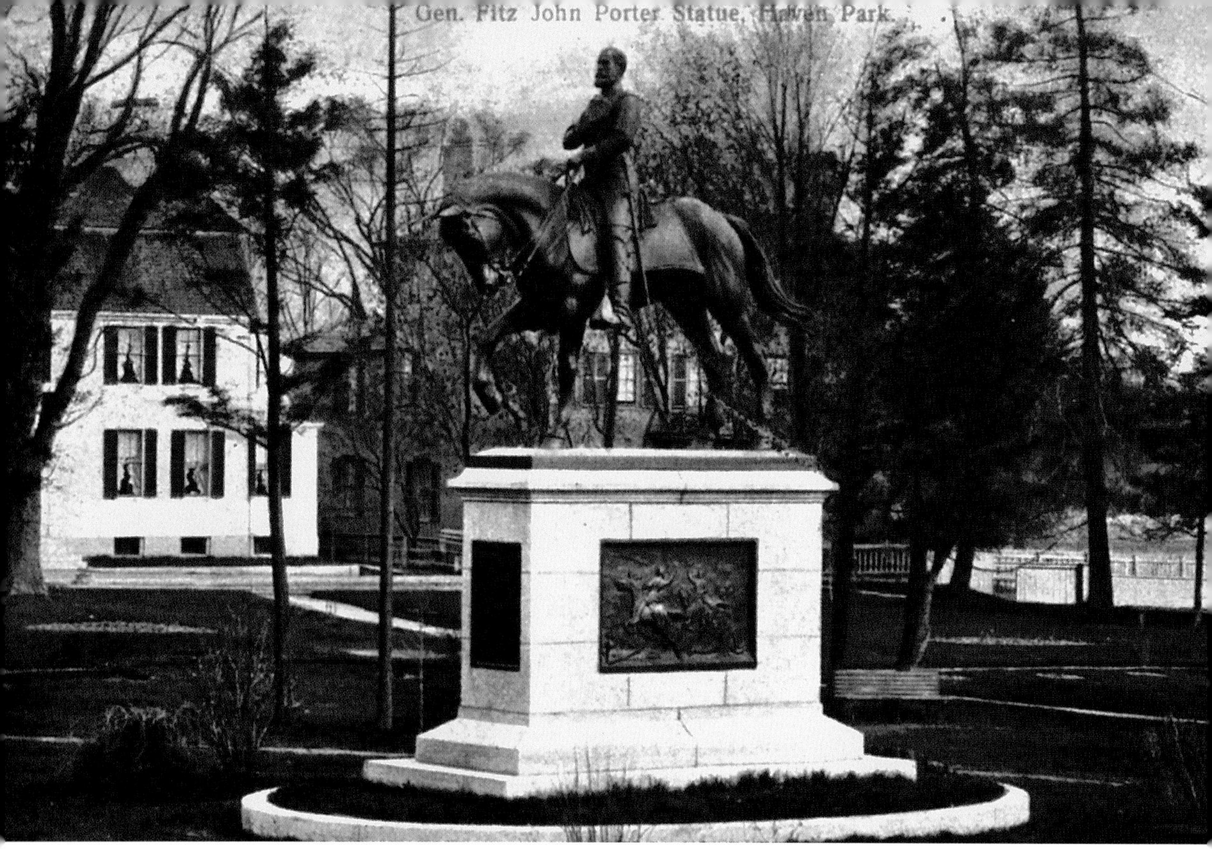

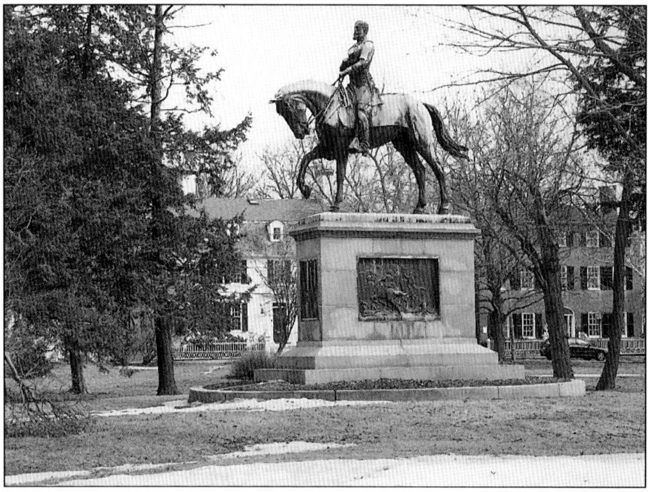

On Pleasant Street there is a monument raised in honor and memory of Gen. Fitz John Porter. It is shown above *c.* 1911. Porter was born in Portsmouth on August 31, 1822. He was a graduate of the Military Academy at West Point. Porter distinguished himself in the war with Mexico in 1846–1847. The plaque on the statue details a long and honorable service to the U.S. Army. Porter died in 1901. Today, this park is one of the beautiful treed areas that help make our city an enjoyable place to live. The white house in the background behind the statue is the Livermore House.

Hovey's Fountain used to be on the corner of State and Pleasant Streets next to the courthouse and post office. It was erected as a memorial to Ens. Charles Emerson Hovey, who was killed in action in the Philippine Islands during the Spanish-American War. Ensign Hovey was the son of the Reverend Henry Hovey and Louise Folsom Hovey. He graduated from the U.S. Naval Academy in 1907. Other monuments to Hovey were a destroyer named for him in 1919 and the Charles Emerson Hovey Post No. 168, Veterans of Foreign Wars, located on Deer Street. Today, the Hovey Fountain can be found in Prescott Park during the summer, mounted on the fountain near the main entrance to the park.

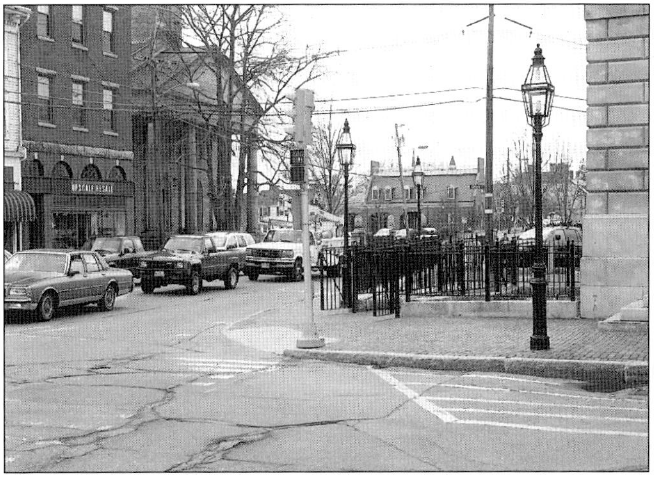

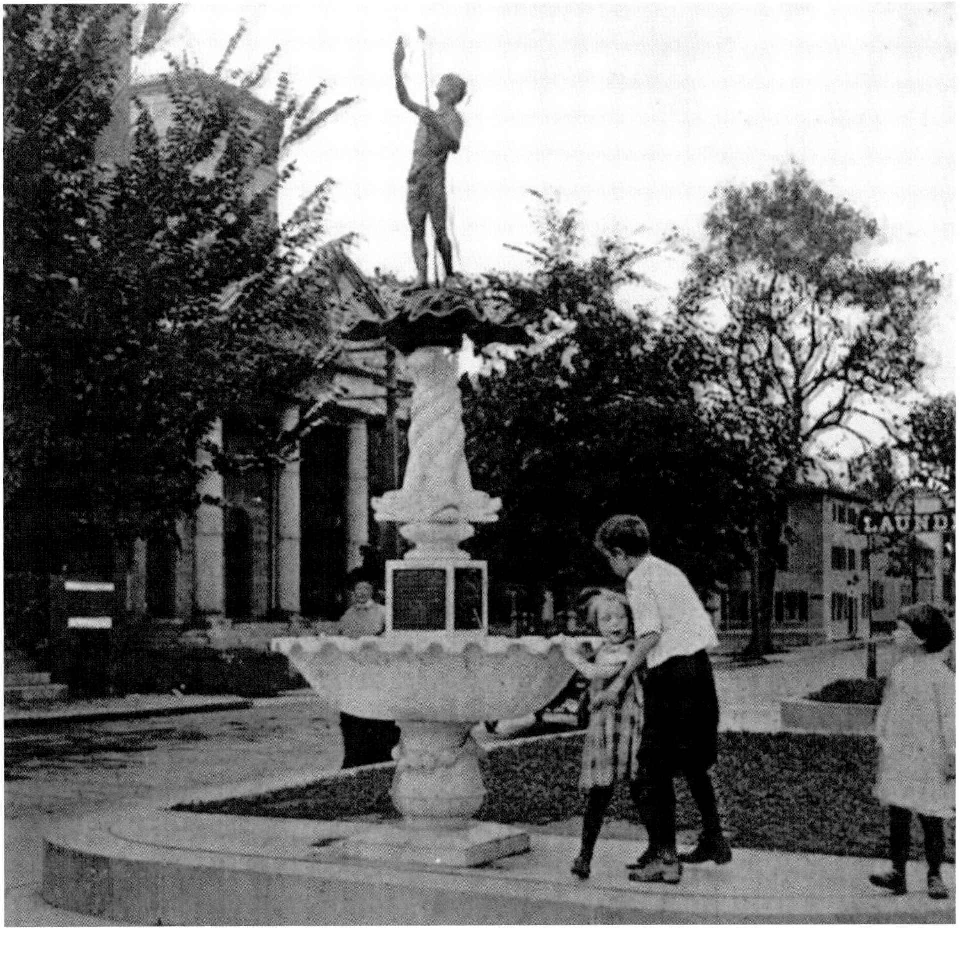

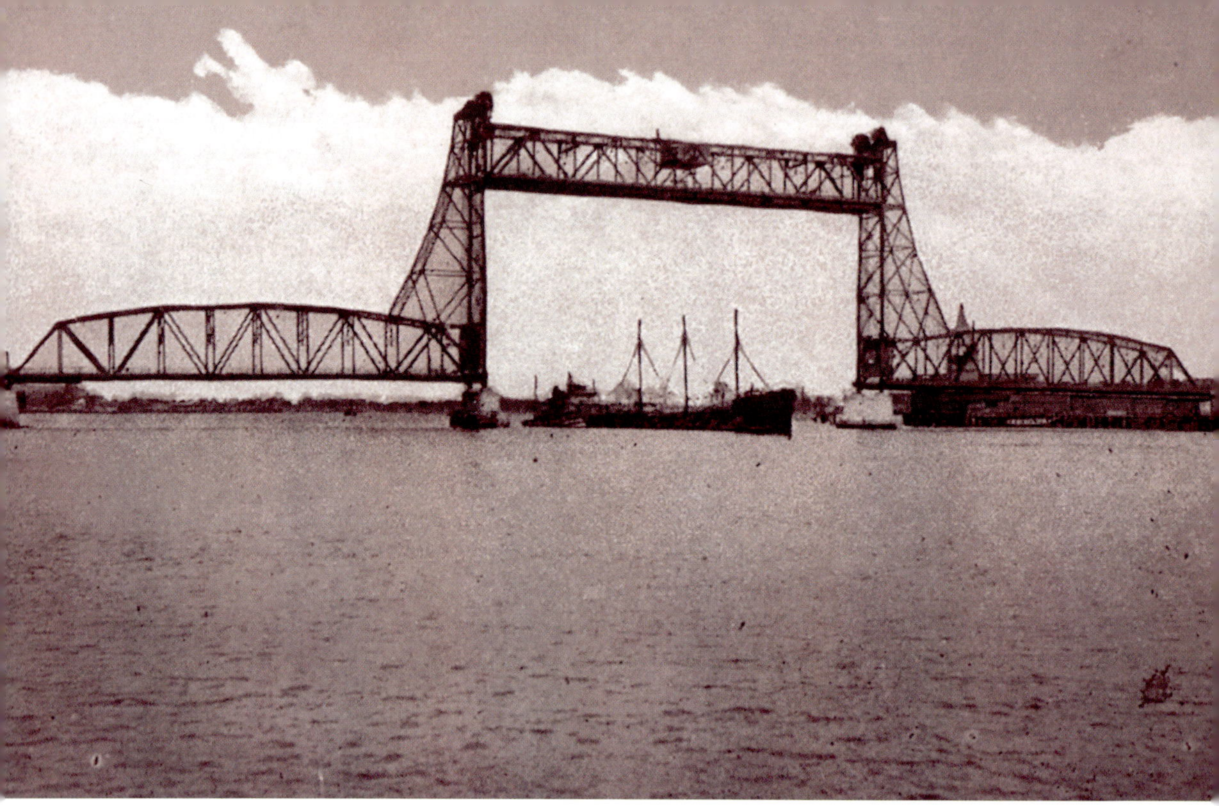

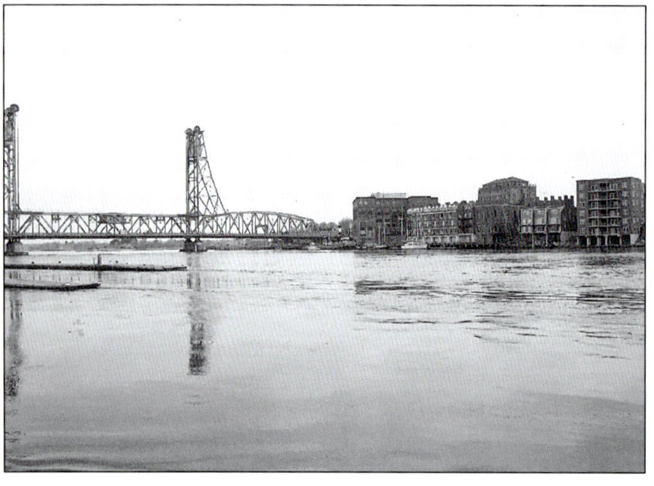

The Memorial Bridge, erected in 1923, was dedicated as a "memorial to the sailors and soldiers of New Hampshire who participated in the World War 1917–1919." The bridge remains as the link most frequently taken between Kittery and Portsmouth.

Chapter 3
Houses and Streetscapes

We are very lucky to have in Portsmouth many old homes. Urban conservation has been well supported by our citizens. Most of the old houses are on their original foundations and are owned by live-in families. Some of the houses belong to historical societies that own and maintain them as museums. We also have a museum of houses at Strawbery Banke. Three of the most famous homes in the museum are the Daniel Webster House, the William Pitt Tavern, and the John Laighton House.

Daniel Webster had more than one address when he moved to Portsmouth. The first home he lived on was at Pleasant Street. This house burned in the 1813 fire (see pages 84–85). The second house, and their last one in Portsmouth, was a smallish home on High Street. Today this is one of the Strawbery Banke houses.

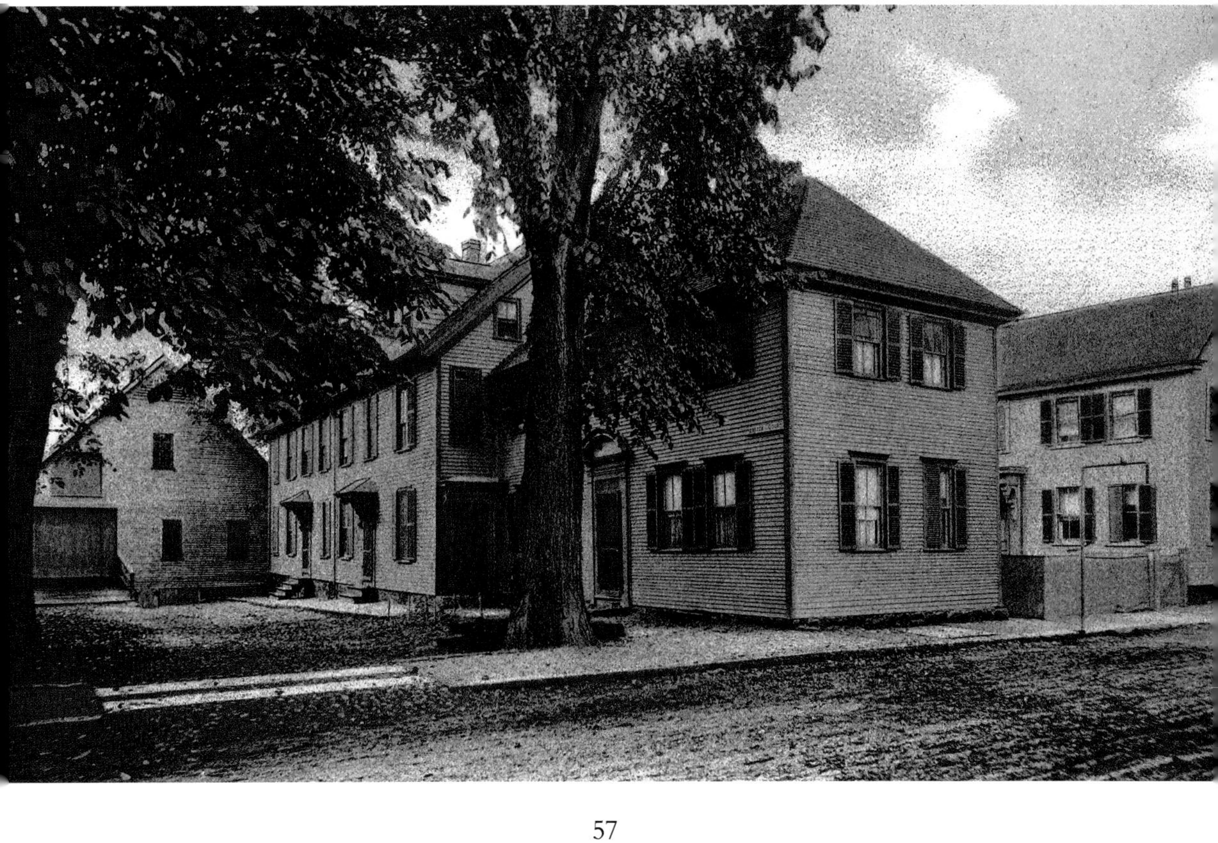

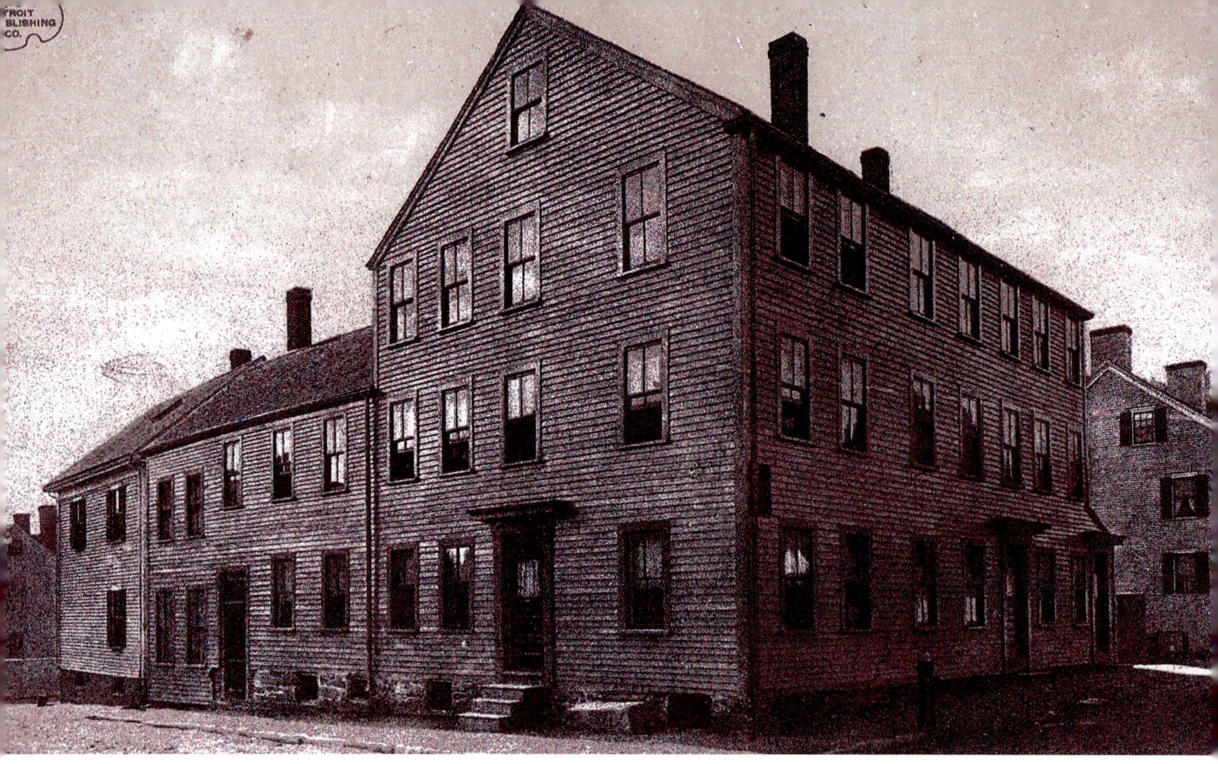

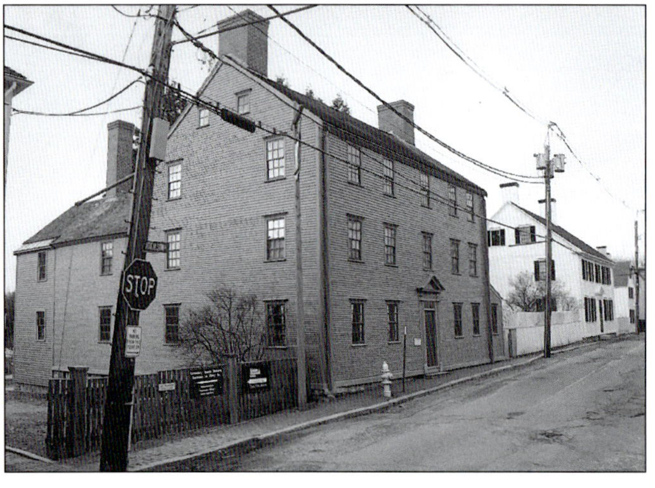

The William Pitt Tavern, *c.* 1890, was built in 1766 by John Stavers. Soon after he began operating his tavern, Stavers offered the uppermost floor to the members of St. John's No. 1 Lodge of Free and Accepted Masons as their regular meeting place. When the tavern opened, it was called the Earl of Halifax Tavern. When renamed, after the signing of the Declaration of Independence, John Stavers chose William Pitt because he was an English Parliamentarian who spoke for the American revolutionary cause. This home is part of Strawbery Banke, which was a renewal and architectural preservation project of the late 1950s. Today, it is a nonprofit educational institution and is named on the National Register of Historic Places.

The John Laighton House, *c.* 1900, is the next house down Court Street from the William Pitt Tavern and was also built by John Stavers. As stated on the postcard, this house is probably better known as the home of Thomas Bailey Aldrich. Thomas Bailey Aldrich, poet and author, wrote *The Story of a Bad Boy,* a semiautobiographical novel on Aldrich's three years (1849–1852) living in his grandfather's house on Court Street. In his book, he called Portsmouth "Rivermouth." The house, which has been open to the public for most of the 20th century by the Thomas Bailey Aldrich Memorial Association, became a Strawbery Banke house in 1979.

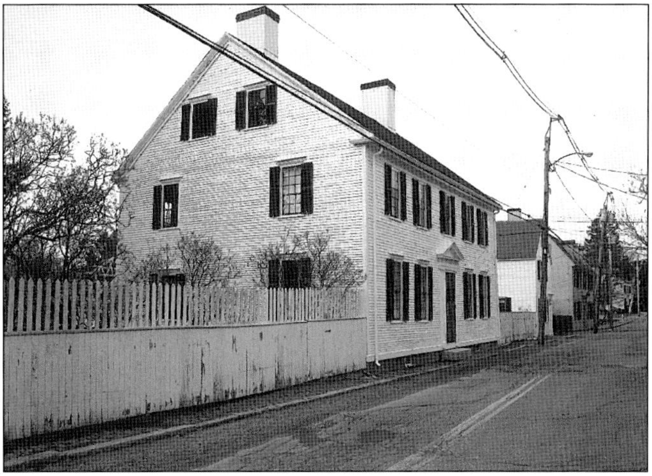

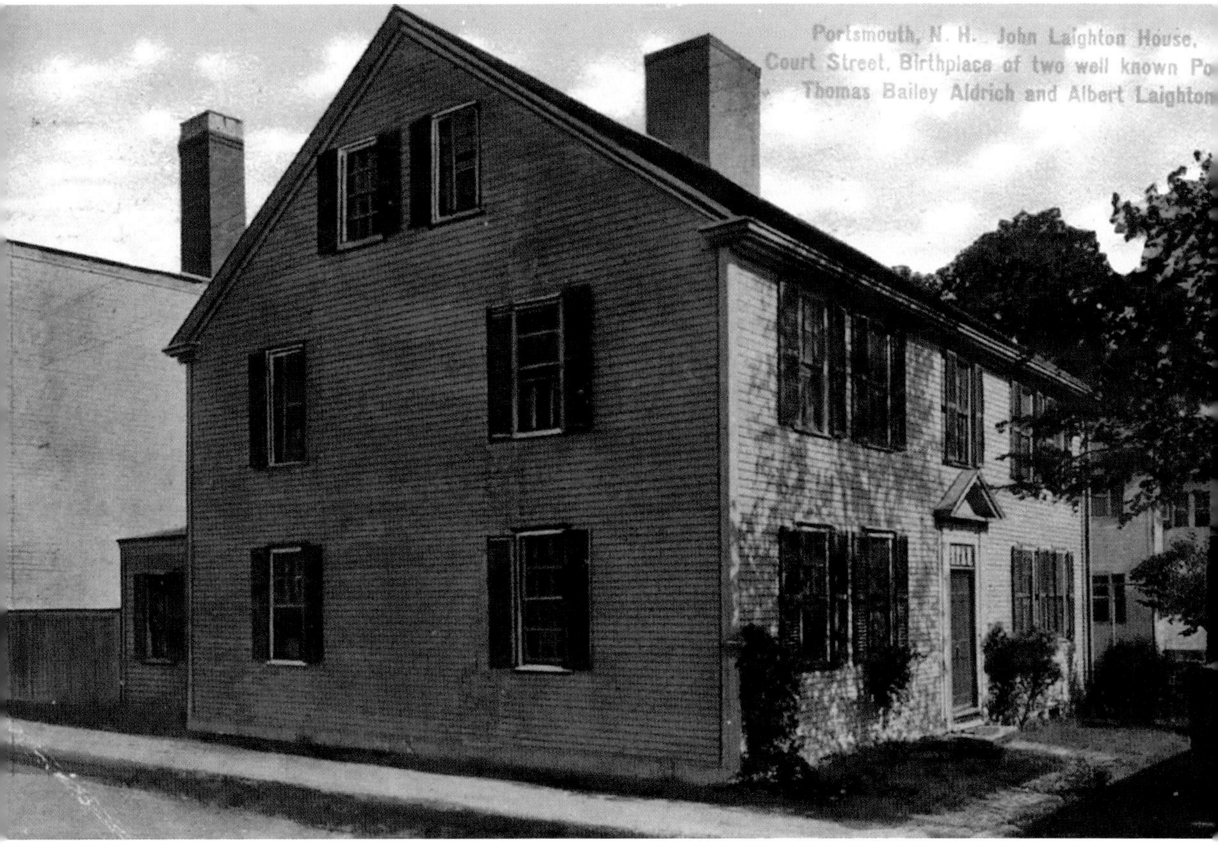

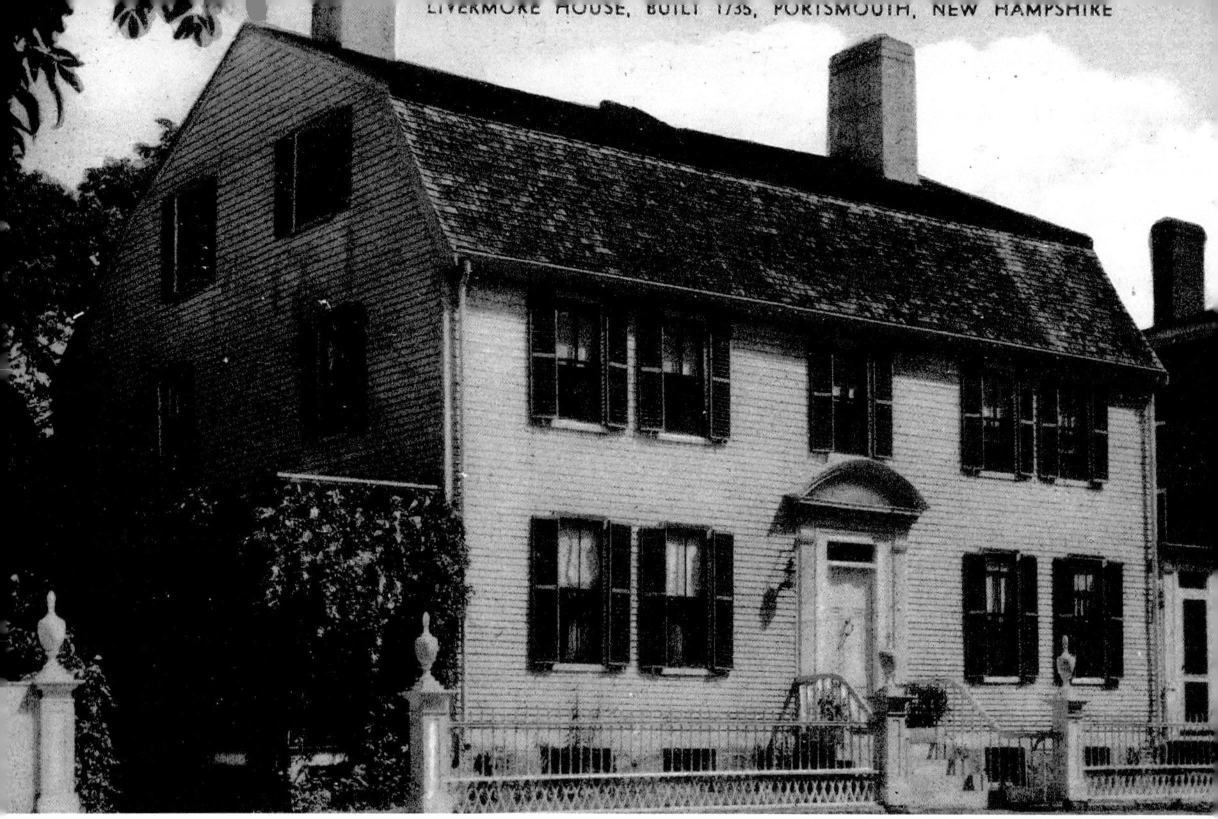

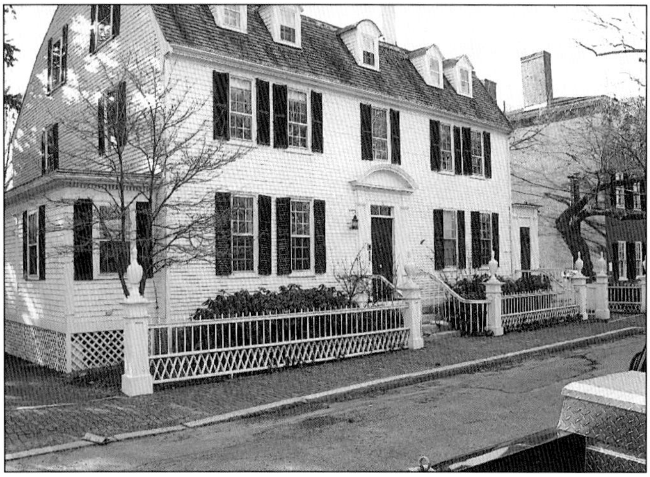

The Livermore House, built *c.* 1735, was named for Michael Livermore. He came to Portsmouth to teach school. He later became an attorney and was appointed, first, as the king's advocate and, second, as the attorney general for the providence of New Hampshire. This house, which overlooks Haven Park, may have been moved to its present location; this is the house that is seen through the trees behind the statue in Haven Park. To reference, look at the 1877 bird's-eye map (pages 90–91) and follow Pleasant Street until just before the intersection with Washington Street. Livermore Street is on the right, and this house is the next to last one on the left.

Stoodley Tavern, *c.* 1910, was on Daniel Street. The building was almost a casualty of urban redevelopment, which cleared half of a city block to make room for the federal building that faces onto Daniel Street and its parking area, which consumes the rest of the block facing Penhallow and Bow Streets. Col. James Stoodley built Stoodley Tavern *c.* 1763. It was considered one of the best places to stay for travelers from around New England.

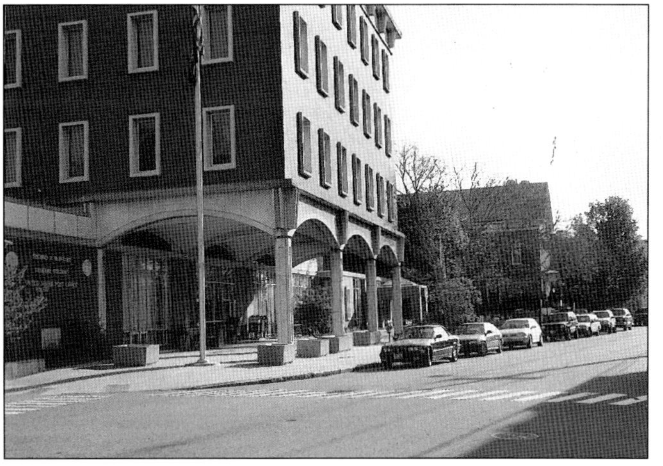

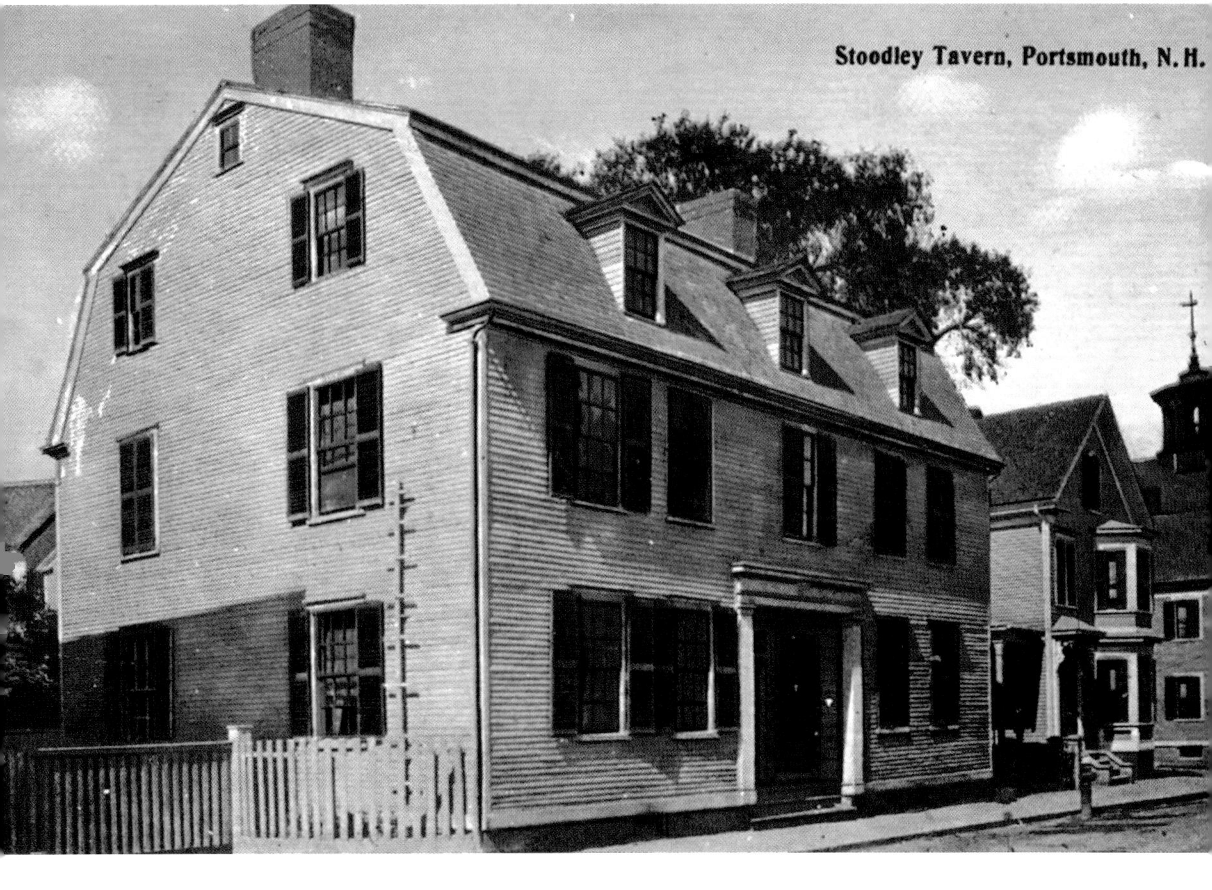

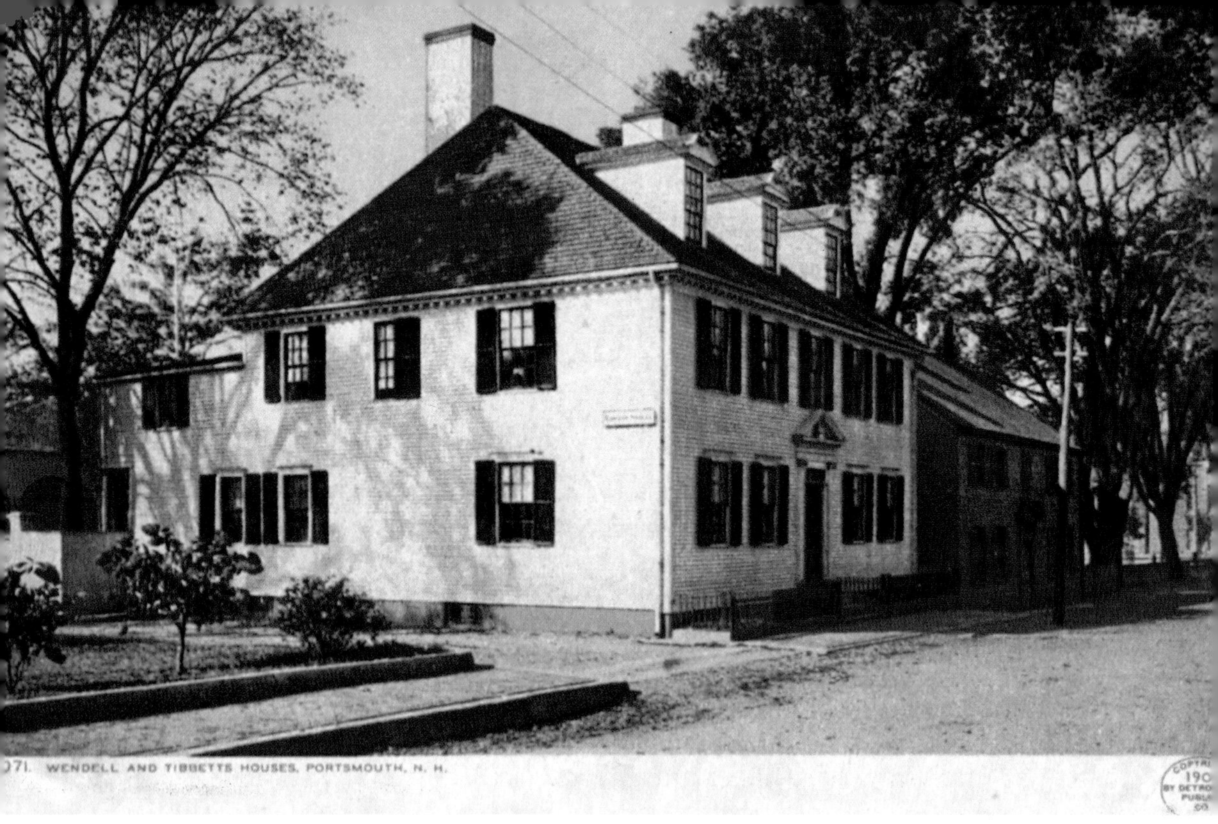

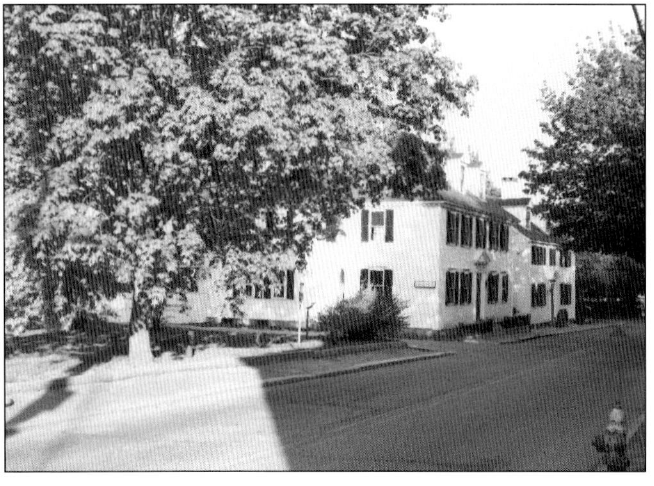

On Pleasant Street, between Haven Park and Junkins Avenue, are two wooden framed houses. The Wendell and Tibbetts houses remain today just as they appeared in the postcard, *c.* 1907. The Wendell house was named for the well-to-do merchant Abraham Wendell, who built it in 1789. The Tibbetts house was named for Richard Tibbetts, who bought the house in 1791. There does not seem to be a date to establish when the house was built.

The Jenness Mansion, *c.* 1920, is on the corner of Court and Pleasant Streets. It was built in 1818 on the site of a building that had burned down in the 1813 fire. The earlier building is believed to have been one of the places where George Washington stayed during his 1789 visit to Portsmouth. The current building was a hotel for many years and was then was purchased by the Elks Club. Today it is privately owned.

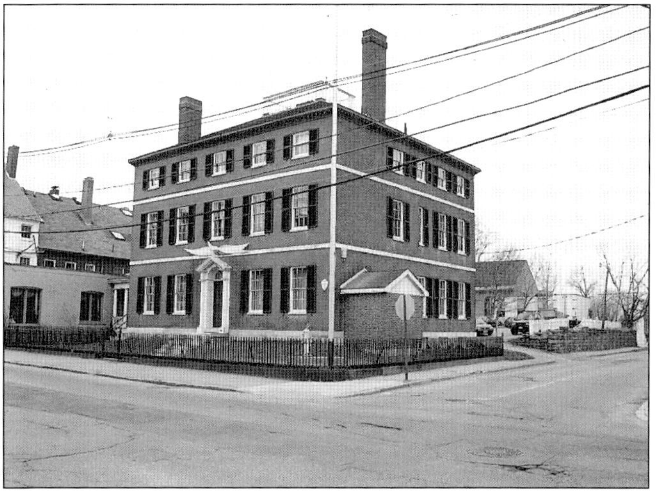

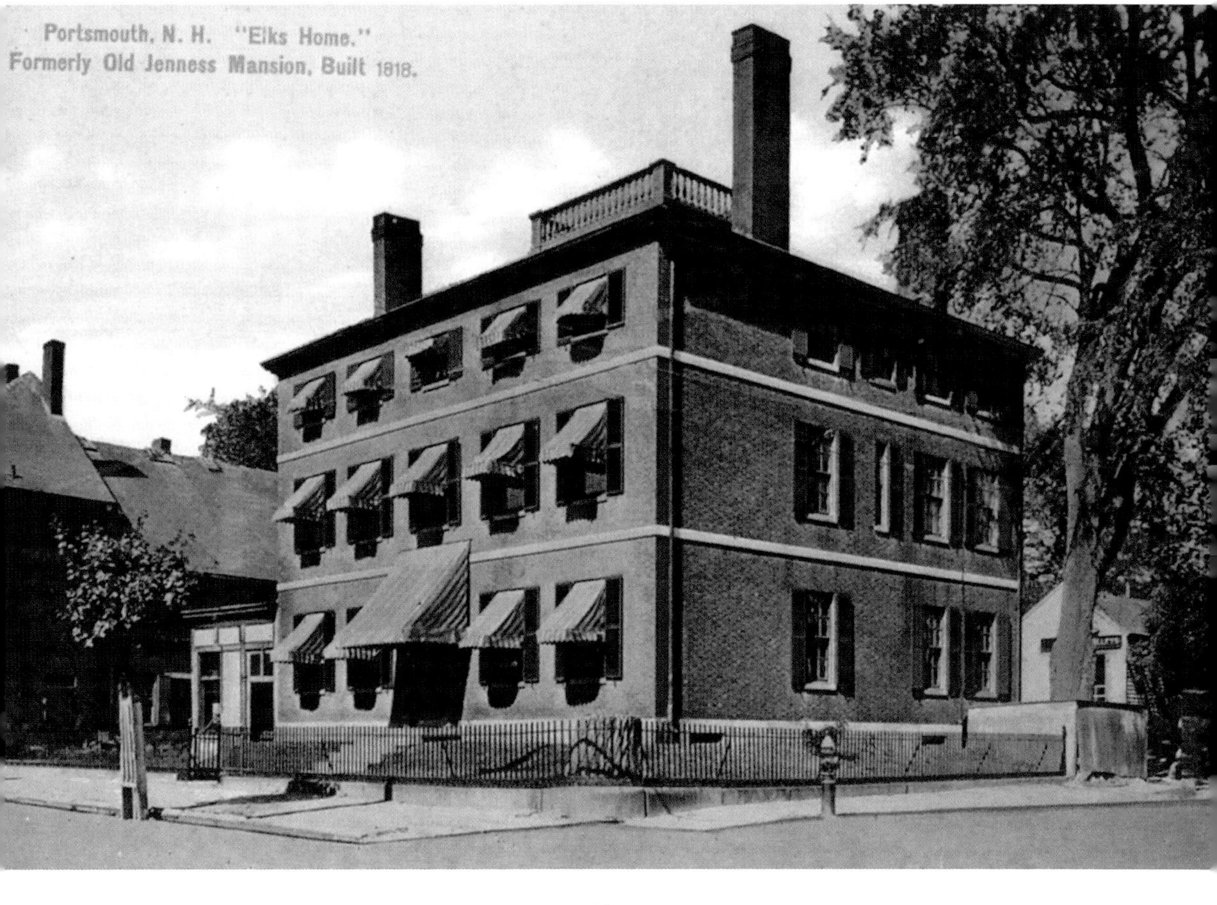

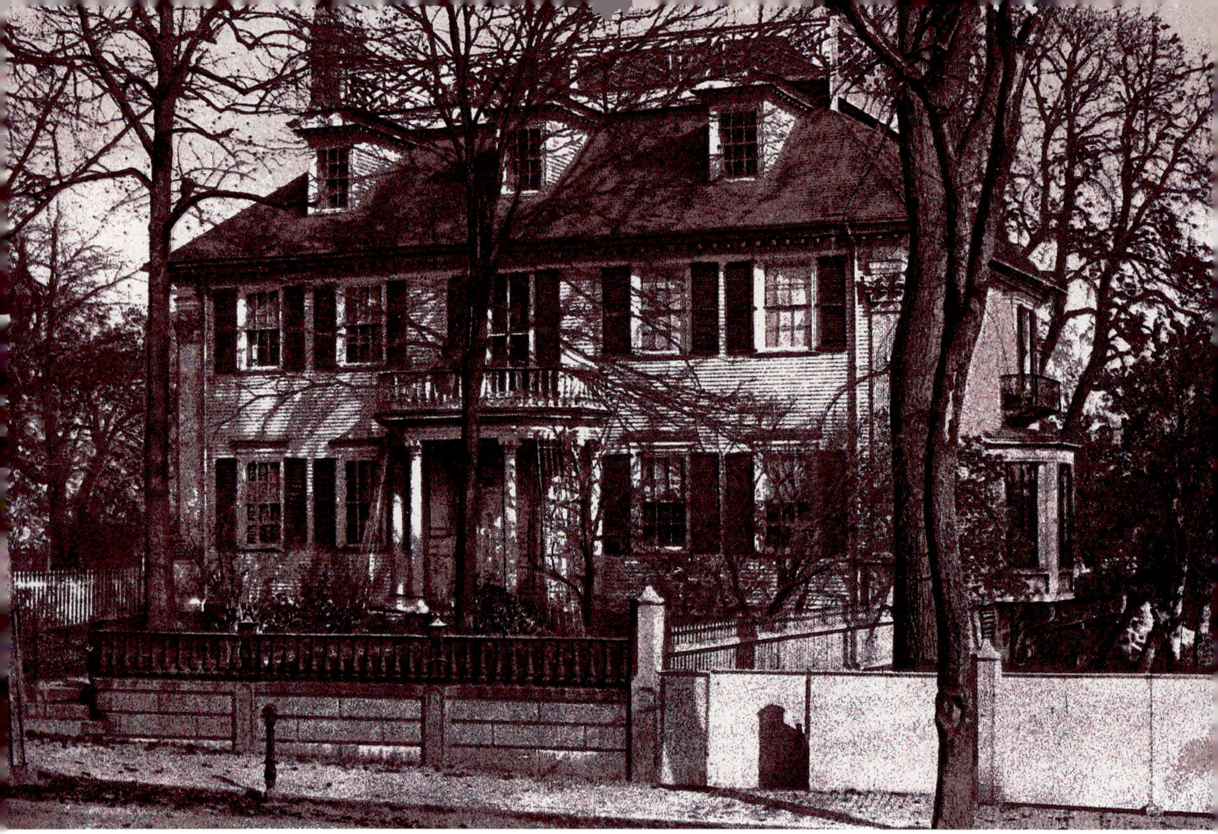

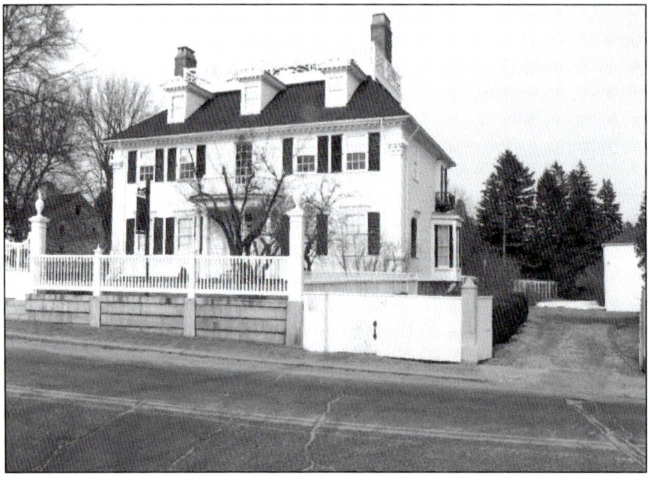

The Governor John Langdon House, *c.* 1907, is on Pleasant Street. The governor built this house in 1784. John Langdon used the Revolutionary War as his stepping stone to wealth and status. Following the war, he represented New Hampshire in Congress. He was the first president of the U.S. Senate. When he returned to Portsmouth, he was elected governor and served several terms.

The Richard Jackson House, built in 1664, is the oldest timber-framed house in Portsmouth. It is owned by the Society for Preservation of New England Antiquities (SPNEA) and sits on a hill overlooking North Mill Pond. This house was extensively renovated in 1930. SPNEA opens the house to the public during the summer months for tours. Portsmouth is known for having a fine collection of 18th- and 19th-century homes, many of which are wooden framed. Old homes are antiques and, as such, have special value. Old wooden homes are rare, as brick or stone are more favored building materials.

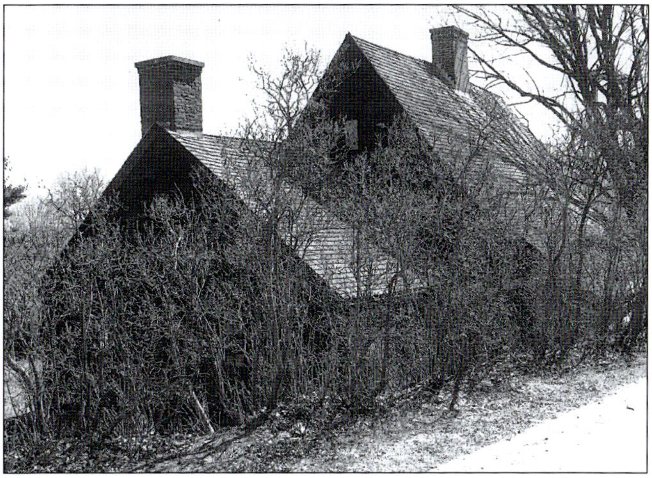

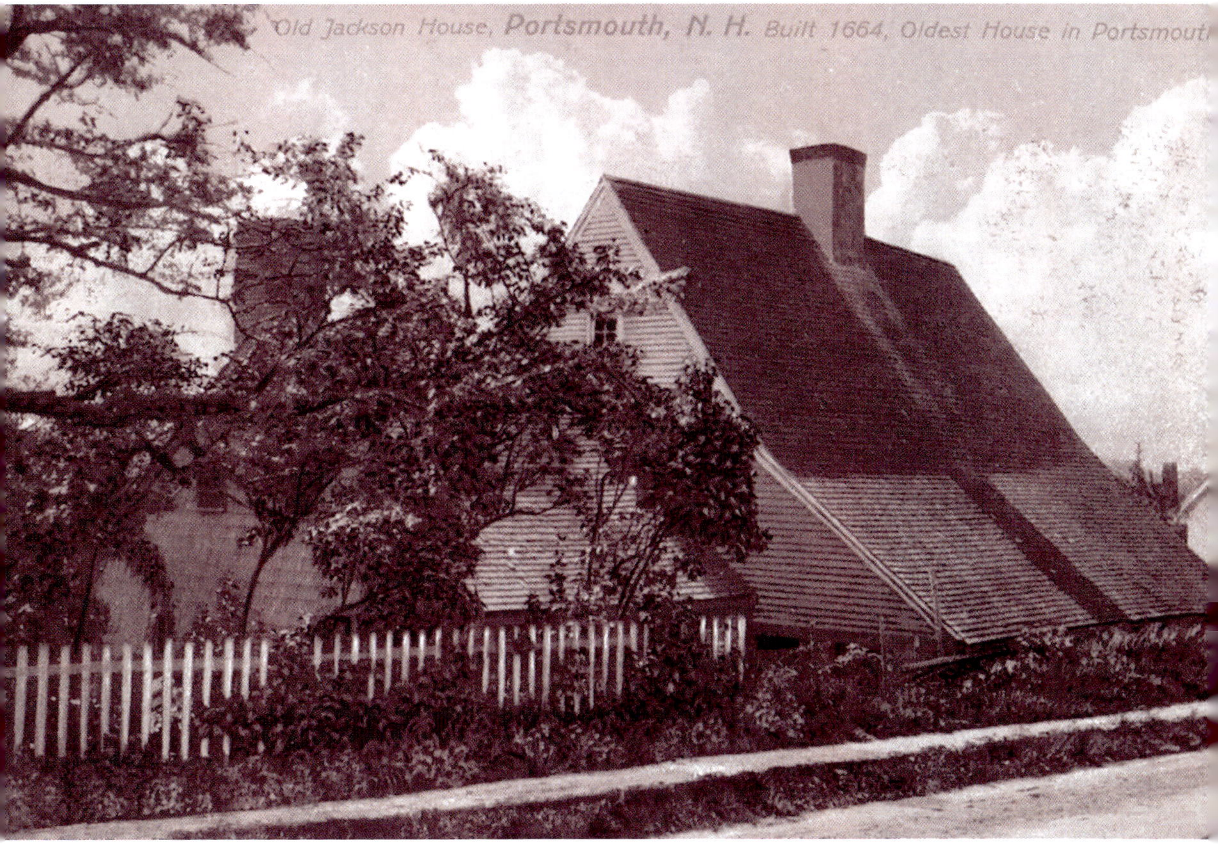

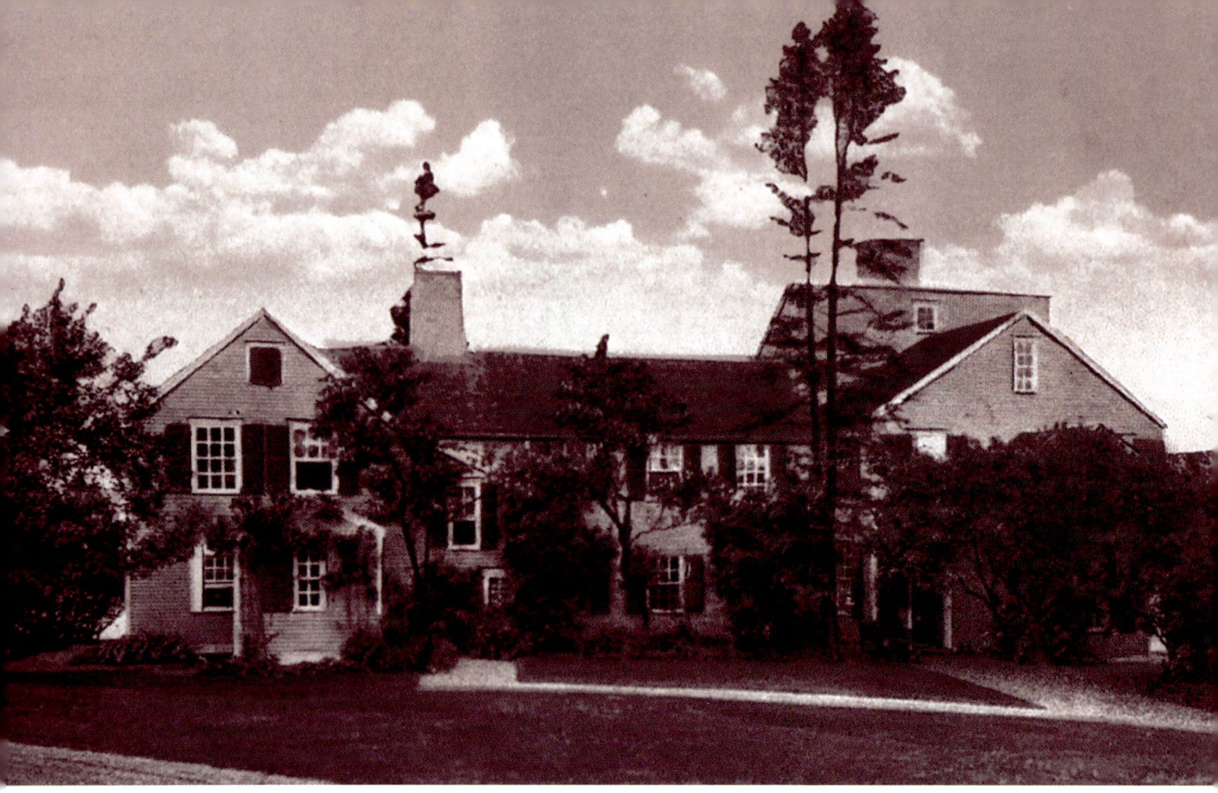

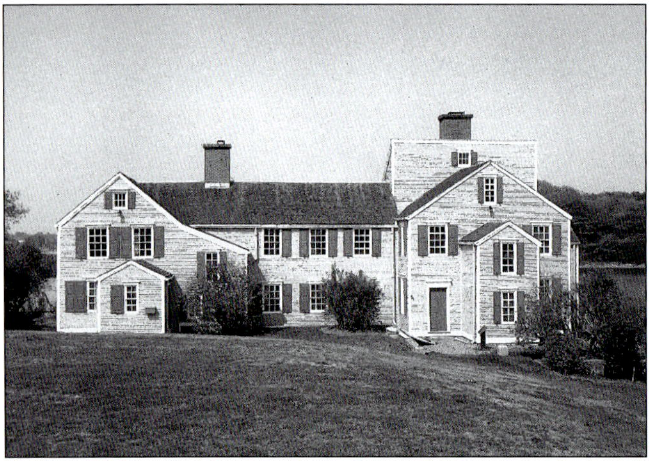

The Governor Benning Wentworth Mansion was built in 1750. Benning Wentworth was the royal governor of New Hampshire from 1741 to 1767. The governor lived here until his death in 1770. This mansion is one of the first homes of famous people to be open to the public. It has been attracting the public since the mid-19th century. It overlooks the island of New Castle and islands in the back channel.

On Middle Street, near Haymarket Square, stands the Samuel Larkin House, built in 1808. It is a fine brick home that stands on a slight hill. Its builder and first owner, Samuel Larkin, was a boat seller and auctioneer who made his fortune selling captured ships during the War of 1812. This is a distinctive house with its fanlight door and arched windows. Other than changes to the trees and shrubs, the Larkin House appears today much as it did *c.* 1900, as shown below.

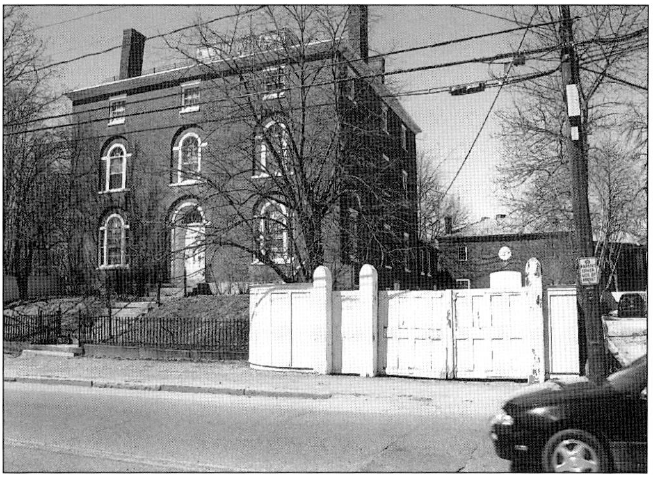

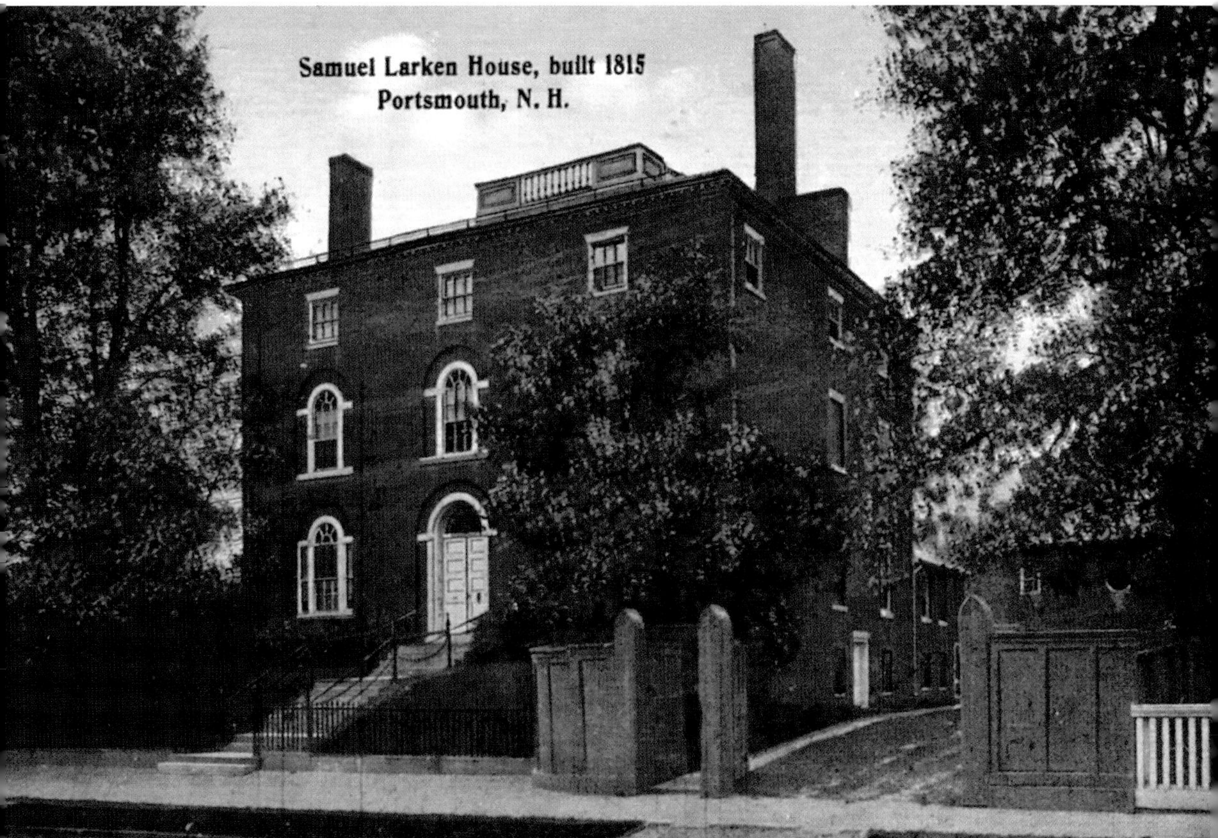

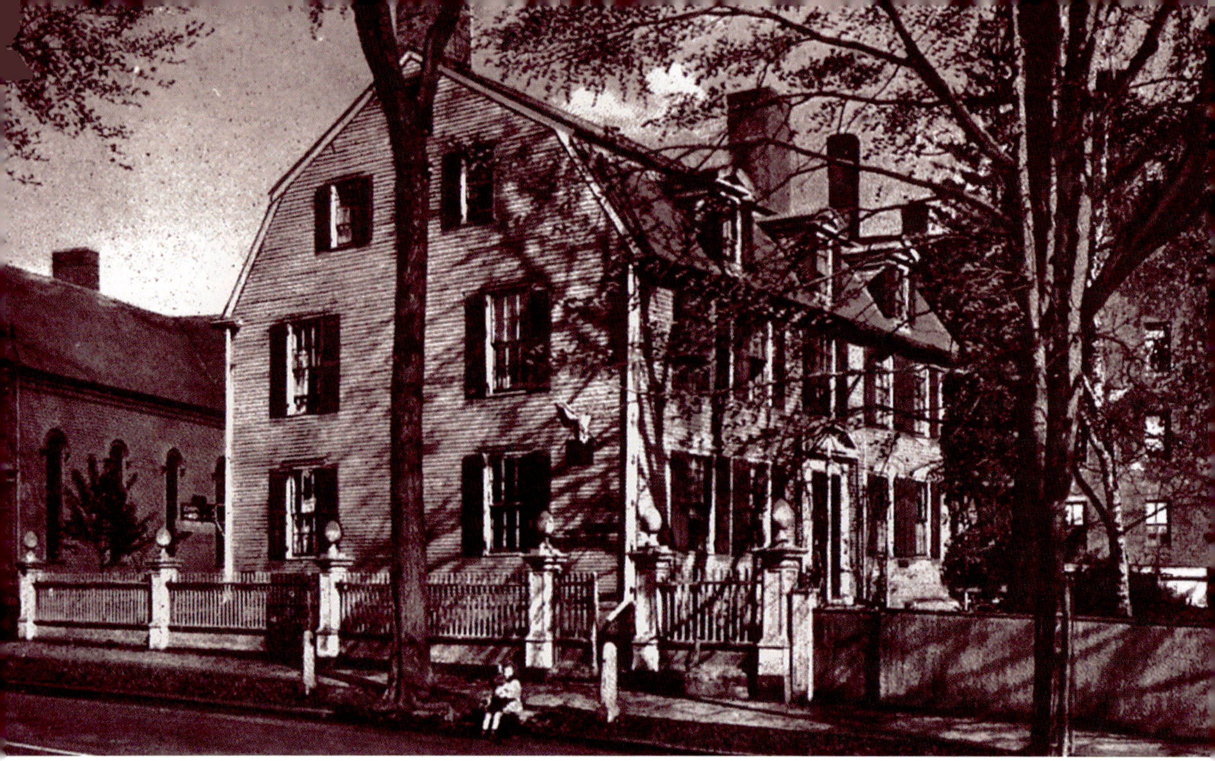

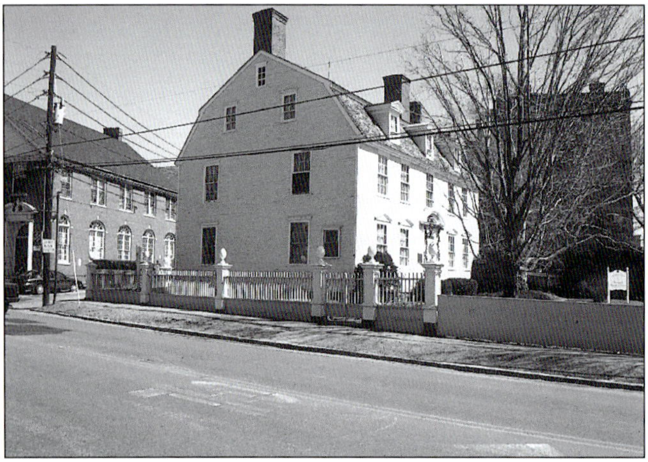

At the corner of State and Middle Streets, opposite the old Middle Street Baptist Church, is the John Paul Jones House, a grand three-story gambrel-roofed house that faces State Street. John Paul Jones was billeted in Portsmouth while awaiting the building of his ship the *Ranger*. The house became a rooming house after the death of its first owner and builder, Capt. Gregory Purcell. The Portsmouth Historical Society now owns the house and has been responsible for its extensive restoration.

On Pleasant Street, across from the intersection with Washington Street, stands the Wentworth House, which was built in 1769 by Gov. John Wentworth, the last of the royal governors. Wentworth was in complete support of the Crown during the onset and battles of the Revolutionary War. At the close of the war, he returned to Great Britain and remained there for the rest of his life. His house, shown below *c.* 1900, was restored and is now a nursing home. At the rear is a new extension that runs down to South Mill Pond.

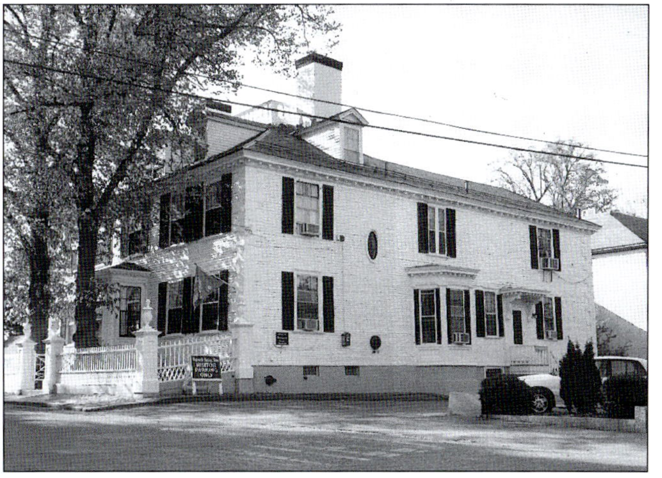

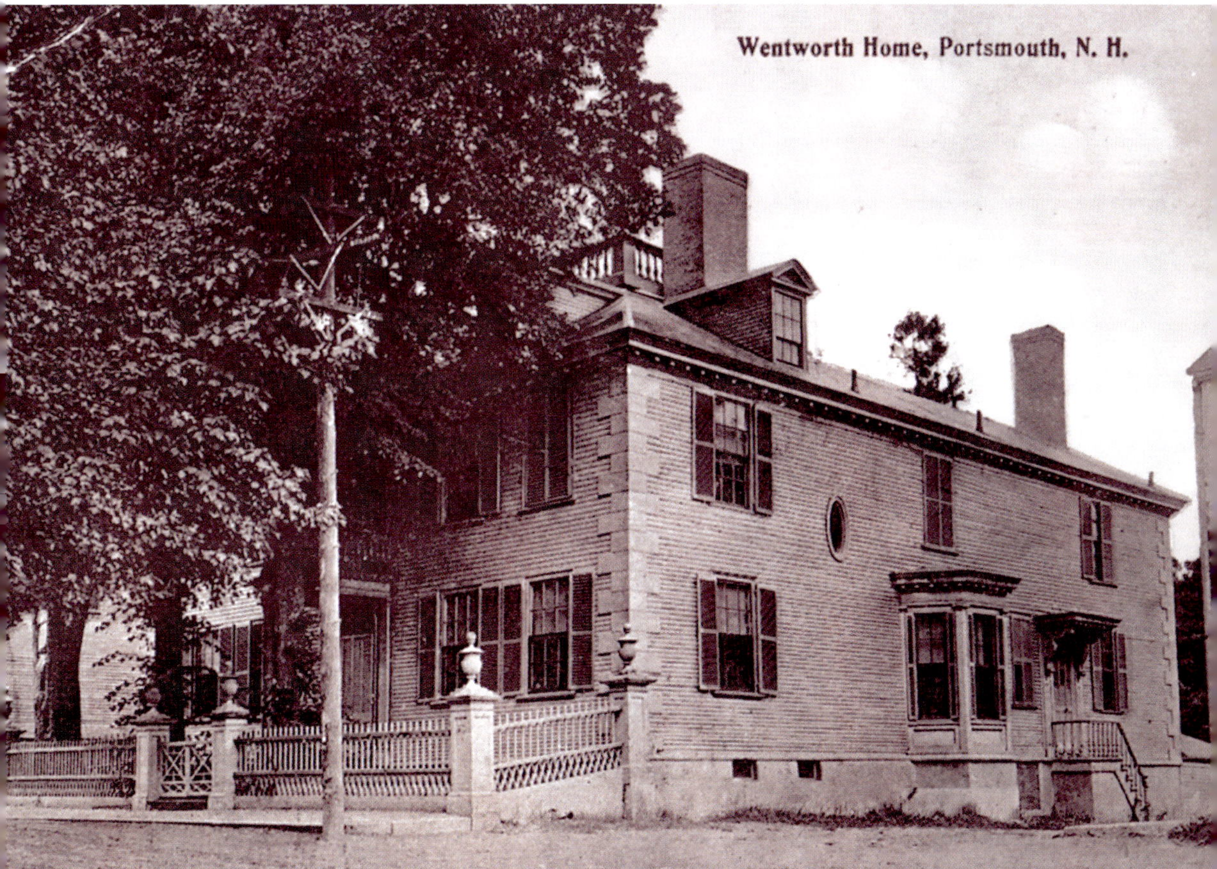

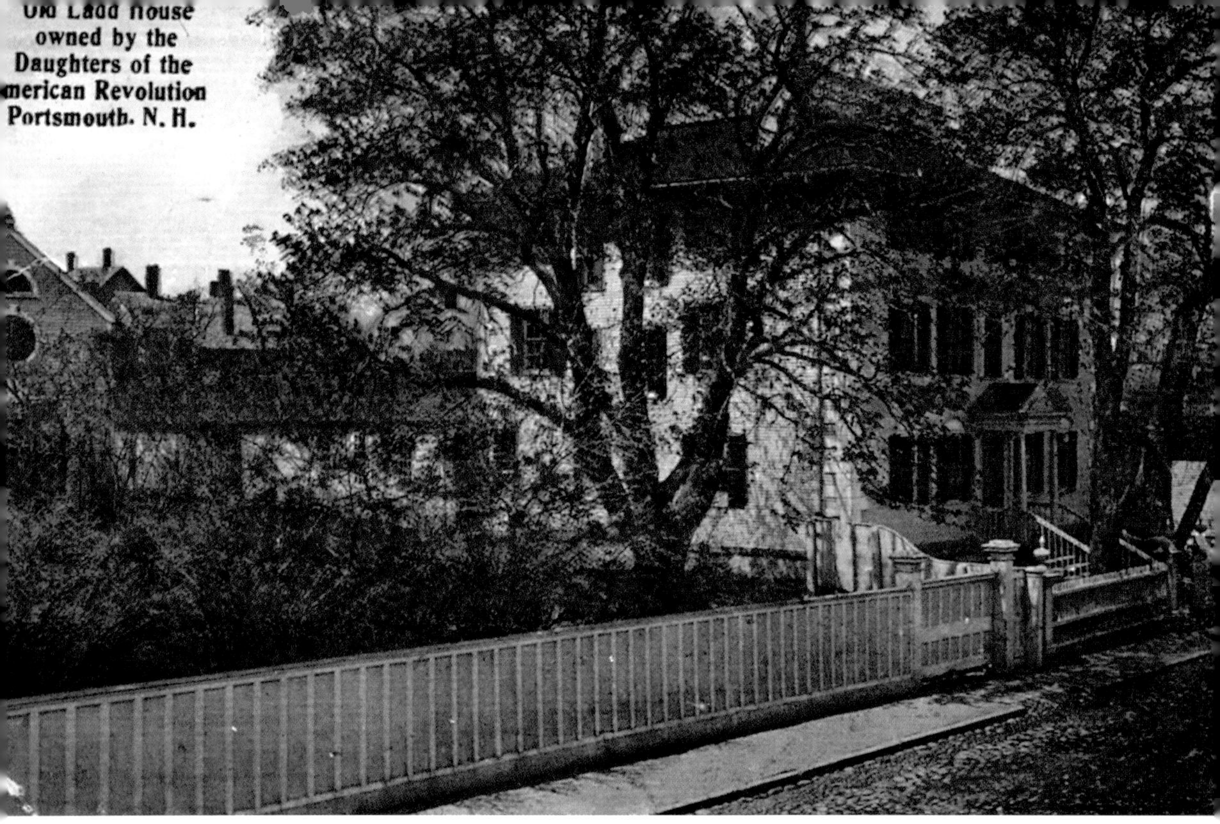

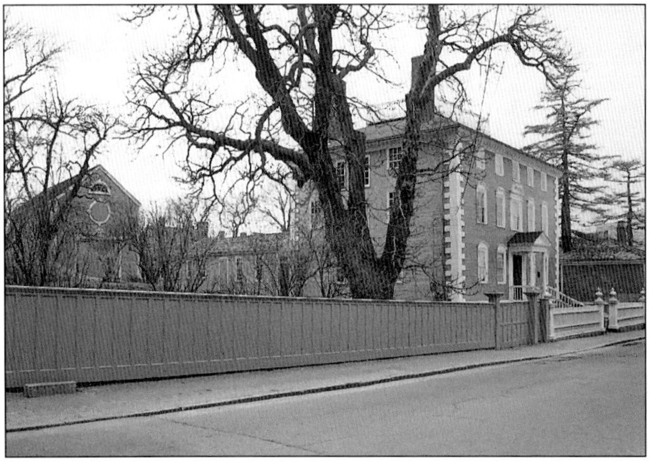

As a gift to his son Samuel, John Moffatt erected the Moffatt-Ladd House on Market Street in 1760. The senior Moffatt arrived in Portsmouth in the early 1720s and married into a wealthy family from Kittery, Maine. When he had this house built, he put a small fortune into its construction. While the father was successful, the son was not. He sold the house in 1819 to Alexander Ladd. Over the years, it has been extensively remodeled. It stands as a great example of mid-18th-century architecture.

The view below, *c.* 1910, was taken from the hill on which stood the Cottage Hospital. From this perspective, there is nothing to be seen of the central business district. There is only the road, crossing South Mill Pond to where it joins Pleasant Street. In the middle background is the Governor John Langdon House. The publishers of the postcard obviously did not know Portsmouth; they misnamed the church to the left of the road. It was the Universalist church, not the Episcopal church, as stated. Today, with fewer trees and a greater number of buildings, more of downtown is visible.

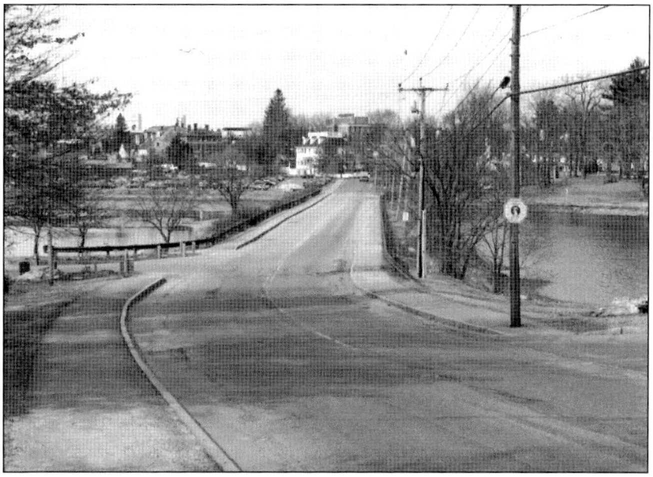

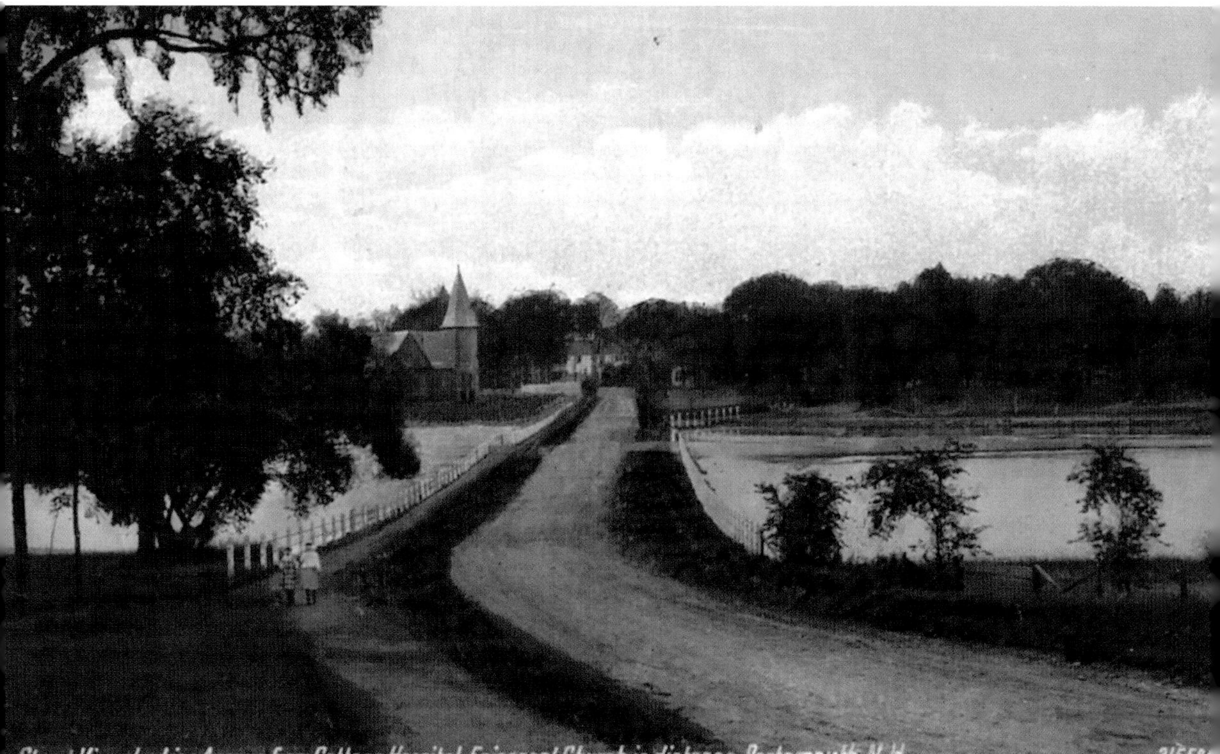

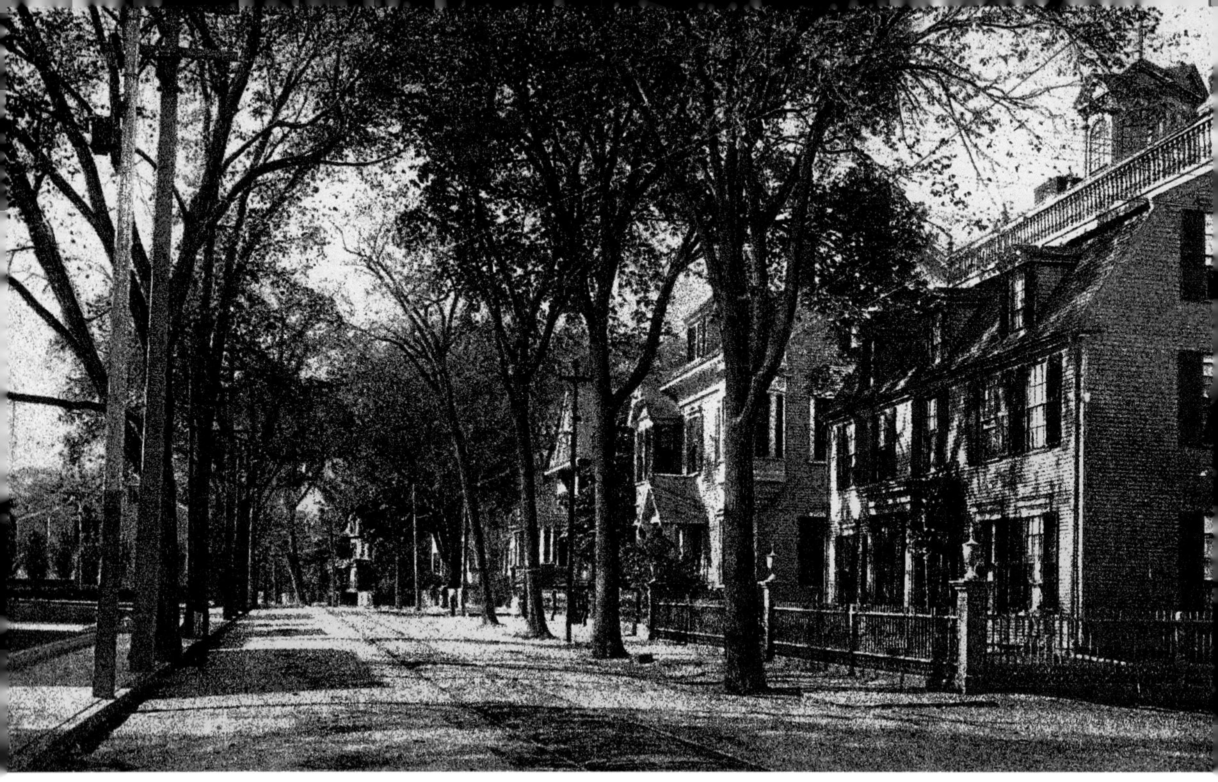

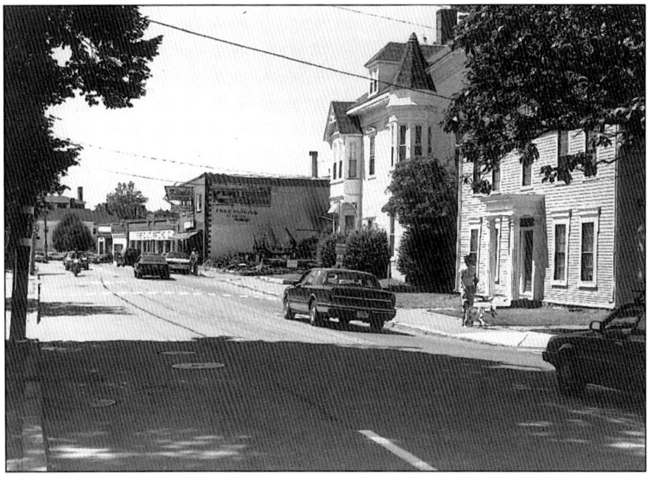

This *c.* 1910 view was taken looking west from the intersection of Congress, Middle, Maplewood, and Islington Streets. At the time, Islington was a residential, tree-lined street with gracious homes on the right side. The first home is the Buckminster House, built in 1720 by Daniel Warner. The house is named for the Reverend Joseph Buckminster, who was one of the 19th-century pastors of North Church. The street in the foreground on the right is Bridge Street.

From the center of Haymarket Square, looking east down State Street *c.* 1900, are homes that were then just outside of downtown. On the left side of the photograph is the fence and front lawn of the John Paul Jones House. Farther up the street, and somewhat visible through the trees is the Rockingham Hotel. In the photograph today, the Rockingham Hotel stands out as the identifying feature.

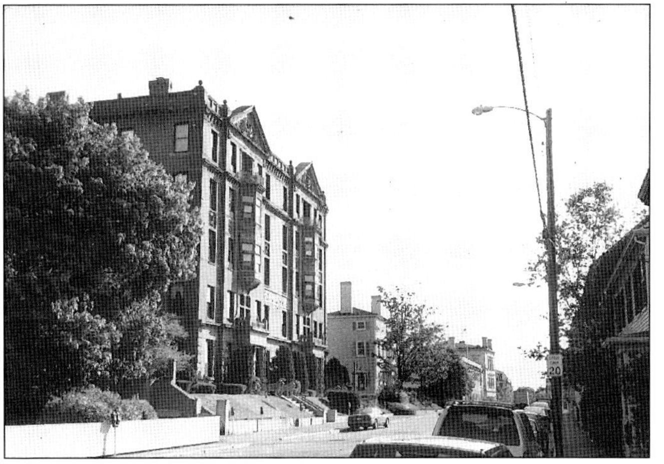

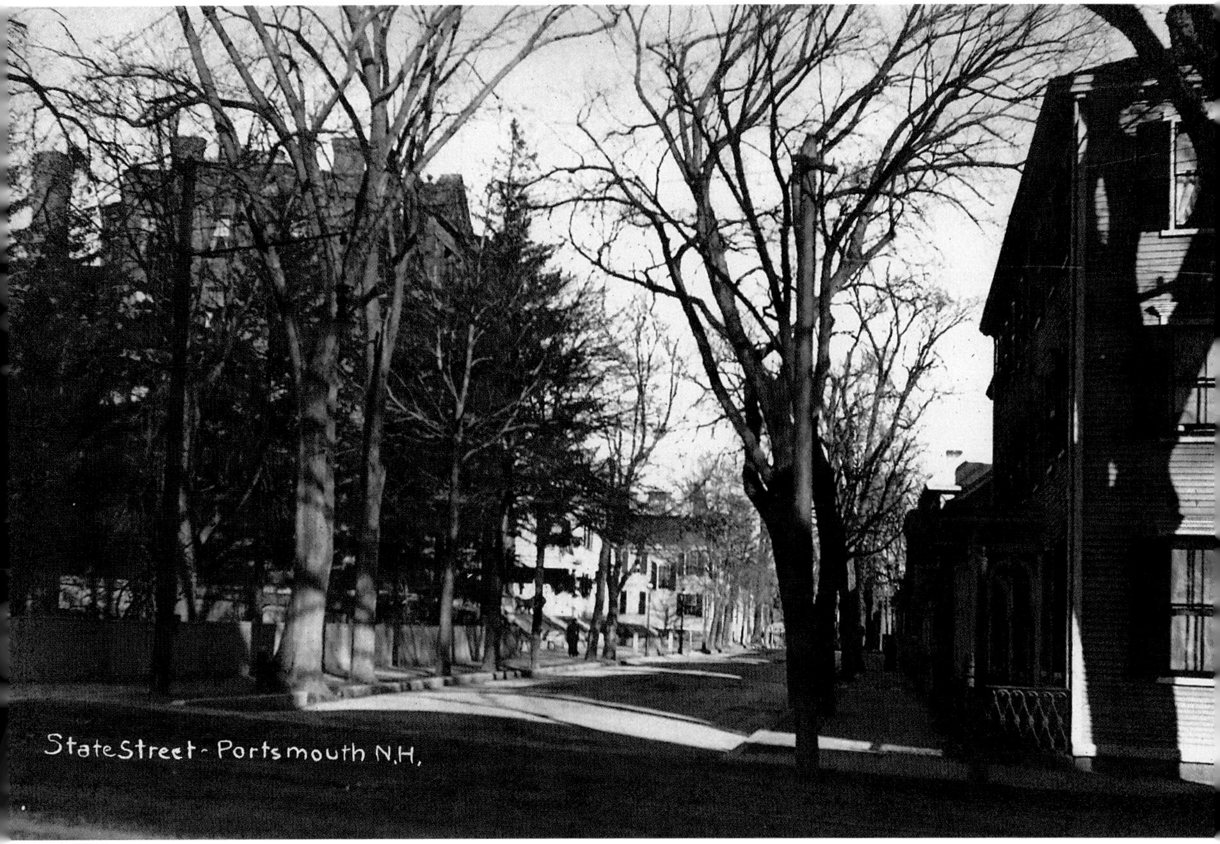

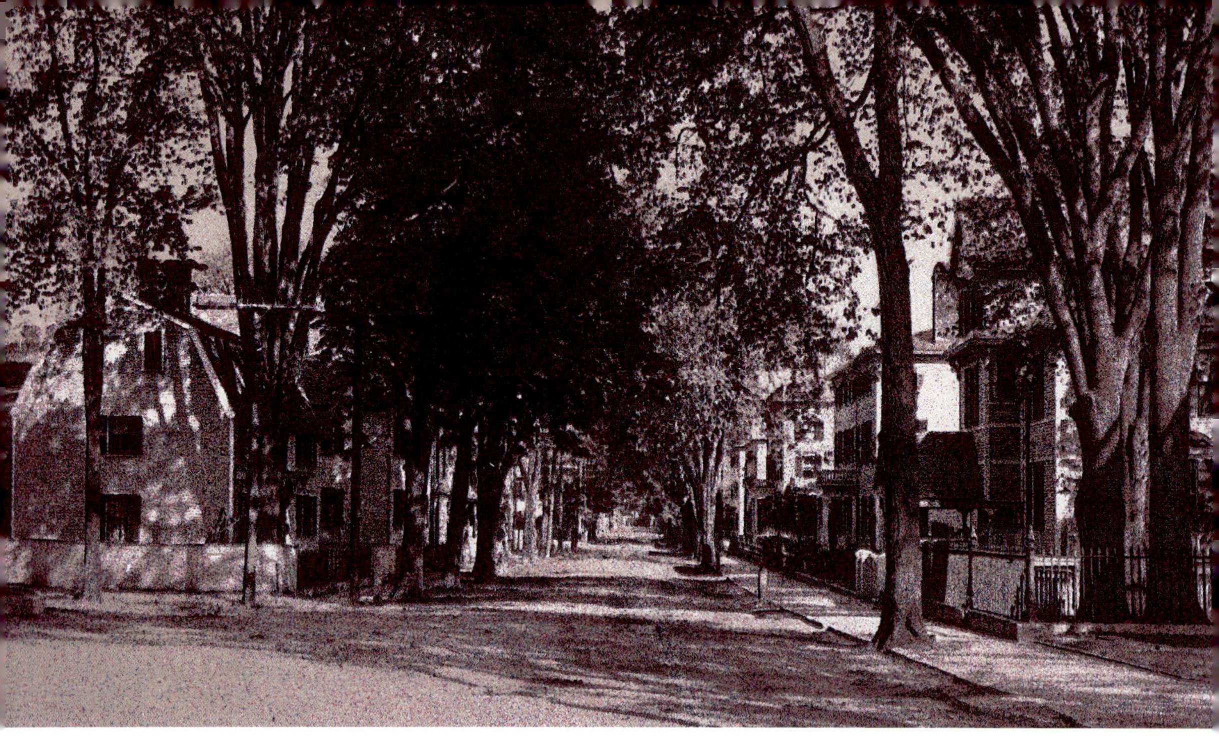

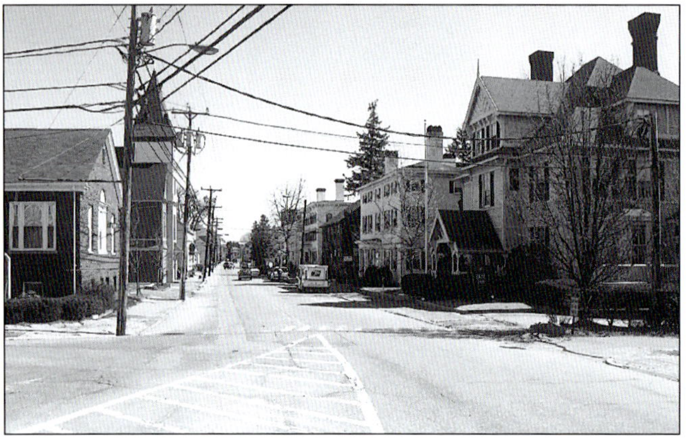

Taken from Haymarket Square, this view looks east down Court Street *c.* 1907. The street was almost all residential at the time. The gambrel-roofed building on the left side of Court Street was the Oracle House, from which Charles Pierce published the *Oracle of the Day* newspaper in 1793. Today the Oracle House is elsewhere. It was removed and replaced by a brick building named the Rufus E. Ross Memorial Building. The building on the right, in the postcard, still stands; it was renovated as the Sise Inn, a modern bed-and-breakfast.

Haymarket Square is shown below as it appeared in 1910. The square gets its name from the place where hay was weighed and valued between 1755 and 1785; the name has carried on ever since. The building on the left is part of the Middle Street Baptist Church. The church was on the corner of State and Middle Streets, across from the John Paul Jones House. In today's photograph the church is the annex to the building.

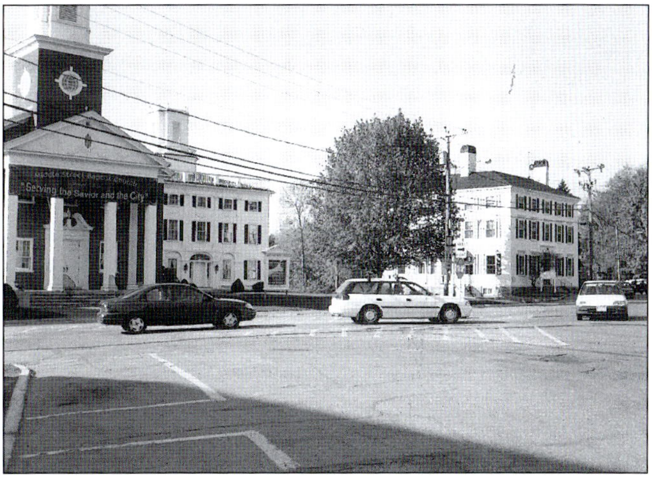

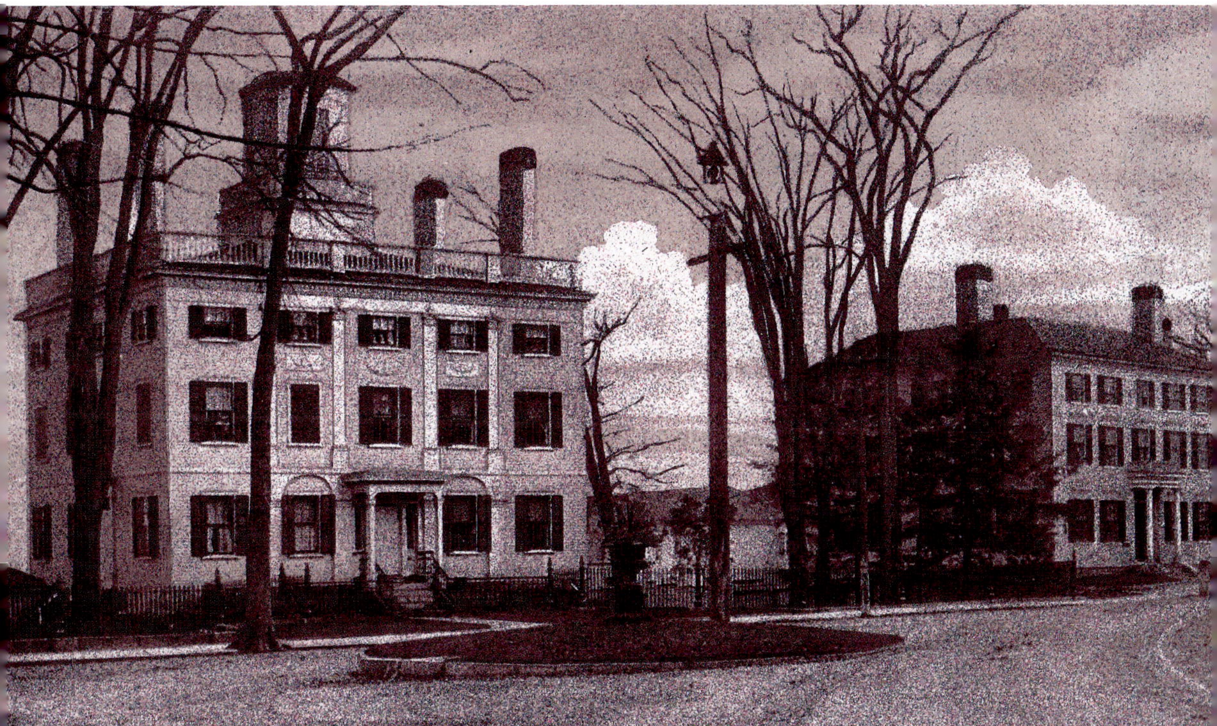

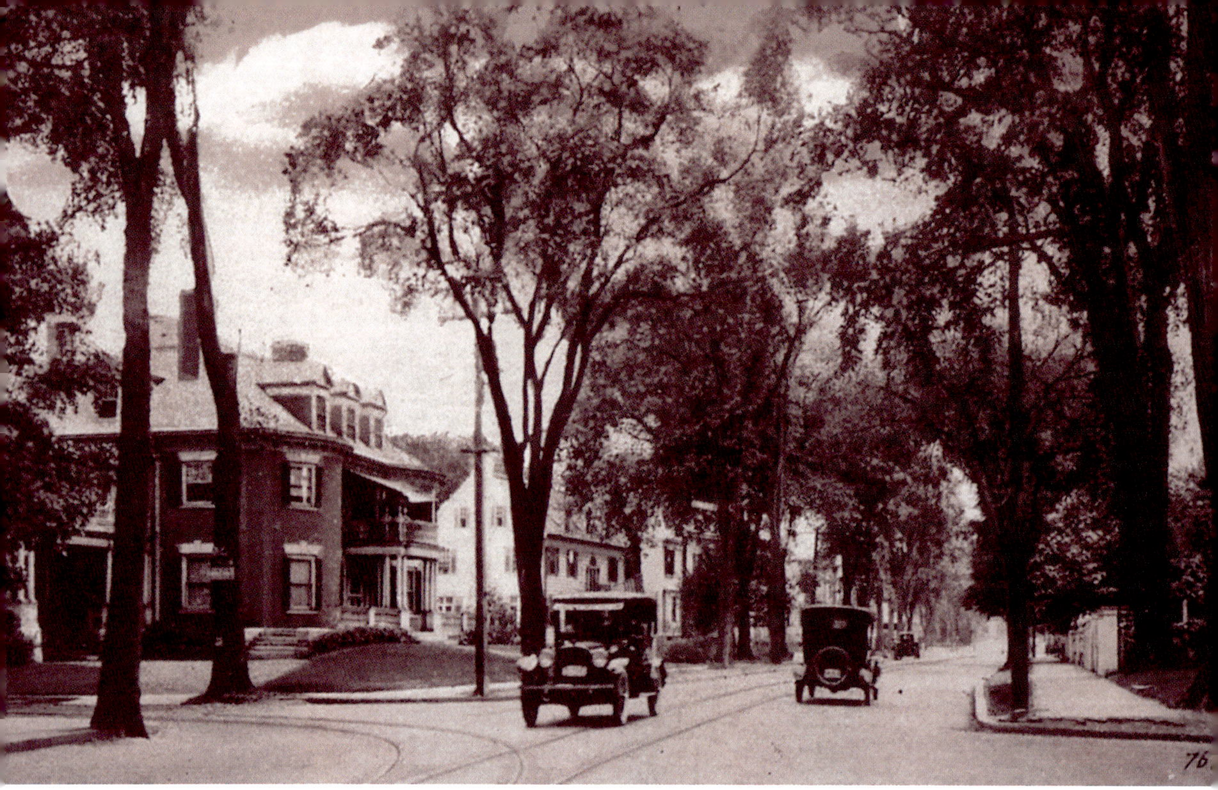

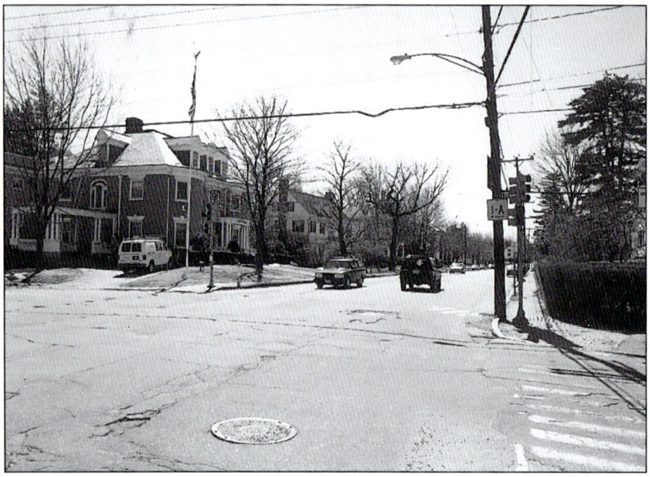

Located 400 yards west of Haymarket Square is the intersection of Middle and Summer Streets and Miller Avenue. In the old photograph, *c.* 1920, the trolley tracks are visible. The ones that turn left and enter Miller Avenue are the tracks for the trolleys that went to Hampton Beach and in-between stops along the way. The prominent building in the left center is the William Hackett house, built in 1892. It is now the Masonic Lodge.

Turning left with the tracks onto Miller Avenue, *c.* 1920, it opens up into one of many residential tree-lined streets. Miller Avenue leads from Middle Street to South Street; at that intersection, the road becomes Sagamore Road. From the South Street end of Miller Avenue, the houses remain pretty much as they were in the 1920s. The only real difference is that the trolley tracks have been removed and the street has been paved.

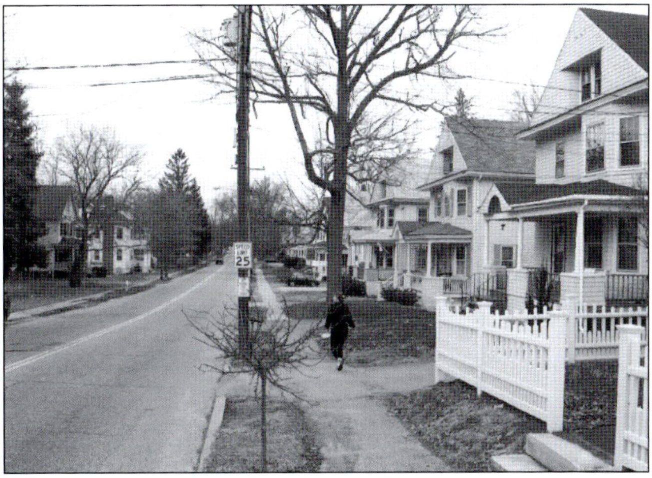

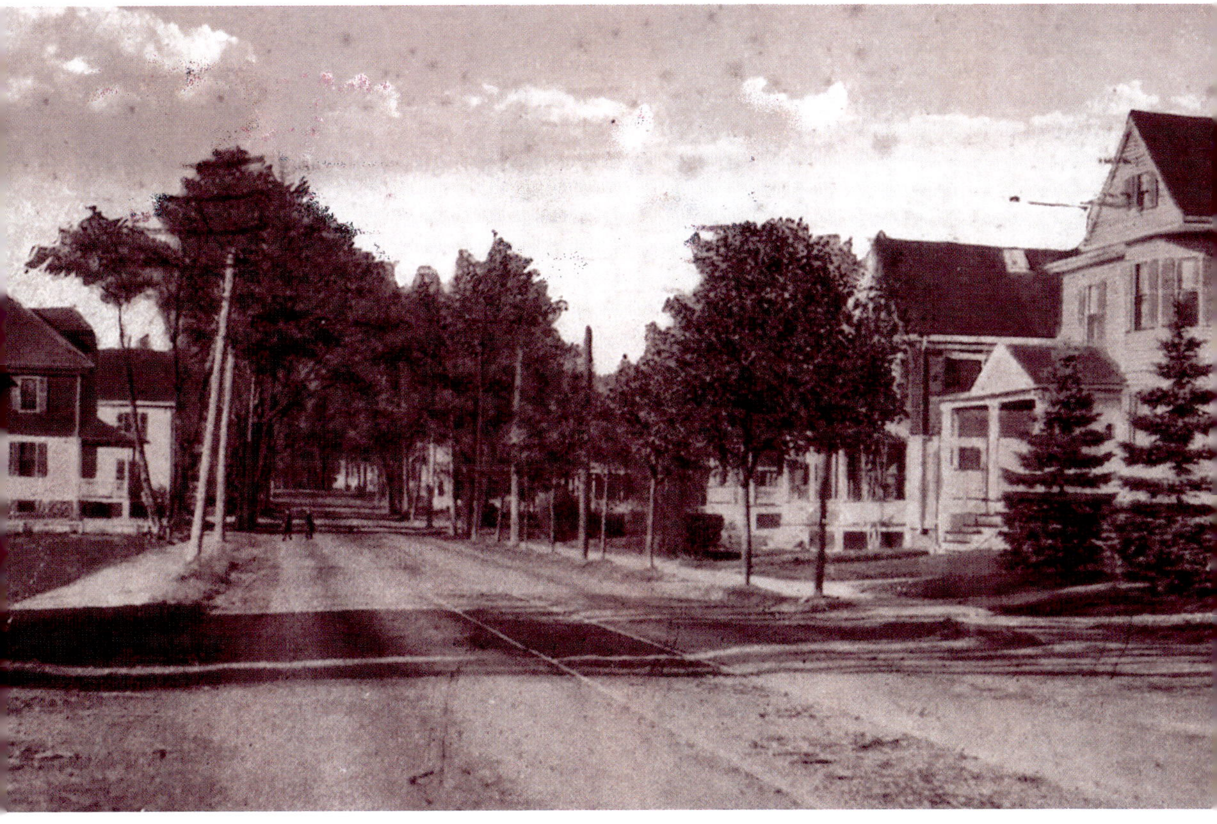

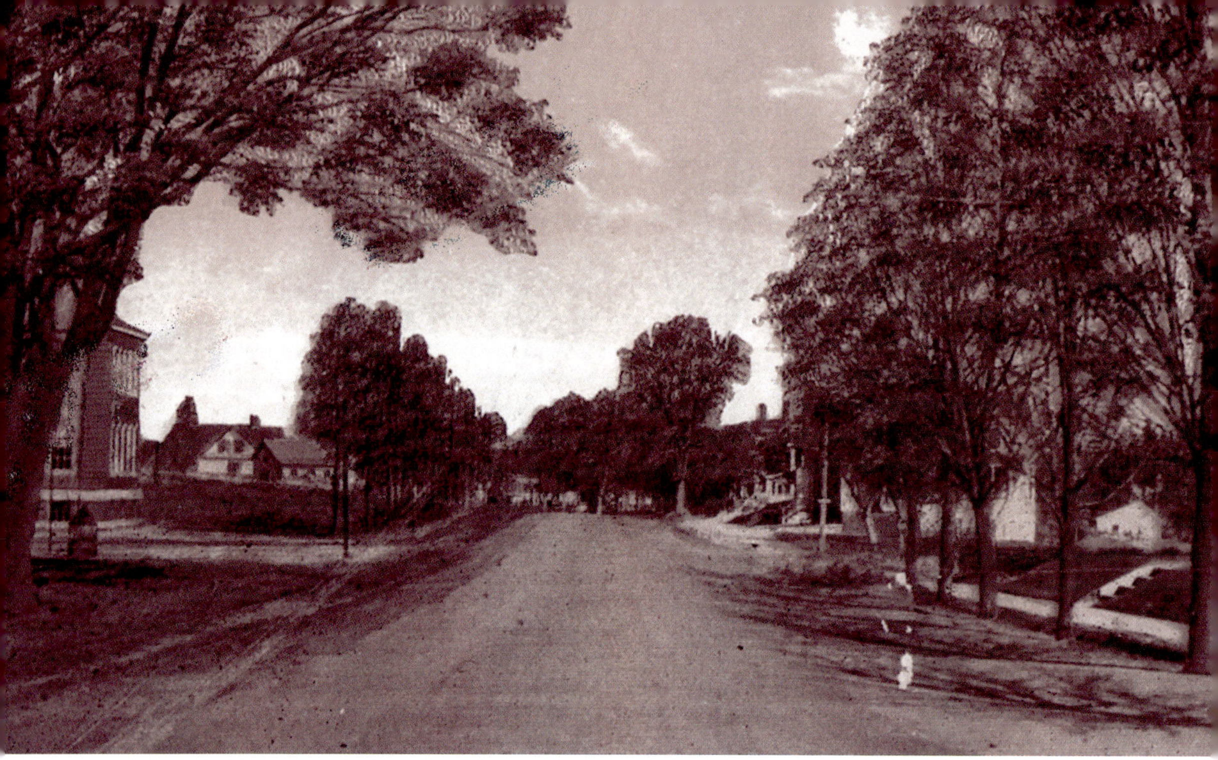

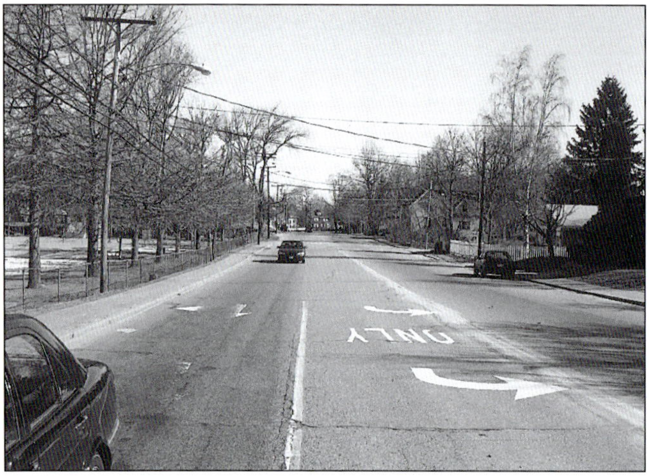

This view was taken *c.* 1920 from the intersection of South and Middle Streets with Lafayette Road and Portsmouth Avenue, looking east down Middle Street. On the left side of the photograph is the Lafayette School. Middle Street was (and still is) the main thoroughfare leading south from Portsmouth.

Farther down Middle Street, where the road makes a lazy S-turn, Middle Street today is almost identical to how the street appeared *c.* 1920. While some of the trees fell victim to Dutch elm disease, Middle Street remains one of the nice, residential neighborhoods in Portsmouth.

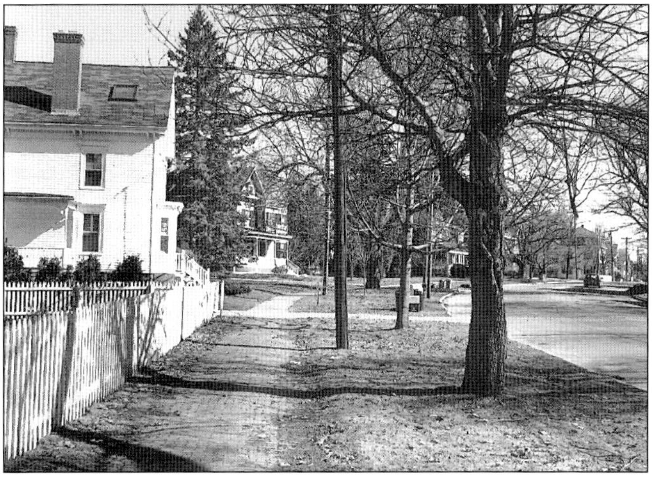

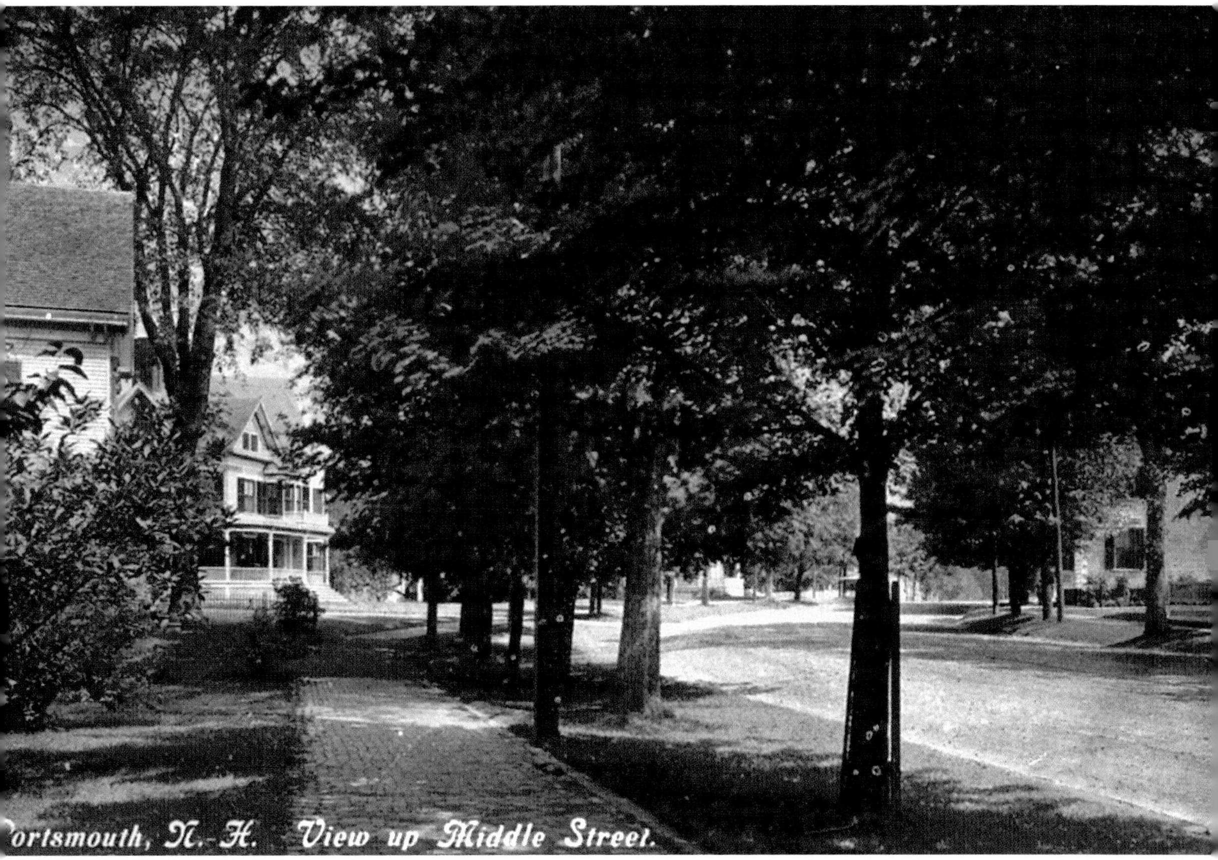

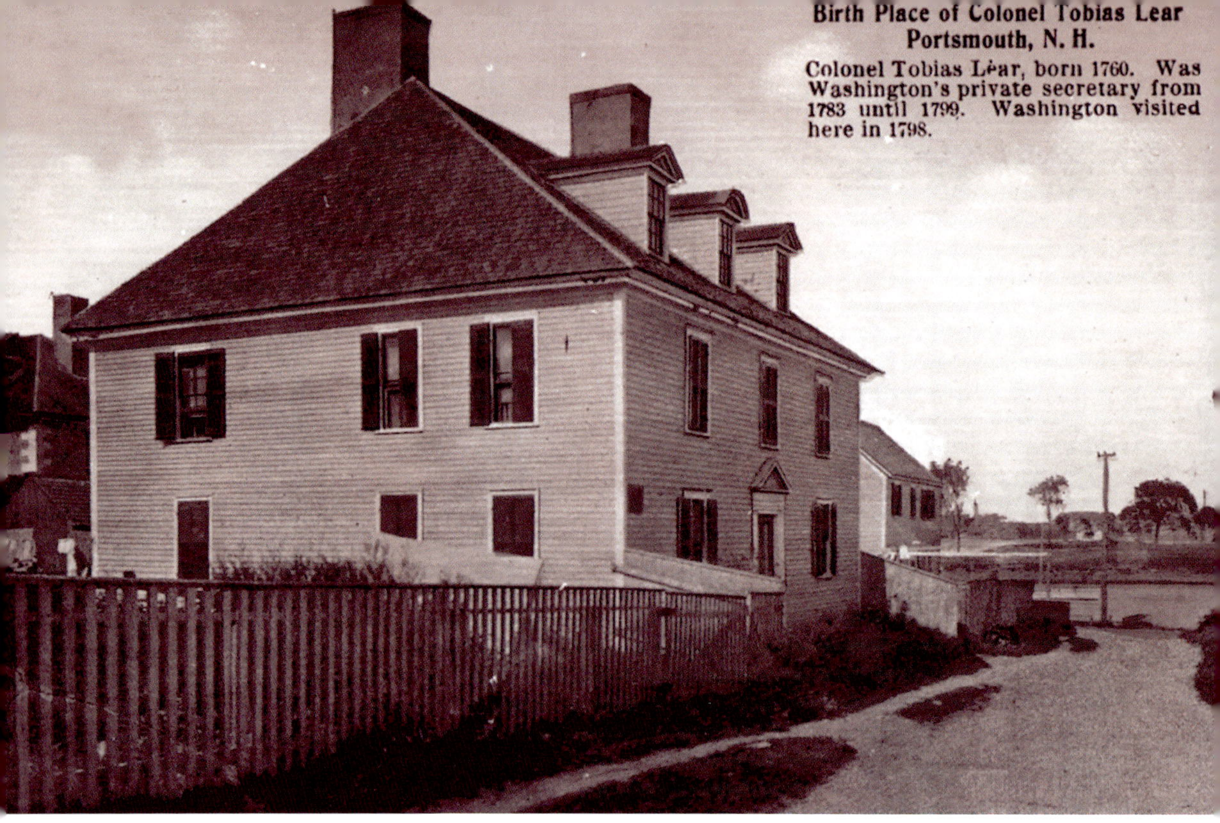

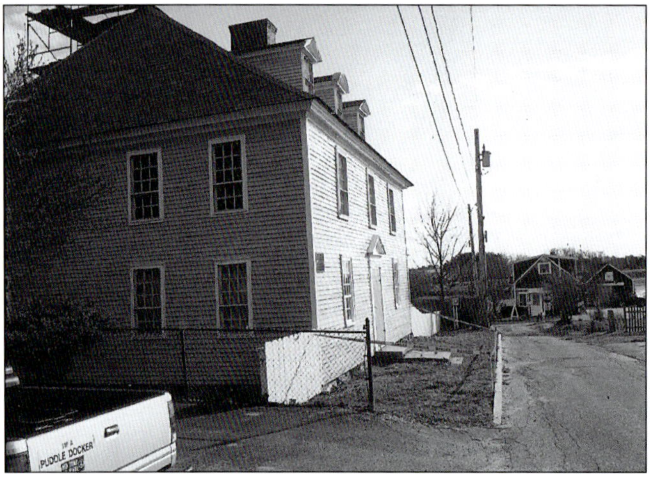

In the south end of Portsmouth, on Hunking Street, *c.* 1910, is the 18th-century Tobias Lear House. Hunking Street leads from Marcy Street to Mechanic Street and then to the waterfront. This returns our pictorial story to our starting point. The Lear House is located on one of many narrow waterfront streets that have been preserved. Many of the buildings have front lawns only a few feet wide, and houses are built very close to one another. Tobias Lear was George Washington's private secretary.

The major road south from Portsmouth is Lafayette Road (Route 1). In the 1950s, the S.J. LaCava Lobster Company built its lobster pound on the banks of the Sagamore Creek where it was crossed by Lafayette Road. The building was erected on a floating concrete pad because the wetlands board regulations did not permit a foundation to be dug. Today, this concrete pad has been extended to form a small shopping center that houses two restaurants as well as several retail stores.

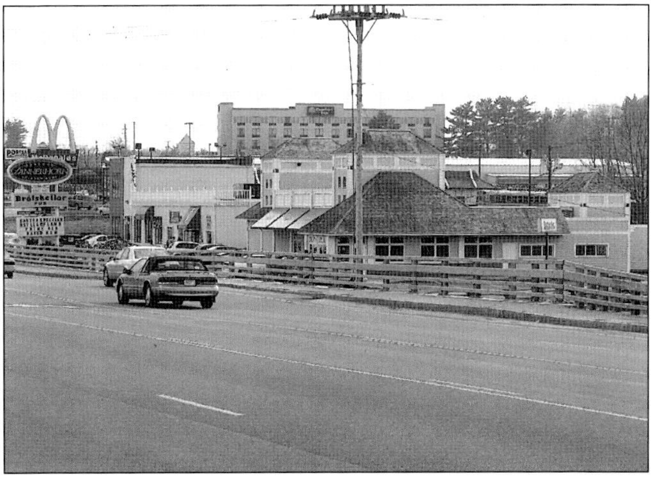

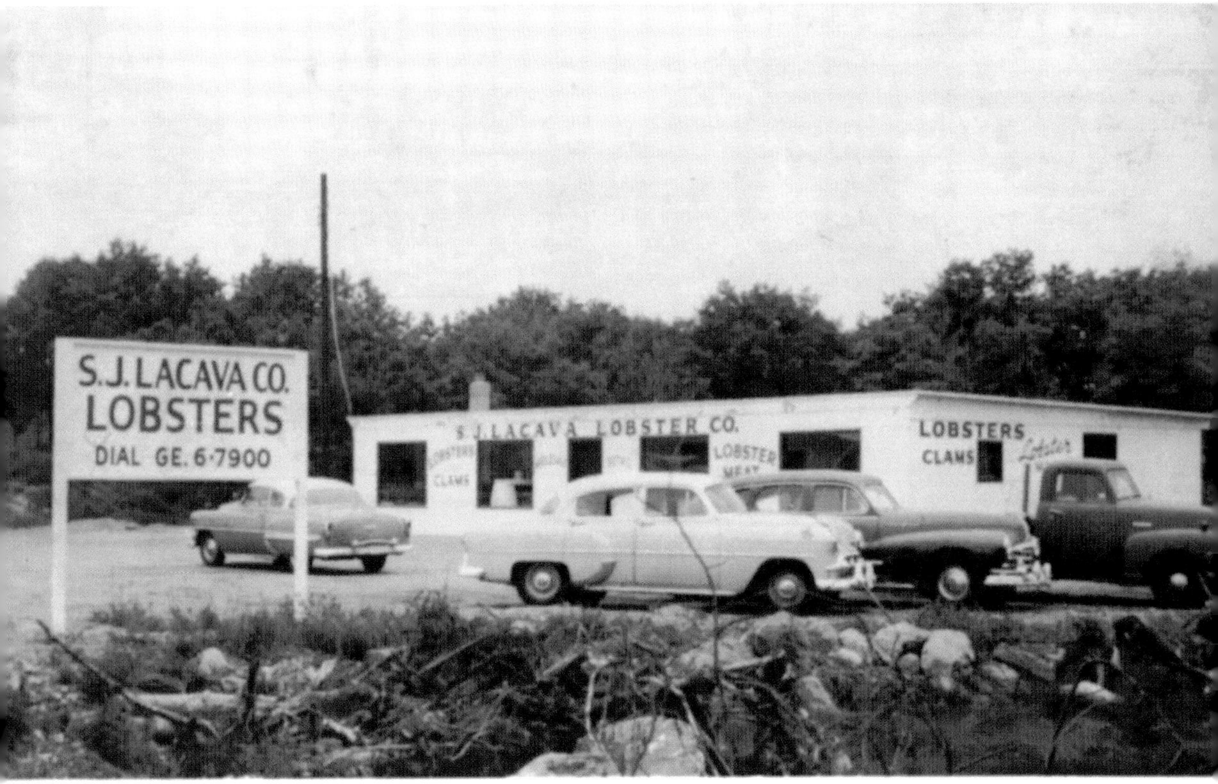

S. J. LaCAVA CO. - Lobsters - 990 Lafayette Road - Telephone GE. 6-7900 - Portsmouth, N.

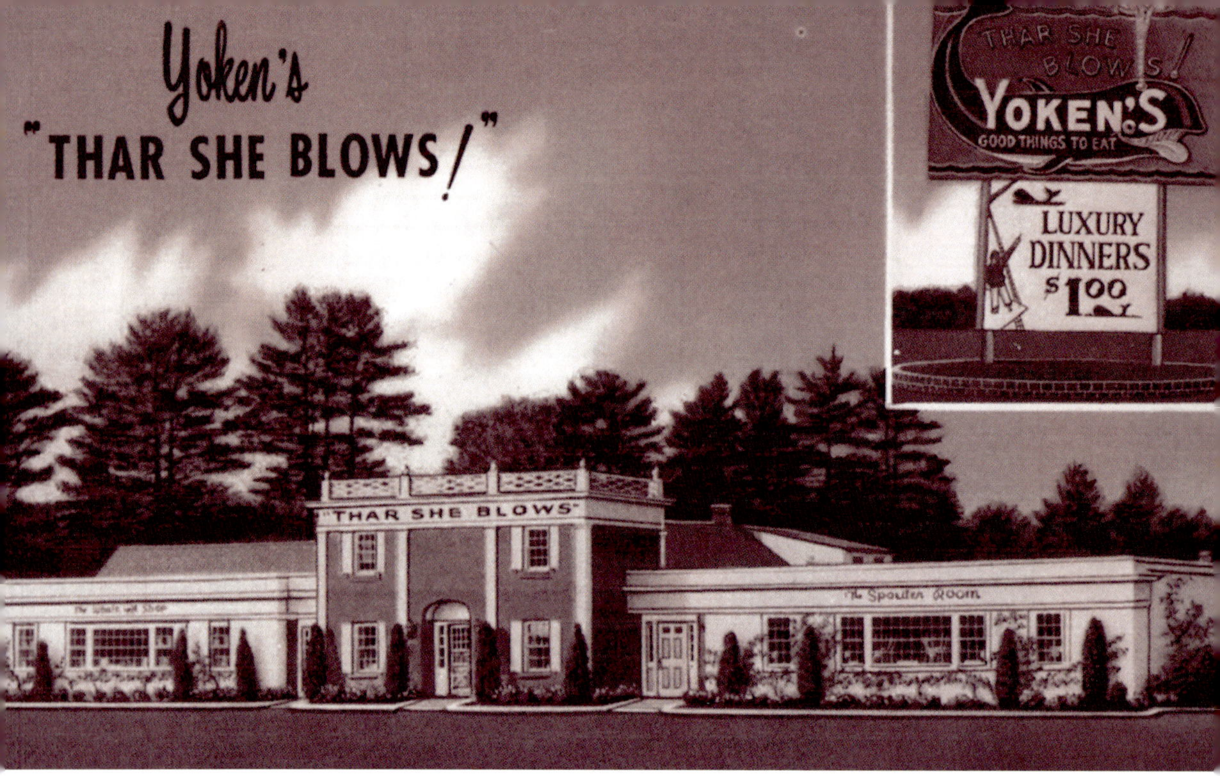

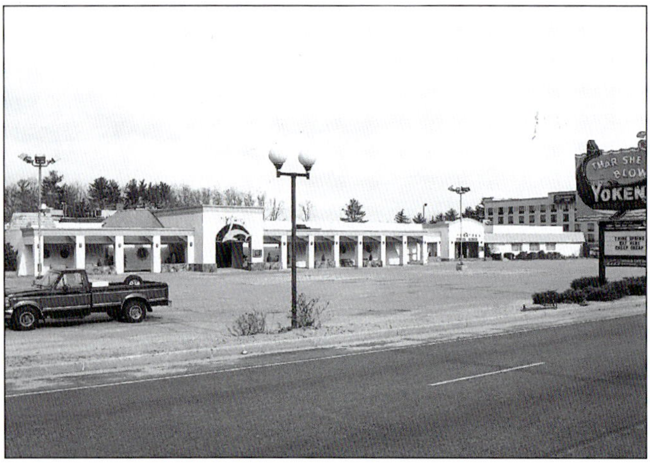

Farther out on Lafayette Road, at the corner of Peverly Hill Road, stands a tradition in family dining in Portsmouth. Yoken's "Thar She Blows" restaurant was purchased by Harry Yoken in 1946. At the time, it was a drive-in called the Parkway. In 1958, Harry MacLeod Sr. became a partner in the business. Since that time, Yoken's has been a family business. Harry MacLeod Jr. ran the business from 1970 to 1989. Today, Kevin MacLeod owns and runs the restaurant. The external Yoken's has changed often, but the good food and the family ownership remains.

Diagonally across from S.J. LaCava was the Foyecliff Inn, the water and marshes in the foreground are those at the end of Sagamore Creek. In the 1940s, the inn was torn down to make room for the radio station and transmitting tower that are still on the site today.

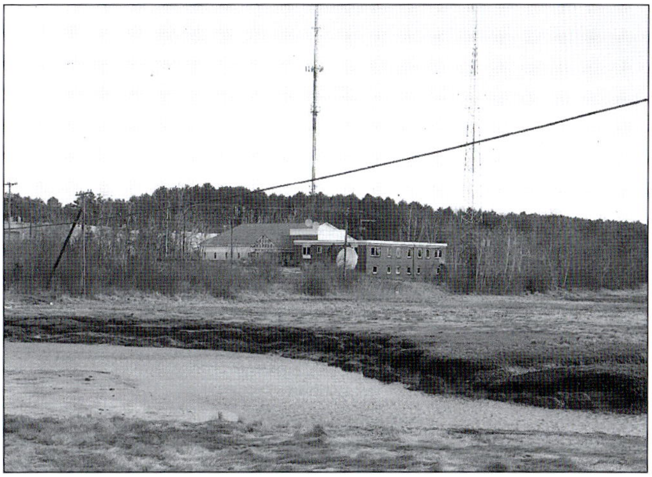

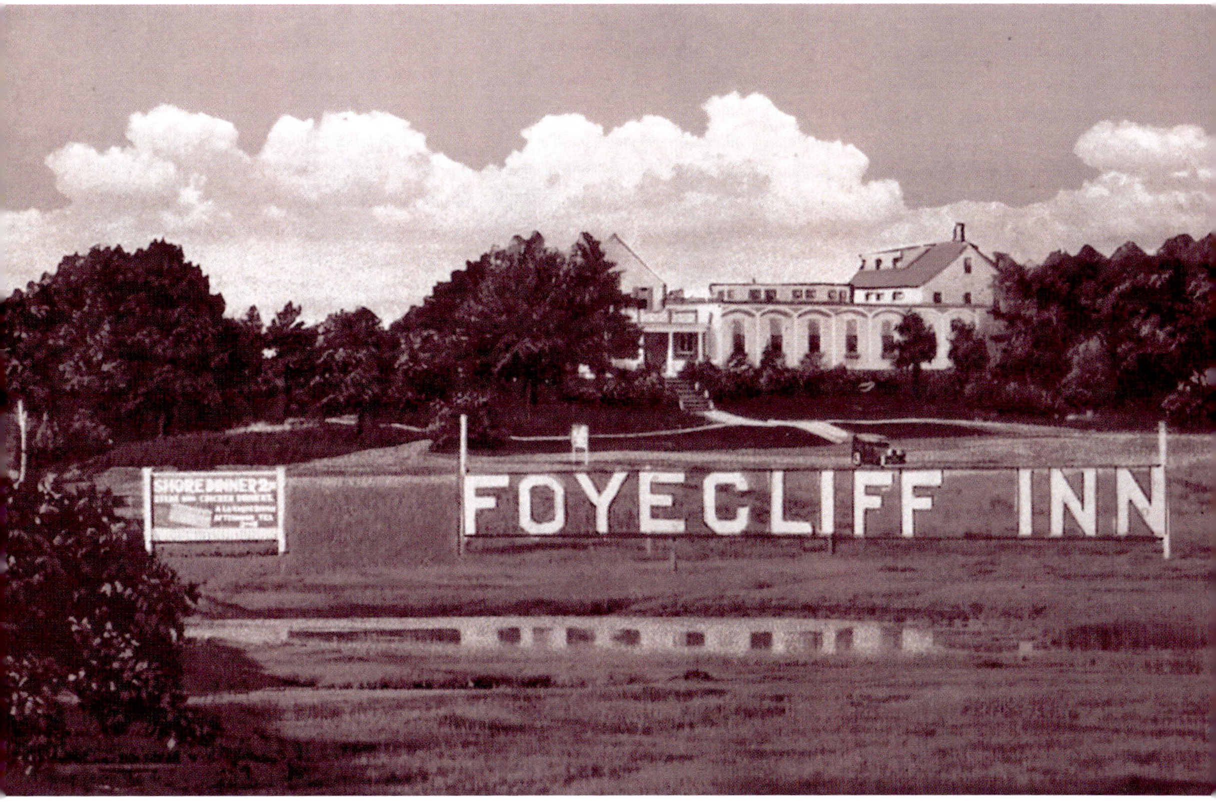

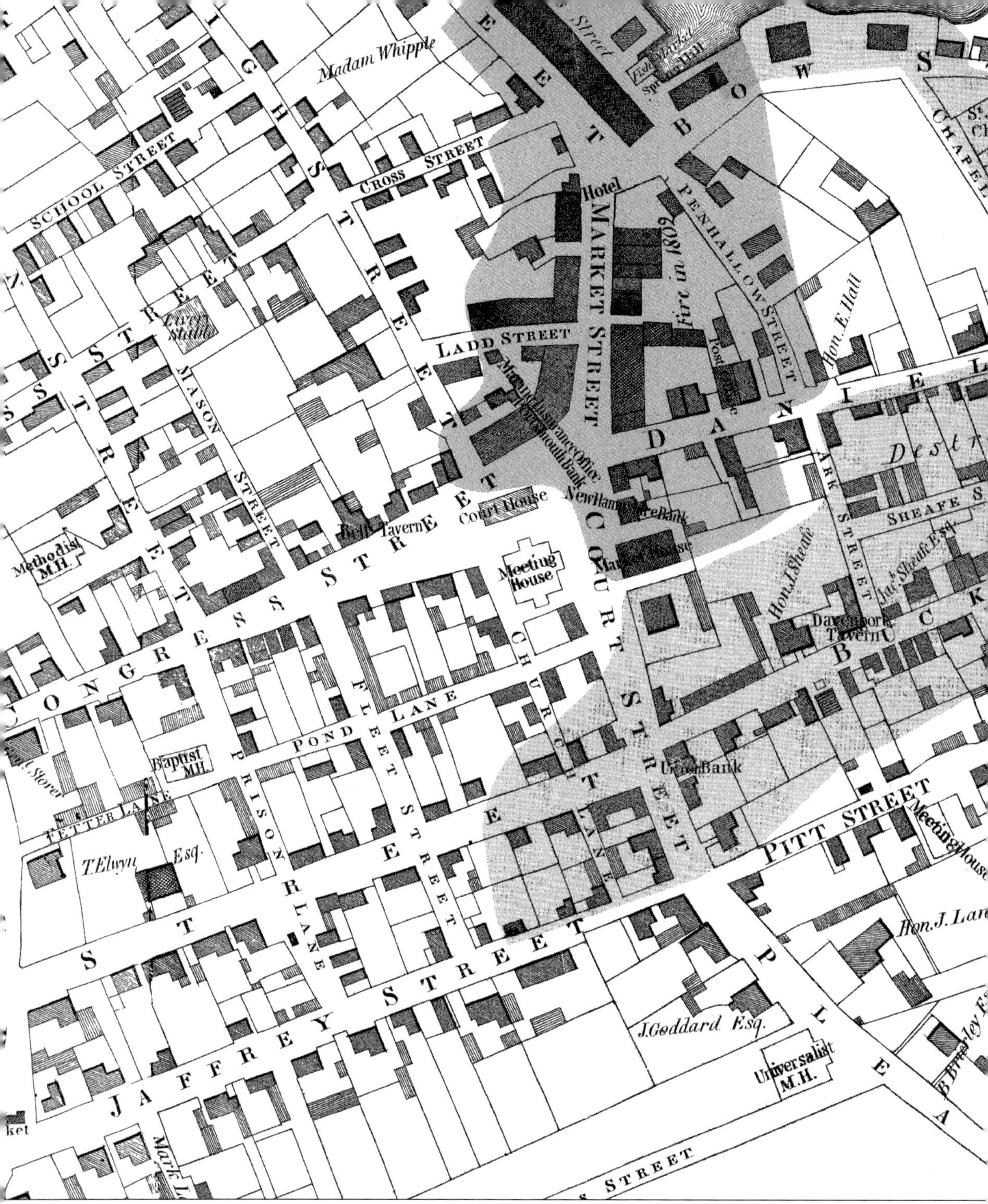

Detail of an 1813 Portsmouth fire map.

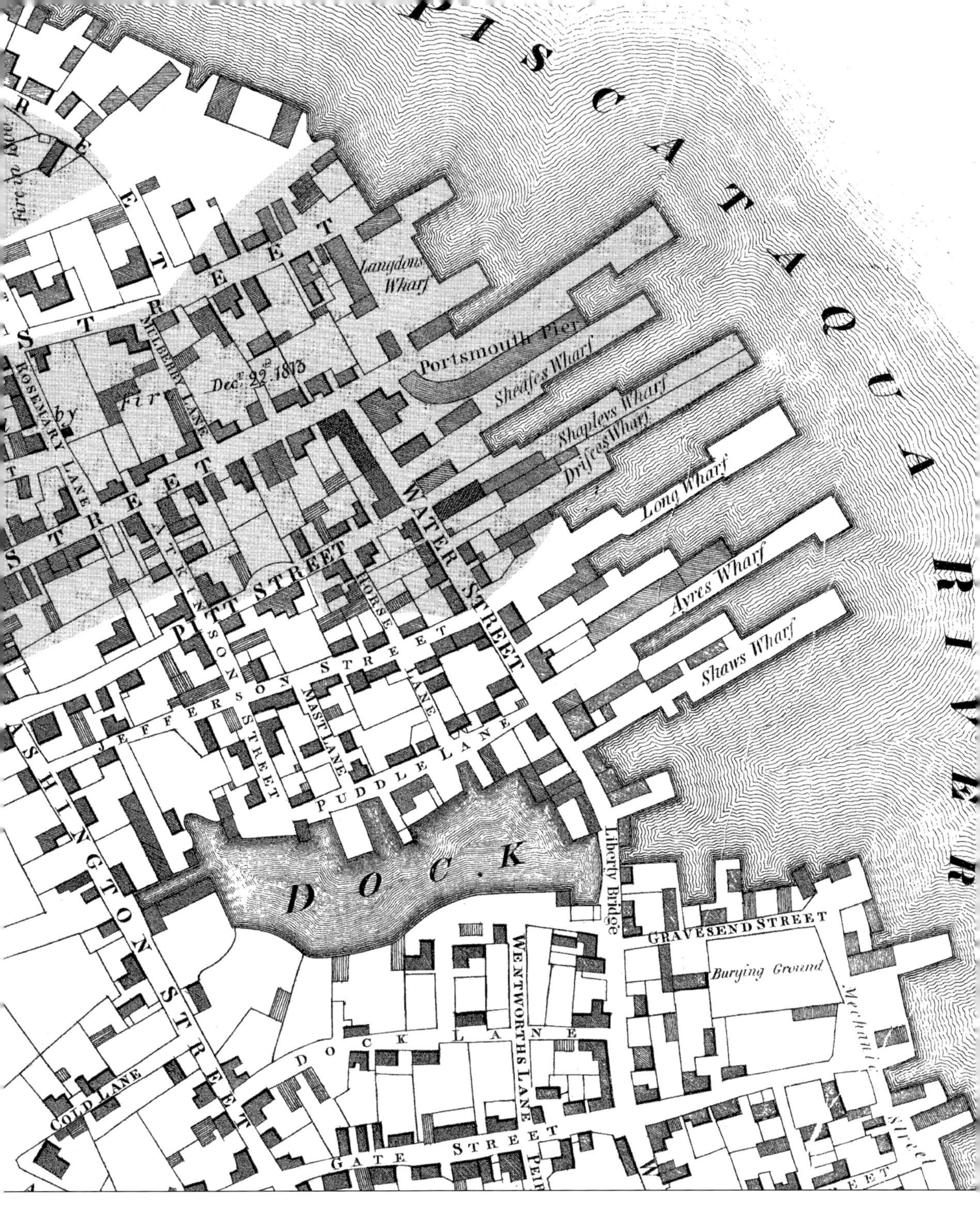
PISCATAQUA RIVER
Langdons Wharf
Portsmouth Pier
Sheafes Wharf
Shapleys Wharf
Drisces Wharf
Long Wharf
Ayres Wharf
Shaws Wharf
Decr. 22d. 1813
ROSEMARY LANE
MULBERRY LANE
PITT STREET
WATER STREET
HORSE LANE
JEFFERSON STREET
MAST LANE
PUDDLE LANE
ATKINSON STREET
WASHINGTON STREET
DOCK
Liberty Bridge
GRAVESEND STREET
Burying Ground
WENTWORTHS LANE
DOCK LANE
COLD LANE
GATE STREET

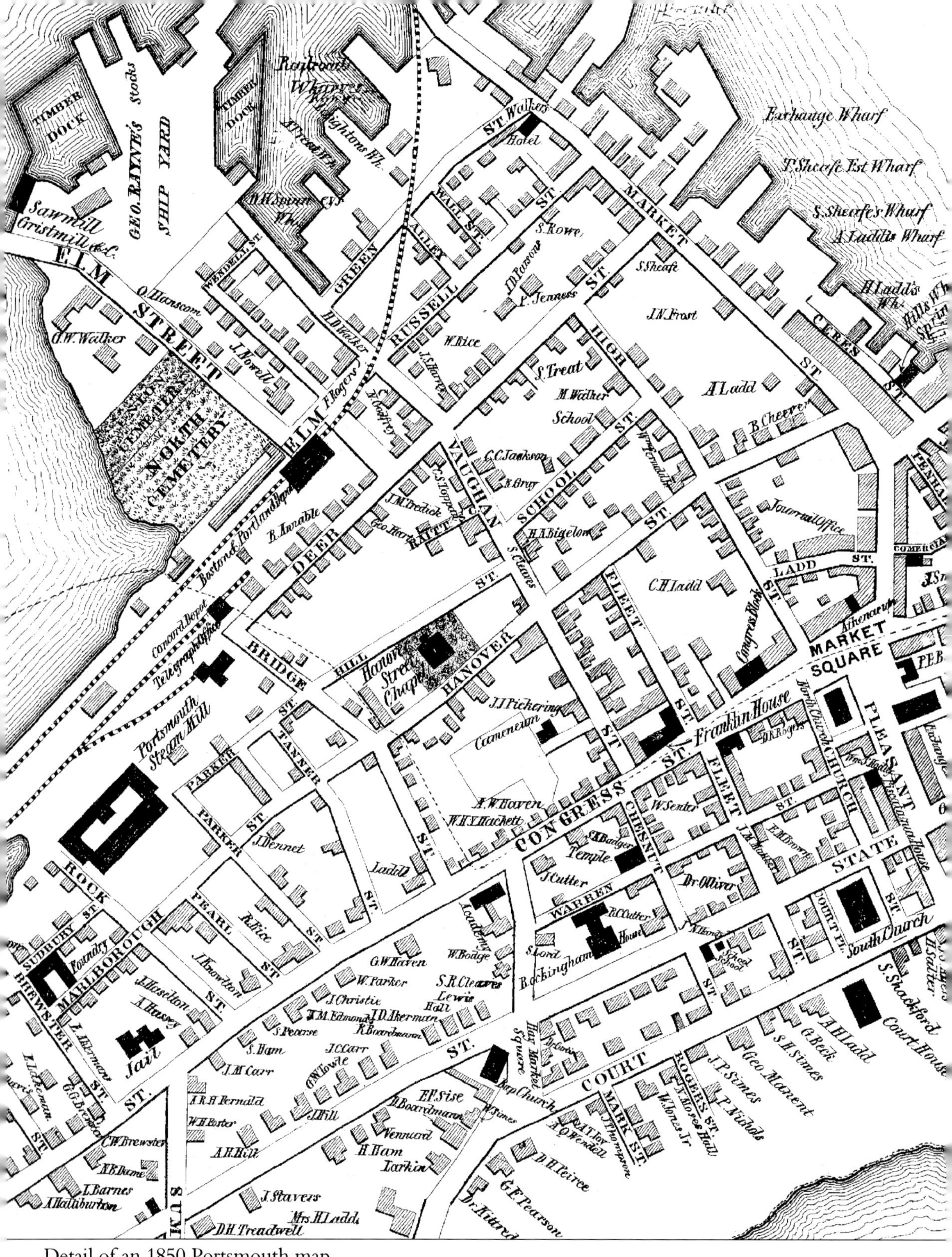

Detail of an 1850 Portsmouth map.

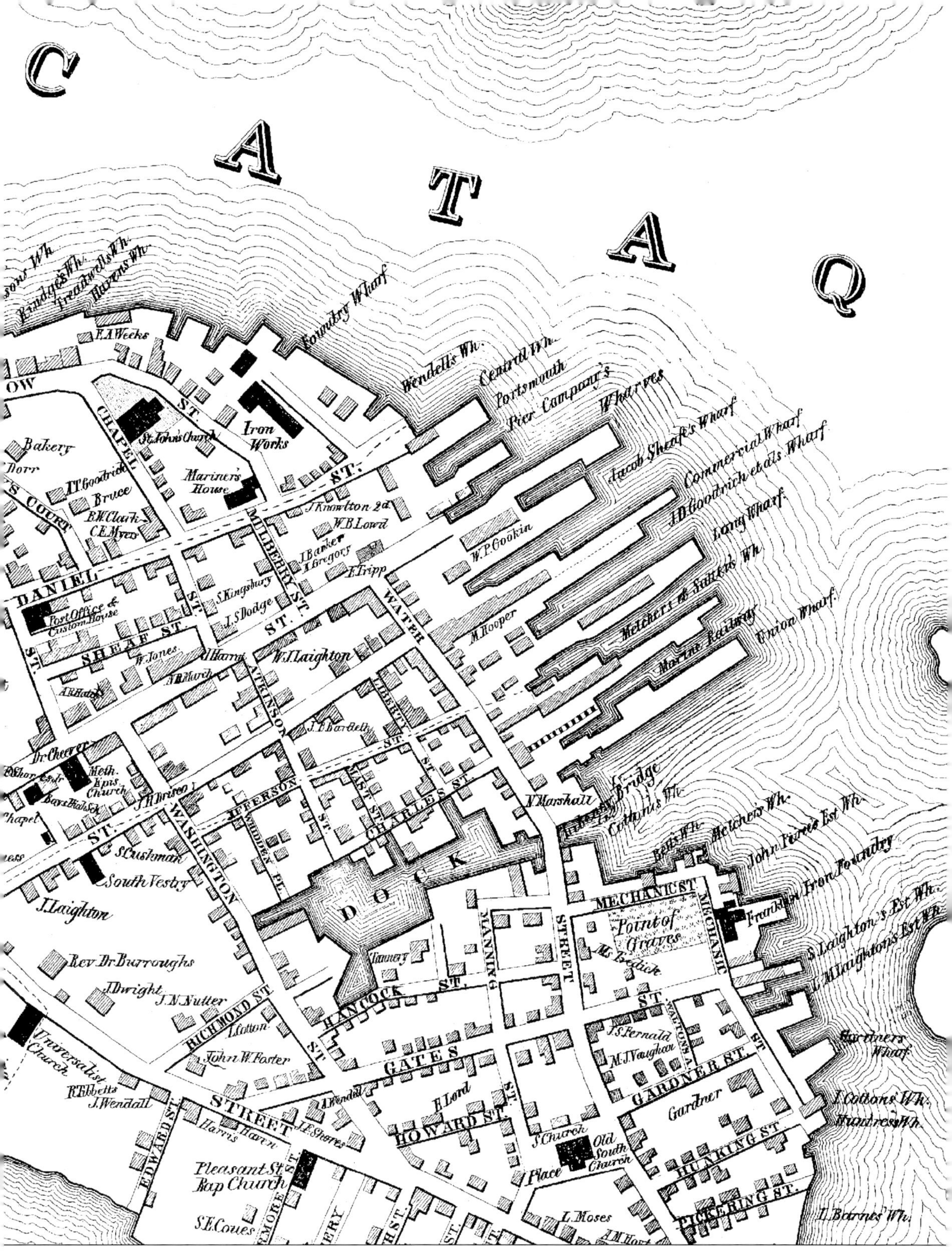
C A T A Q
Bridges Wh.
Treadwells Wh.
Havens Wh.
E.A.Weeks
Foundry Wharf
Wendell's Wh.
Central Wh.
Portsmouth Pier Company's Wharves
Jacob Sheafe's Wharf
Commercial Wharf
J.D. Goodrich et als. Wharf
Long Wharf
Union Wharf
Marine Railway
Iron Works
St. John's Church
Mariner's House
CHAPEL ST.
Bakery
DANIEL ST.
Post Office & Custom House
SHEAF ST.
MULBERRY ST.
WATER ST.
ATKINSON ST.
W.P. Gookin
M. Hooper
W.J. Laighton
J. Knowlton 2d
W.B. Lord
E. Tripp
S. Kingsbury
J.S. Dodge
W. Jones
Meth. Epis. Church
Chapel
JEFFERSON ST.
WASHINGTON ST.
CHARLES ST.
S. Cushman
South Vestry
J. Laighton
DOCK
N. Marshall
Liberty Bridge
Cottons Wh.
Fletchers Wh.
John Pierce's Est Wh.
Franklin Iron Foundry
MECHANIC ST.
Point of Graves
MANNING ST.
S. Laighton's Est Wh.
Gardners Wharf
Rev. Dr. Burroughs
J. Dwight
J.N. Nutter
RICHMOND ST.
John W. Foster
HANCOCK ST.
GATES ST.
GARDNER ST.
Universalist Church
J. Wendall
STREET
HOWARD ST.
E. Lord
J.S. Fernald
M.J. Vaughan
Old South Church
S. Church Place
HUNKING ST.
PICKERING ST.
J. Cottons Wh.
Pleasant St. Bap Church
S.E. Coues
EDWARD ST.
L. Moses
J. Barnes Wh.

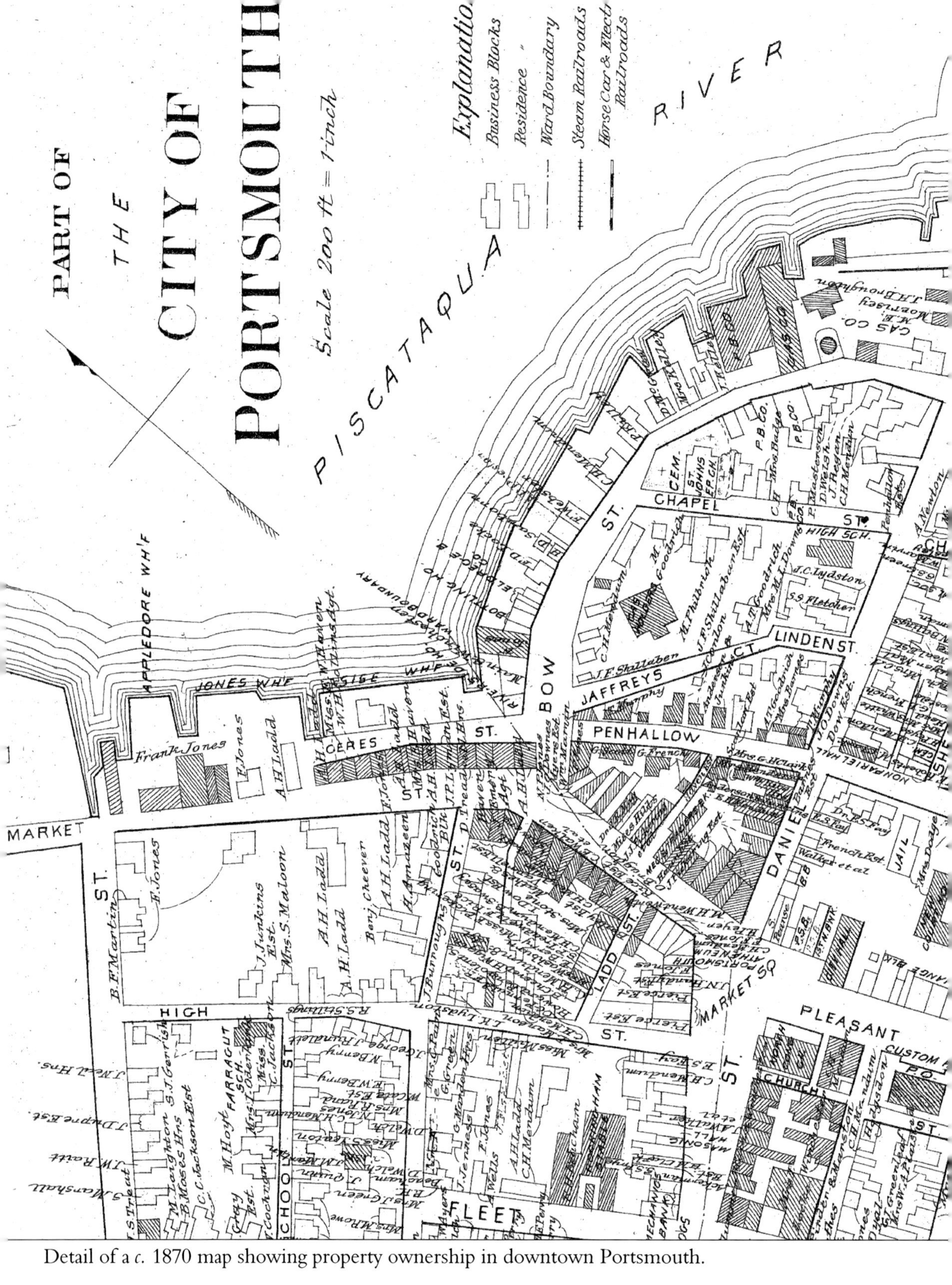

Detail of a *c.* 1870 map showing property ownership in downtown Portsmouth.

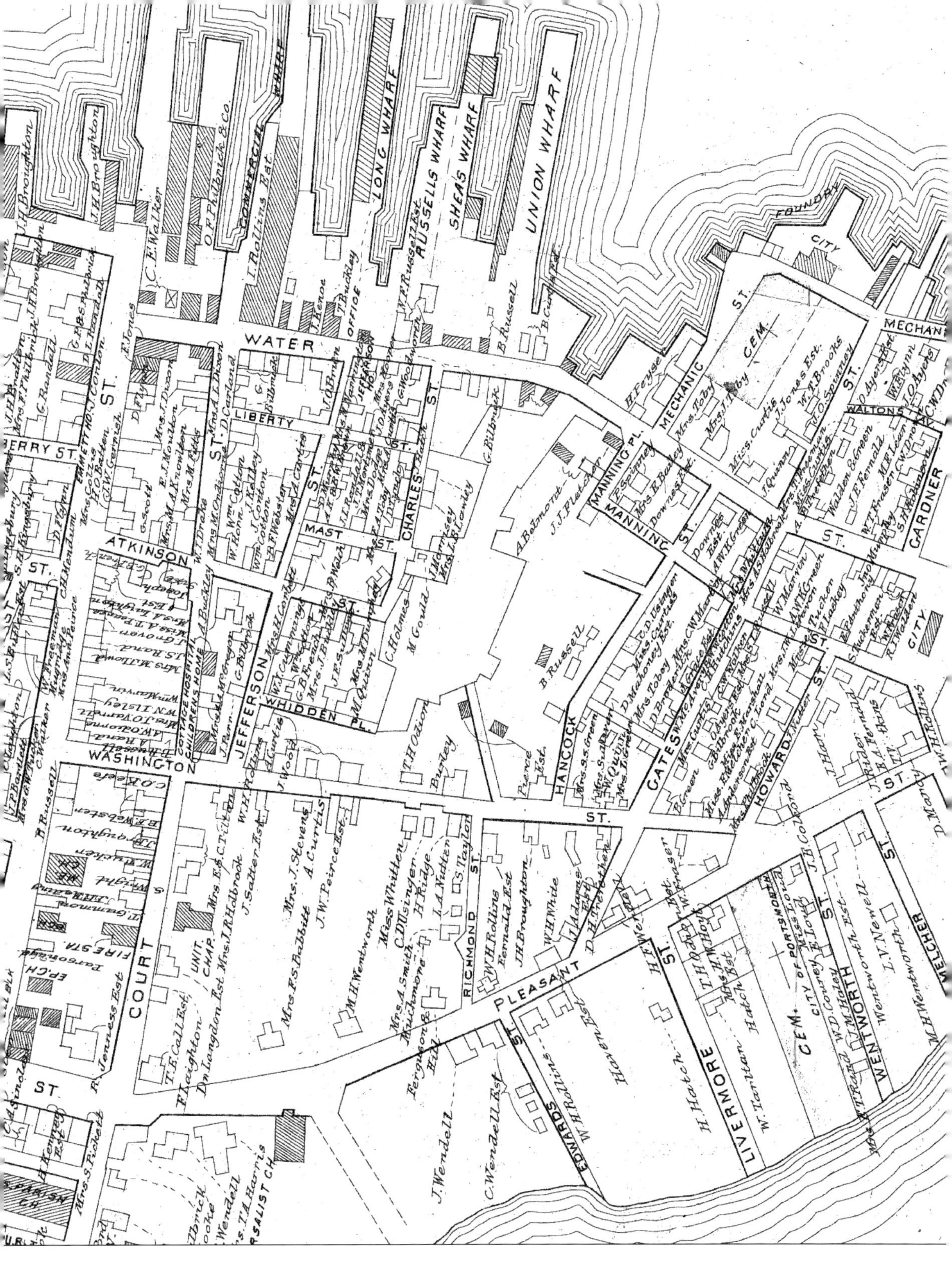
WATER ST.
LONG WHARF
RUSSELLS WHARF
SHEAS WHARF
UNION WHARF
COMMERCIAL WHARF
LIBERTY
CHARLES ST.
MAST ST.
ATKINSON
JEFFERSON
WHIDDEN PL.
WASHINGTON
COURT ST.
RICHMOND ST.
PLEASANT ST.
EDWARDS ST.
LIVERMORE
WENTWORTH
MELCHER
HANCOCK
GATES
HOWARD ST.
MANNING ST.
MANNING PL.
MECHANIC ST.
GARDNER
CITY CEM.
FIRE STA.
CITY FOUNDRY
UNIT. CHAP.
COTTAGE HOSPITAL CHILDRENS HOME

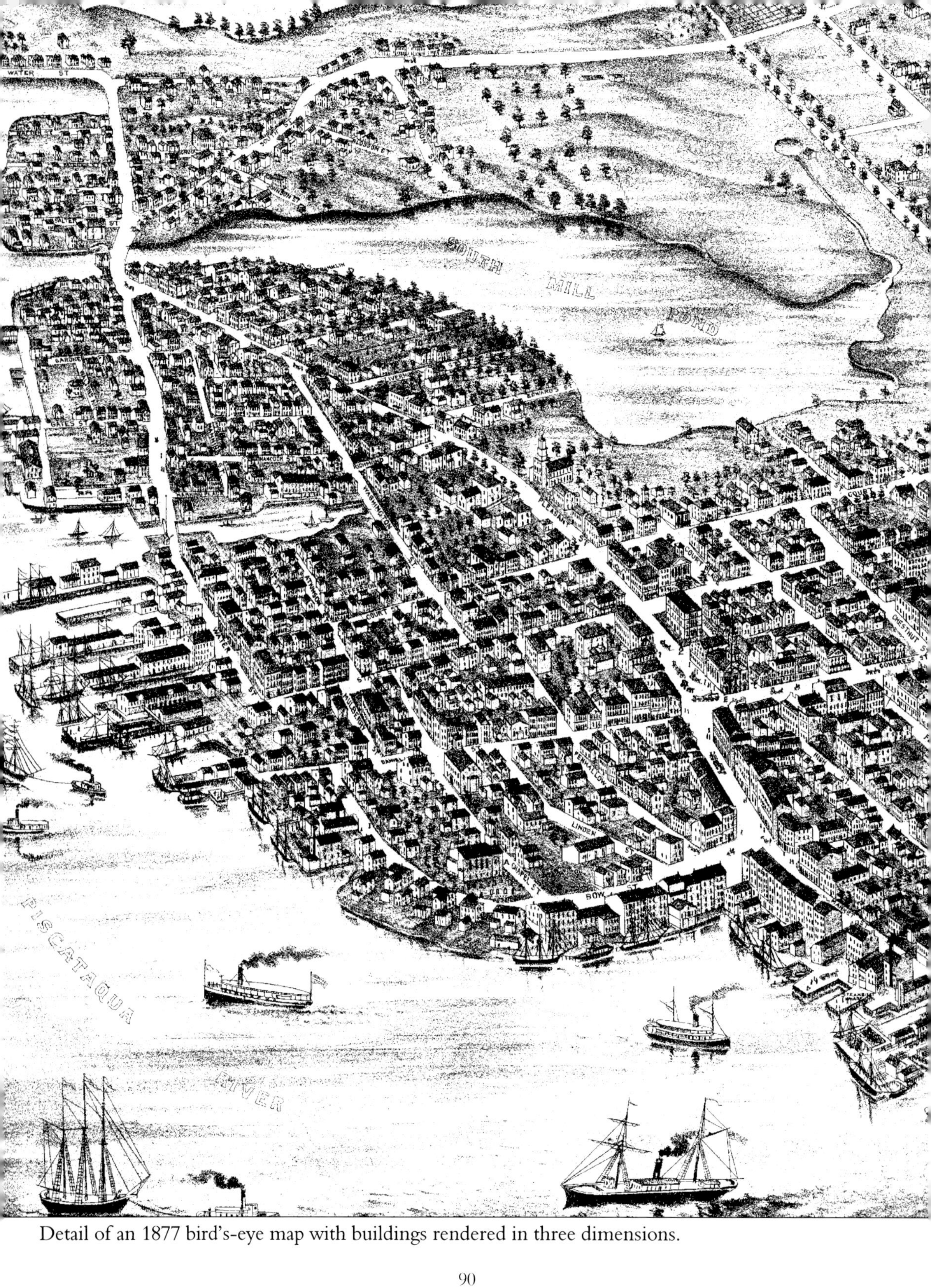

Detail of an 1877 bird's-eye map with buildings rendered in three dimensions.

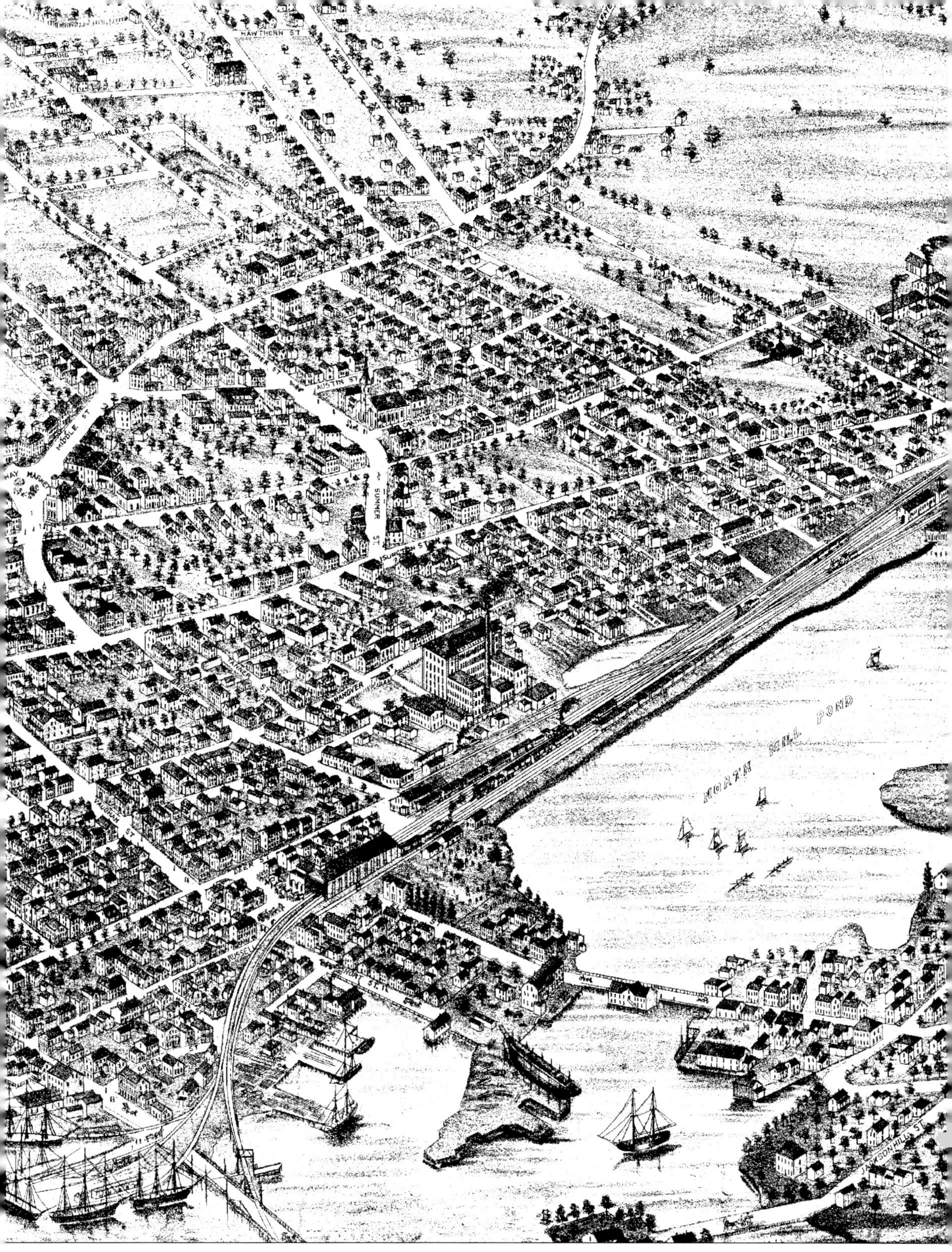
HAWTHORN ST.
HIGHLAND ST.
MIDDLE ST.
HAY MARKET
SUMMER ST.
AUSTIN ST.
SUMMER ST.
HANOVER
NORTH MILL POND

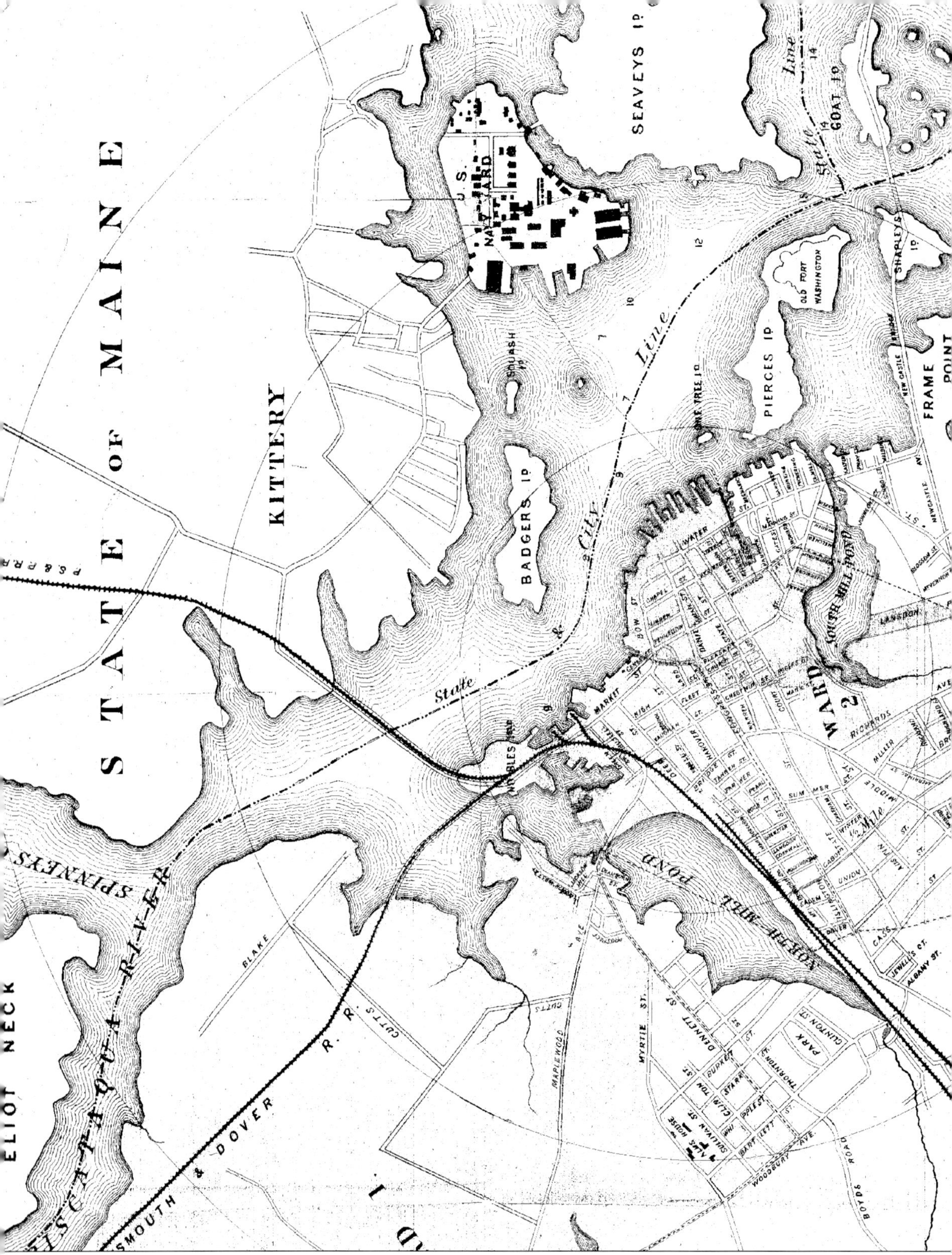

Detail of an 1888 map showing ward zones.

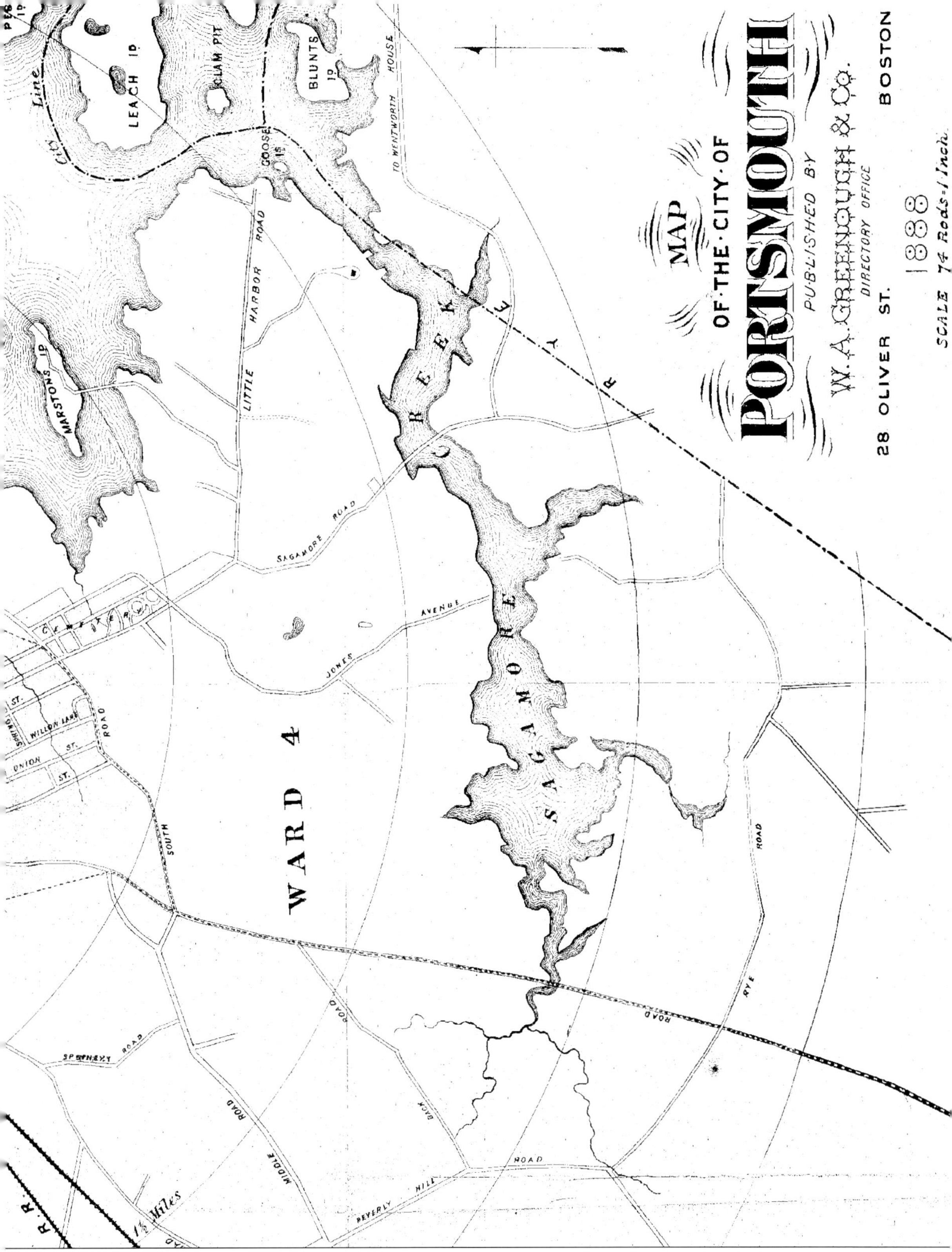
MAP
OF THE CITY OF
PORTSMOUTH
PUBLISHED BY
W. A. GREENOUGH & Co.
DIRECTORY OFFICE
28 OLIVER ST. BOSTON
1888
SCALE 74 Rods=1 Inch.
WARD 4
SAGAMORE CREEK
LEACH ID
CLAM PIT
BLUNTS ID
GOOSE IS
MARSTONS ID
City Line
TO WENTWORTH HOUSE
LITTLE HARBOR ROAD
SAGAMORE ROAD
JONES AVENUE
CEMETERY
WILLOW LANE
UNION ST.
SOUTH ROAD
RYE ROAD
BACK ROAD
MIDDLE ROAD
BEVERLY HILL ROAD
1½ Miles
R. R.

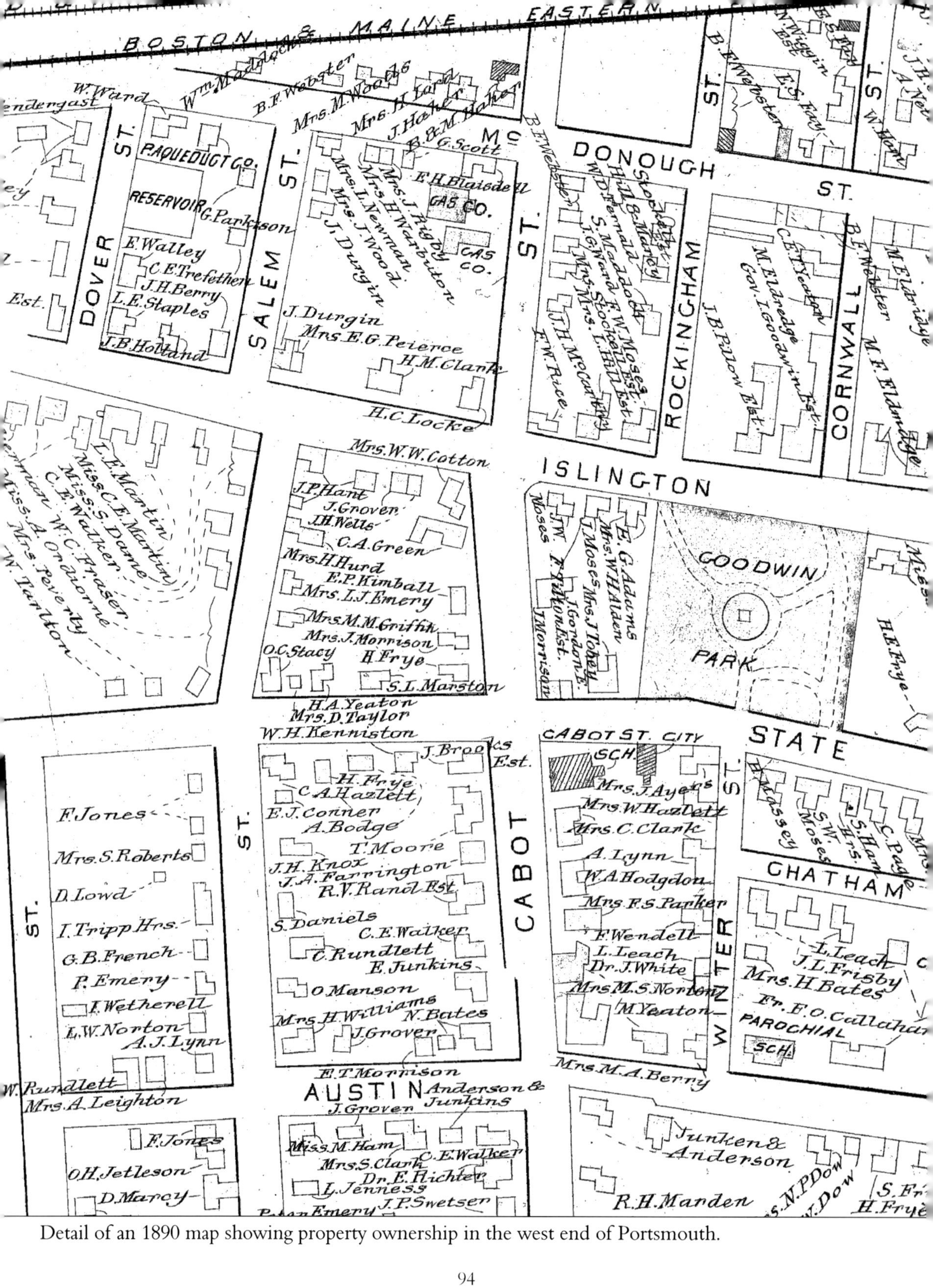

Detail of an 1890 map showing property ownership in the west end of Portsmouth.

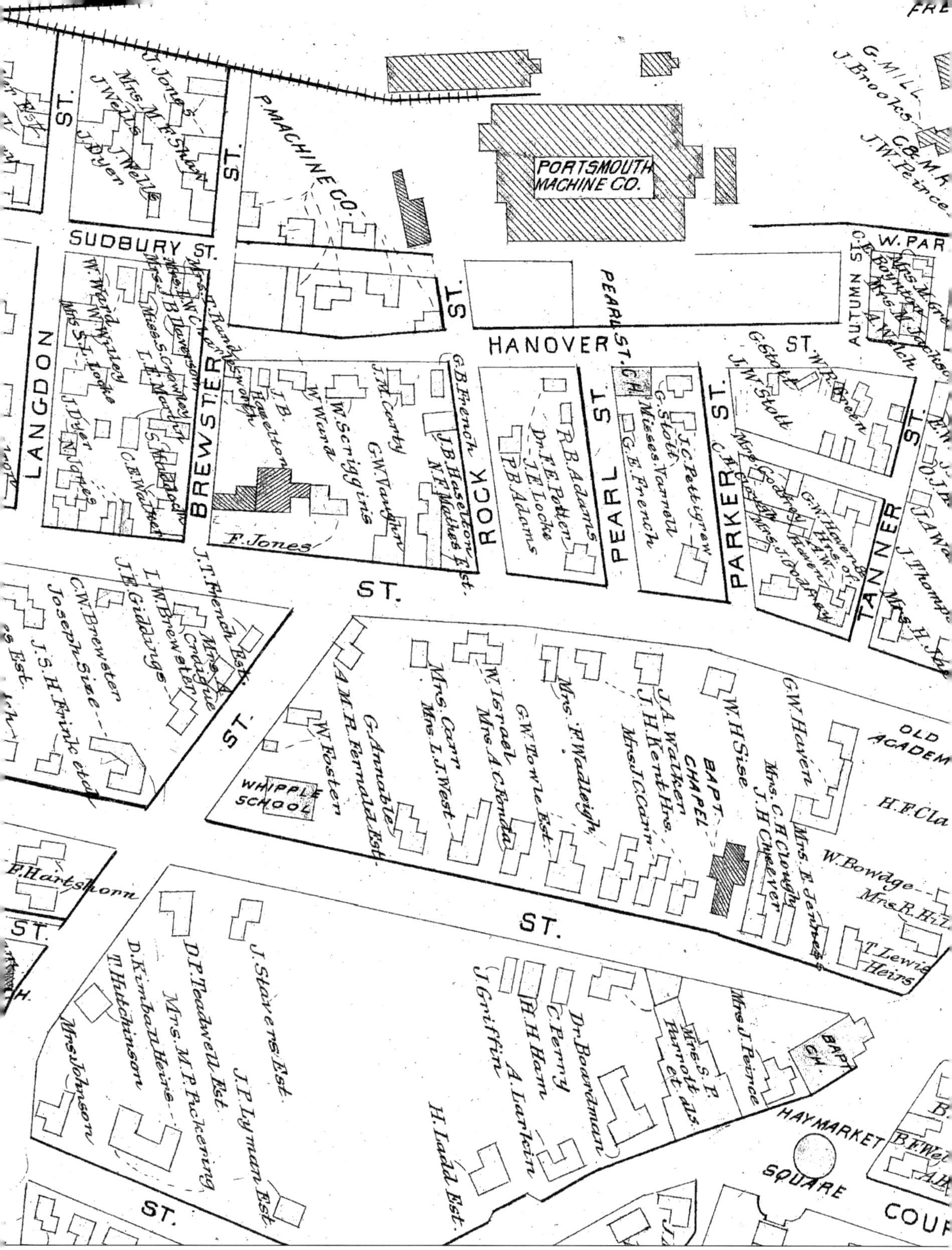
PORTSMOUTH MACHINE CO.
P. MACHINE CO.
SUDBURY ST.
LANGDON ST.
BREWSTER ST.
HANOVER ST.
PEARL ST.
ROCK ST.
PARKER ST.
TANNER ST.
AUTUMN ST.
ST.
WHIPPLE SCHOOL
BAPT. CHAPEL
OLD ACADEMY
BAPT. CH.
HAYMARKET SQUARE
COURT
F. Jones
F. Hartshorn
G. W. Haven
W. H. Sise
J. A. Walker
G. W. Towle Est.
Mrs. F. Waddleigh
G. Annable
W. Foster
J. H. Cheever
W. Bowdge
H. F. Cla
T. Lewis Heirs
J. Stavers Est.
J. P. Lyman Est.
D. P. Teadwell Est.
Mrs. M. P. Pickering
T. Hutchinson
Mrs. Johnson
H. Ladd Est.
A. Larkin
H. H. Ham
C. Perry
Dr. Boardman
J. Griffin
Mrs. J. Peirce
J. W. Peirce
J. Brooks
J. W. Stott
G. Stott
R. B. Adams
P. B. Adams
Dr. F. E. Potter
J. E. Locke
G. E. French
G. B. French
J. C. Pettigrew
Misses Vannell
W. Scriggins
G. W. Vaughn
J. B. Haselton
C. W. Brewster
I. W. Brewster
J. E. Giddings
Joseph Sise
J. S. H. Frink et al.
J. T. French Est.
C. E. Walker
J. Dyer
J. Wells
Mrs. S. J. Locke
Mrs. J. C. Carr
Mrs. C. H. Clough
Mrs. E. Jenness
Mrs. R. Hill
W. Israel
Mrs. A. C. Fonda
Mrs. Carr
Mrs. L. J. West
A. M. R. Fernald Est.

BIBLIOGRAPHY

Brewster, Charles W. *Rambles about Portsmouth.* Portsmouth, New Hampshire: Portsmouth Journal Office, 1873.

Candee, Richard M. *Building Portsmouth.* Portsmouth, New Hampshire: Portsmouth Advocates Inc., 1992.

Chamberlain, Samuel. *Portsmouth, N.H.* New York: Hastings House Publishers, 1940.

Dolph, James and Ronan Donohue. *Around Portsmouth in the Victorian Era.* Charleston, South Carolina: Arcadia Publishing, 1997.

Foss, Gerald D. *Portsmouth.* Charleston, South Carolina: Arcadia Publishing, 1994.

Foster, Joseph H. *The Portsmouth Guide Book.* Portsmouth, New Hampshire: Journal Steam Press, 1876.

Garvin, James L. *Historic Portsmouth.* Portsmouth: Strawbery Banke Inc. Second Edition, 1995.

Gilmore, Robert C. and Bruce E. Ingmire. *The Seacoast New Hampshire.* Norfolk, Virginia: the Donning Company, 1989.

Glimpses of Portsmouth and Vicinity. Portsmouth, New Hampshire: Brewster & Wilson Publishers.

Gurney, C.S. *Portsmouth . . . Historic and Picturesque.* Portsmouth, New Hampshire. 1902.

The Portsmouth Book. Boston: George H. Ellis, Printer, 1899.

Portsmouth New Hampshire. Portsmouth, New Hampshire: City of Portsmouth and Portsmouth Board of Trade and Merchants Exchange Publishers.

Sammons, Mark J. *Strawbery Banke: Official Guidebook.* Portsmouth, New Hampshire: Strawbery Banke Inc., 1997.

Thomas, Matthew E. *Rockingham County.* Charleston, South Carolina: Arcadia Publishing, 1994.